TRADITIONAL SPOONCARVING
IN WALES

WELSH
CRAFTS

Traditional
Spooncarving
in Wales

Gwyndaf Breese

Gwasg Carreg Gwalch

Published by Gwasg Carreg Gwalch in 2006.
All rights reserved. No part of this publication
may be reproduced or transmitted, in any form
or by any means, without prior permission.

ISBN: 0-86381-046-0

Gwasg Carreg Gwalch,
12 Iard yr Orsaf, Llanrwst, Conwy, Cymru (Wales)
LL26 0EH.
Tel: 01492 642031 Fax: 01492 641502
e-mail: books@carreg-gwalch.co.uk   website: www.carreg-gwalch.co.uk
Printed and published in Wales.

Acknowledgements
(page references)

Museum of Welsh Life:
6, 31(A), 42, 44, 57, 58, 71, 77, 84, 88, 91, 93

Dorothy Wright, Museum of Welsh Life collection:
9, 22

Author:
11, 13, 14, 16, 18, 21, 24, 25, 27, 29, 30, 31(B), 32, 33, 51, 53, 61-3, 65-7, 73, 75, 79-81,
83, 87, 95

Gwasg Carreg Gwalch:
34-41, 43, 45-8, 97-103, 107-9, 112

Mike Davies:
104-5

Cadwyn:
106

Siôn Llewellyn:
110

David Western:
111

Contents

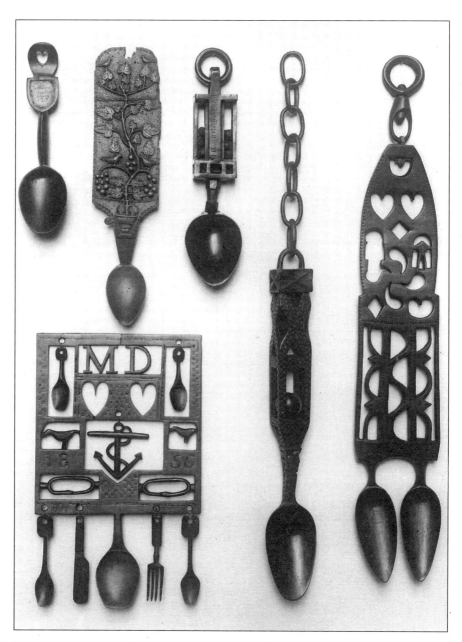

A fine selection of traditional Welsh lovespoons

Introduction

Today the Welsh lovespoon is synonymous with Wales: every year lovespoons are produced in their hundreds to satisfy an ever increasing demand by overseas visitors. A survey of the development of the lovespoon from a crude courting gift through to the cheap mass-produced item found in retail outlets, along with the superb work of the specialist carver has hitherto not been attempted in any detail. Nor has the making of lovespoons been placed properly in the context of domestic utilitarian spoonmaking, out of which it appears to have developed. The tradition of making domestic spoons is of course not unique to Wales, but the quality of what was produced ranks with the finest. However, its development into the lovespoon tradition is indeed a unique Welsh phenomenon.

As Trevor Owen documents in *Welsh Folk Customs* and Catrin Stevens in *Welsh Courting Customs*, the young suitors of Wales followed the pattern that prevailed throughout western Europe and beyond, and gave decorated trinkets to their loved ones as tokens of their affection. By doing so they were no different from suitors everywhere, and yet the objects they made were unique: they have not been made in such a wide range of design and techniques anywhere else in the world.

A great deal of misleading information about lovespoons has been and still is given to local people and tourists alike, and this work is an attempt to set the record straight, even if it means being accused of shattering what has become a national myth. The amount of reliable information on the history of the lovespoon is scanty, but this account attempts to trace the rise and decline of this unique Welsh courting custom, and its revival during the second half of the twentieth century into what became a flourishing small rural industry and a satisfying pastime, and to place the love spoon in the context of its development out of domestic spoon-making.

During the past forty odd years I have had the privilege of meeting the majority of the lovespoon carvers referred to in this book, as well as many more besides who are too numerous to mention by name. I have encouraged and advised beginners, exchanged ideas and techniques with the more advanced, and stood in awe at the work of the recognised experts. It was at the insistence of many of them, who felt they could not put pen to paper themselves, that this account has been written.

The story begins with the making of domestic spoons, a tradition of spooncarving out of which the uniquely Welsh tradition of the lovespoon developed.

Domestic spooncarving

Crudely made wooden spoons intended for the preparation of food have been in existence since prehistoric times, but it was not until the seventeenth century that they began to be used for eating semi-liquid food from a bowl. The word 'spoon' is derived from the Anglo-Saxon 'spon', meaning chip or spatula, which suggests such objects were in use centuries earlier.

The habit of sipping liquid from a bowl remained among the poor long after pewter spoons and, later, silver spoons were in common use among the gentry. Although many eating spoons from the eighteenth and nineteenth centuries were based on the design of such pewter and silver spoons, there is ample evidence from the fragments of well-designed spoons from as far back as 150 BC that patterns produced by Welsh spooncarvers as late as the 1930s were in fact based on designs from some two thousand years earlier.

Wooden domestic utensils in general, and spoons in particular, had only a limited life span, and few if any complete examples have survived from much earlier than the beginning of the eighteenth century. Most of the wooden spoons made in the British Isles were intended for day-to-day practical use, and are considered crude when compared with the fine workmanship that may be seen on those from central Europe that were given as christening presents, or were used for various ecclesiastical ceremonies.

During the period when most of the domestic objects found in the humble home were made of clay or wood, there was a constant demand for such items because of the relatively short life span of both these materials. Most of the domestic spooncarving undertaken in Britain was carried out on a part-time basis, with men spending many hours of the long winter months whittling away to produce a wide range of domestic ware for their needs. Gradually the practice of using spoons for eating as well as for cooking became more widely accepted. In Wales in particular, part-time workers were unable to fill the demand, and full-time craftsmen began to take up the work.

The bulk of the domestic wood-ware required by the Welsh economy prior to the arrival of mass-produced factory-ware, which followed in the wake of improved road and rail links, was produced by the woodturner. He differed considerably from his English counterpart, the chair 'bodger', not only because of his superior skills and the versatility of his work, but also because he completed all stages of the work without resorting to the

*James and John Davies turning and carving spoons
at their Aber-cuch workshops, 1929.*

sophisticated machinery normally found in factories.

Domestic spoons were not turned on a lathe (with very few exceptions, and only for some stages of the work, such as rounding the handle), but were shaped out of a solid block of wood without the use of any machinery. This was a slow, labour-intensive process. In the case of domestic wooden spoons, the better the quality of the object, the shorter its life span was: a rough heavy spoon would outlast a carefully made delicate and well-designed object. Eating spoons were particularly vulnerable: a spoon with a delicate thin bowl was the most comfortable to eat with, but it would soon become chipped and damaged. It was customary among farming communities to replace their eating spoons once a year, generally before shearing or harvest time, when the arrival of seasonal workers meant that there were extra mouths to feed.

The two main staple semi-liquid foods in rural Wales in the eighteenth and much of the nineteenth century were variants of vegetable and oatmeal dishes such as *cawl* and *llymru*. Eating spoons fell into one or the other category, differing only in the shape of their bowls: a rounded bowl was preferable for eating broth, and a more pointed version was preferable for porridge. Ladles, which were larger versions of such spoons, and often had a hook on the end of the handle for storage, or to prevent the ladle falling into the cooking pot, were used to transfer hot food from the cauldron to the eating bowl.

All rural crafts depend on a suitable supply of raw material, and the Welsh woodturners established their cottage industry in an area of west Wales where the old counties of Carmarthenshire, Ceredigion and Pembrokeshire met, and where the deep sheltered valleys grew a profusion of sycamore – a stainless, odourless, and taste-free timber, which was the ideal choice for a utensil likely to come into contact with food. Sycamore is also easy to work and wears well without splintering.

The village of Aber-cuch and its surrounding area became one of the main centres of spooncarving, and the craft continued to flourish there until its gradual decline in the mid-1930s. Members of one particular family, James and John Davies, were among the last of the traditional Welsh wood-turners and spooncarvers who had become well known far beyond their rural workshop. During the latter years, when local trade was in decline, their work was still finding a market in some of the large London stores.

Another well-known producer of domestic wood-ware was William Rees from the small village of Henllan, who developed his craft to a high artistic and technical standard.

The decline in the habit of eating with a wooden spoon, together with the introduction of new metal designs for all types of cooking spoons, led to a rapid decline in spooncarving from the late 1920s onwards. Those who still considered wooden spoons to be best for cooking were able to buy mass-produced ones at a fraction of the price. This did not prevent the older generation from insisting that *cawl* did not taste the same without a wooden spoon and bowl, but they eventually got used to burning their lips with the metal version, which, as they recalled, was something that had never happened with the old wooden spoons.

From time to time eating spoons made from bone, ivory, whale-bone and walrus tusk appear in antique shops. These are not the work of rural domestic carvers, but were mostly made by sailors on long voyages. Other spoons, made of hard dense woods such as box and lignum vitae are also considered to be very collectable and command a high price. Most of these are based on metal spoons, however, and although they may have been originally made as eating spoons, they are now generally considered in the same category as presentation rather than utilitarian spoons.

1. Types of spoon

Eating spoons

Spoons designed and made for the consumption of food fall into two categories, depending on the type of semi-liquid nourishment they were intended to convey from bowl to mouth. In Wales these were generally known as broth and porridge spoons, the design and shape of the bowl of each one being considered suitable for that particular type of food. Those intended for broth had a rounded bowl, but a perfect circle was never attempted, perhaps because it was almost impossible to achieve such a shape by hand-carving, but also because a slightly oval form fits better into the mouth. The preferred shape of porridge spoons, on the other hand, was pointed and narrow.

Broth spoons were by far the most popular, and to make them well called for a high degree of skill. They had to be well balanced, light, deep enough to hold a mouthful of broth, and yet fit comfortably in the mouth. The lip had to be thin, but thicker towards the back where the handle joined the bowl and extra strength was needed.

Ideally, the back of the handle would curve gracefully upwards: flat spoons were considered to be the worst, and were viewed with contempt by skilled makers. The handle ends were cut square, rounded, or chamfered to a point. Regional variations, of which there were only three or four types, showed in the shape of the handles. Unlike many continental designs, particularly Swiss and Tyrolean, these spoons were not decorated with chip-carving designs (which involved using a sharp knife to cut shallow, usually geometric patterns in a flat surface) and did not have hooks.

One slight modification that developed in the latter years of the trade was the rounding off of the area where the handle joined the bowl. In earlier

Traditional Welsh spoons used in the butter-making process.

11

spoons a shoulder was cut in at this point, which could cause cracking and also collected dirt. Unnecessary surface decoration was also viewed with uncertainty, because of the question of hygiene, which is probably one reason why chip-carving was never used on Welsh domestic spoons, as they were for use rather than display.

Pointed eating spoons were not considered to be as comfortable to use as the traditional broth variety, and were most probably a later development that had been influenced by metal spoons. All of them had flat handles, and however well made they were, they never seemed comfortable to use. Eating spoons varied slightly in length, most makers using as a rough measurement the distance between the outstretched thumb and little finger of their hand.

Ladles and cooking spoons

There was very little regional variation to be found among cooking spoons and ladles. *The Oxford English Dictionary* defines a ladle as 'a large spoon with cup-shaped bowl and long handle for transferring liquids'. Some ladles had a turned bowl, whereas others were shaped entirely by hand. Most ladles had a roughly shaped bowl and a flat or rounded handle, and the larger types almost invariably had a hook attached to the underside of the handle. Cooking spoons were much lighter and a little smaller, with the bowl varying from square front to oval. Those with square fronts were preferable, as they were better for reaching the bottom of a cauldron or saucepan.

These items were intended for hard wear, and unless they were burned or charred so badly that they were no longer useable, they would last for years. Even those made for everyday use by skilled craftsmen had a rough, heavy appearance, with more emphasis on practicality than on aesthetic design.

The most notable feature that distinguished these ladles from eating spoons was the incorporation of a hook at the end of the handle. This was to allow them to be suspended from a shelf or rack when they were not in use, or to hook them over the side of the pot or cauldron to prevent them from falling into whatever was being cooked.

Cooking spoons came in a wider variety of shapes and sizes than ladles. There was often a thin demarcation line between the two sorts, but on the whole cooking spoons were lighter. Oval ones were called jam-making spoons although square ones were more practical for making jam. Those similar to miniature ladles sometimes had a pouring lip carved into the side, which made them suitable for pouring liquid into a smaller receptacle.

The shapes of the hooks have changed little over a period of two thousand years. It was only during the 1920s and 1930s, when ladles became popular competition pieces, that makers attempted to introduce a more elegant form of hook, which was often at the expense of strength.

Pair of eating spoons based on metal counterparts

Butter spoons

There were two types of butter spoons: those used in butter-making, and those known as crock-spoons. The butter-working spoon was of a flat shallow design with a bowl about 5 inches (150 mm) in diameter, and a short handle terminating in a circular disc on which was carved a simple reverse design. This was used to imprint a decoration on the finished butter (each family had their own pattern). Other butter-working spoons had hooked handles with indented grooves cut into the front of the bowl, and both were used to remove butter from the churn and to press out the surplus moisture – the butter-milk – on a turned device called a butter-worker.

The butter-crock spoon is an odd-shaped object that has baffled many an antique dealer not familiar with Welsh domestic wood-ware. Normally it was a long shallow bowl, curved on the left side (on the assumption that everyone was right-handed) where a serrated edge was cut, and with a hook on the end. Its purpose was to hack salted butter from a crock where it had been placed in readiness for the winter shortage of fresh butter. By this time the butter would be so hard that a small indentation was carved on the face of the spoon in order to allow added leverage for the thumb.

These were the first types of wooden spoons to become obsolete, but they remained popular competition pieces long after butter-making on farms had fallen into decline. The most skilled of competitors took great pride in shaping the hook to form an elegant swan's neck. They were also a popular choice for decorating during the nineteenth century and were given as love tokens alongside the better-known lovespoon.

Salad servers and mixers

Salad servers were not produced by traditional spooncarvers until the late 1940s, when they became popular competition pieces. Most were based on metal or, later, on plastic servers, and included two spoons joined in the middle in the form of a pair of scissors.

. Some English carvers made forks, but this was never a custom in Wales. These followed metal versions closely, were painstaking to make, and required a stronger timber than the traditional sycamore in order to be practical to use.

A device that became very popular in the 1950s and 1960s, when the few remaining spoon makers began to attend craft fairs, was a flat spatula used for mixing pastry and cakes. Mixers sold in the craft fairs of the early 1950s for 1/6 (about 18p), and at one time they were so much in demand that mass-production was considered. At this time they were made from any sawn thin strips of wood. Needless to say, these were of an inferior quality, and it was not long before the more discerning customer began to demand the proper cleaved versions shaped by hand. Eventually they priced themselves off the market, but during the years that followed it was not uncommon to see an elderly lady going around the craft fair circuit clutching a burnt and badly worn 'mixer', almost pleading for a replacement.

Traditional large sycamore soup ladles

2. Materials

Traditional domestic spooncarving was carried out using only six basic tools, most of which were home-made or readily available. Small eating spoons could easily be produced using a small axe for the rough shaping, a wooden spokeshave (a small wooden shaping tool with two handles), some straight knives for smoothing, and a bent tool, known as a *twca cam* for hollowing the bowl. The word *twca*, now obsolete, was at one time the name given for a general purpose knife, and *cam* is the Welsh word for 'bent'. Larger ladles and cooking spoons would require a bowl adze or a gouge for the initial hollowing out of the waste from inside the bowl.

Most of the early domestic spoons were made from timber that was readily available, regardless of its overall suitability. Over a period of time it was discovered that certain woods contained stains, or gave off obnoxious smells that tainted the food, while others proved difficult to carve, or cracked when in use, and spooncarvers became more selective in their choice of materials. The English carvers favoured beech and lime, while in Scandinavia the main woods used were birch and juniper. In the Alpine regions white poplar was the favourite, and in the heavily afforested eastern states of America, where most of the early emigrants settled, maple proved to be an ideal choice. The Welsh turners and carvers, however, used only sycamore for all domestic ware and coopered dairy utensils, but as this wood was not introduced into Britain until the sixteenth century, and would have taken another hundred years to become established, they too must have used a wide range of woods in earlier times.

Sycamore is without doubt the ideal choice: free of taste, stainless and odourless, this timber carves well, wears without splintering, and was so readily available in the sheltered west-facing valleys of Wales as to become known as 'The Welsh Weed'.

There was a common belief both among makers and users that the salt-laden air which blew continuously from the sea gave a distinct taste to the wood, although some makers would add to this by boiling their produce in salt between the roughing out and finishing processes.

Sycamore, if properly seasoned, should be of a milky-white appearance, which could be easily achieved in spooncarving, as the timber was always used in its unseasoned condition. Unlike harder, dense woods such as holly, box, elder, or fruit woods, which were often used for decorative spoons, sycamore could be worked unseasoned without danger of it cracking as it dried. For spooncarving, sycamore was always used 'green'.

Unknown Ceredigion spooncarver at work using a bowl adze and 'twca cam' hollowing knife. Probably early 1920s.

In deep sheltered valleys sycamore attained considerable height, due to its fast growth and continued struggle towards the light, and it was these trees that were the ideal material for the spooncarvers. The timber was often obtainable in long clean lengths, with a straight grain, and above all a soft easy working nature. The trees were felled as required throughout the year, although summer-cut wood discoloured quickly and became hard to work after a few weeks. Too much winter-felled wood was also avoided. Spooncarvers worked on an as-needed basis, making frequent visits to the woods for fresh supplies, much of which was grown as coppice timber.

Some spoons could be worked from the branches of larger trees that were felled for planking, but this was generally considered to be brittle and of poor standard. Trees grown in exposed places were also avoided. Easily recognisable by the roughness of their bark, they were considered tough, as were the bottom few feet of any tree regardless of where it had grown. Such timber was usually turned into bowls, although some carvers who were more skilful than others would put it aside for making large ladles or exhibition spoons; with these, a certain degree of hardness was an advantage to achieve a fine finish.

Each log was carefully selected for a particular type of spoon, and although sycamore was plentiful enough it was a matter of principle among spooncarvers to keep waste to a minimum. A clean, knot-free billet of about 18 inches (46 cm) in length was required for a ladle, while about half that size would provide for an eating spoon. Twisted and bent branches were much sought after by spoon makers in other countries, but Welsh carvers always used to shape their spoons from straight timber rather than take advantage of the added strength and shape available in naturally curved and unusual growth.

Although some spooncarvers and domestic bowl turners boiled their wares for a period of time from a few minutes to about half an hour, none of them appear to have used this method in order to soften the wood and allow it to be bent into a variety of shapes, as was common in the chair-making industry. Perhaps it would have been a pointless exercise, as further heating and washing of the bowl or spoon when it was in practical use would have soon returned it to its original shape.

Following the brief revival in rural crafts during the 1980s, those who took up spooncarving no longer felt it necessary to restrict themselves to the use of sycamore, and more decorative woods have begun to appear. Here there has been an emphasis on figure and colouring, rather than traditional practical reasons determining the choice of material.

3. Preparation and working practices

Most Welsh woodturners ran their business as a small family concern, and any apprentices who were taken on were usually young relatives who had chosen, or been forced, to learn the trade. Although treated with slightly more respect than the average learner, they started like everyone else on preparation work, ending a long day with a stiff back and often blistered and bloodied hands.

Once cut, the billets (pieces of wood) dried quickly, although it was possible to retain some of the moisture by covering them with wet sacks. Alternatively, it was possible to keep them in water, although the latter method was not favoured, as soaking wet wood is difficult to hold and is therefore considered to be dangerous, particularly during the initial chopping-out procedure. In any case no amount of soaking could bring back the original 'green' state to dry timber.

The practice of working wood in its unseasoned condition was well known in many aspects of rural woodworking, and this technique enjoyed a considerable revival during the later part of the twentieth century. The great advantage of green wood is that it works well, and it cleaves without the need of using undue force. Cleaved timber is much stronger than sawn timber, as it follows the natural line of the fibres, unlike sawn planks which often cut across it. Because of this, cleaved wood is far less likely to crack and warp during drying. Basket and hurdle makers also find it more pliable.

The revival period in rural crafts saw a considerable change in the traditional roughing out methods of spooncarving. This was among the most difficult of skills to master, and consequently most

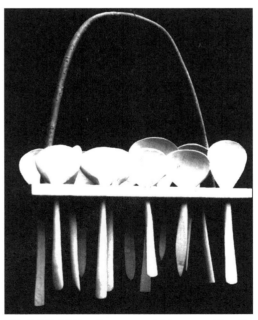

'Tooled finish' broth spoons with bentwood handle in a traditional rack

enthusiasts resorted to the use of a band-saw, or a bow-saw if they worked in a workshop with no electricity. Having cut out the rough shape in a matter of minutes, they attempted to save more time by resorting to fast-cutting conventional shapers. Such tools have no respect for the natural form of the fibres, and movement during drying increases considerably when these tools are used.

Selecting the wood

Preparation work was important, as it is in all aspects of craft work, and suitable logs were cut to length avoiding as many small knots as possible. The experienced carver could see if knots could be removed during the initial shaping stages; having to discard a partly-finished spoon later on because of the appearance of a knot would be a waste of valuable time. Selected logs, once cut to length, were cleaved, usually with steel wedges or a 'froe' – a general-purpose splitting tool much used by many rural woodworkers. Depending on the diameter of the log and the number of spoons required from it, four, six or eight billets were split, but ladles were usually made from the two halves cleaved down the middle. For making small spoons it was customary to aim for half-round or triangular-piece billets, as this lessened the amount of waste to be removed during the initial cutting out work.

Traditional spooncarvers used neither templates nor measurements: spoons were sold as individual items, and even if 'sets' were made for a specific order, they were only restricted to a basic size and design, and there was no great attempt to make them identical.

Chopping out

A small hand axe was the only tool used by carvers to shape in the initial stages. The weight and pattern of the axe depended on preference, and around a pound and a half was a good average. More weight resulted in less effort, but was offset by bulk, and once factory-made products began to find their way into the rural areas, spoon makers soon discovered their favoured type of axe from the number of regional patterns available.

It is surprising that other traditional shaping tools such as the clogger's knife were never adapted for shaping spoons, although this one would have been very effective in the hands of a skilled worker. Clog-makers seldom made spoons, and it would have been an interesting experience to watch a skilled clog-maker and spooncarver compete against one another.

Some continental spooncarvers used a draw-horse with remarkable dexterity for shaping their spoons, but Welsh makers chose to ignore this versatile holding device, although it was well adapted by many other rural craftsmen.

Chopping out the rough shape of a spoon required skill, patience, and a remarkable eye for balance and form. As much waste as possible was removed at this stage, which reduced the labour with smaller tools during later stages. Chopping out was no job for a learner, and the work was undertaken by the master, who would often shape enough in a couple of hours in the morning to keep his apprentice occupied for the remainder of the day. I recall being told by a spoon maker who learned his craft from an uncle in the 1920s, about the heart-breaking task of having to finish a pile of roughed-out spoons before the end of a day. He claimed he was swamped under an ever-increasing mountain of blanks and was not allowed to put any left over in water to keep moist until the next morning.

The chopping-out followed a set pattern, regardless of the type of spoon being made. First the back of the bowl was shaped, then the handle, followed by the front. Good shaping was critical; the tendency among poor makers was to leave the spoon too flat, either by not using a thick enough billet in the first place, or by taking too much off the back. There was a tradition that Welsh eating spoons (and the same is true of all well-designed spoons) would touch at three points when laid face down on a flat surface: the front of the bowl, halfway up the handle, and at its tip. This last criterion, however, only applied to the 'fishback' handle that was popular in north Wales.

As it was a rather featureless timber, sycamore on the whole did not offer any great challenge when it came to the balancing out of the colour and figure frequently found in more decorative woods. For run-of-the-mill work this was of no importance, but if the bowl was hollowed out from the outside of the log (that is, through the bark) the annual rings could be balanced into attractive diminishing rings within the bowl. This technique was not lost on bowl turners either. It came into its own when more decorative timbers began to be used for spoons, and a distinct contrast was obtained between the heart and sap woods.

Hollowing

After chopping-out, the next stage was to hollow out the bowl, and here a unique tool came into operation: the bent knife. In skilled hands it was the most effective way of cleaning out waste from within the bowl. On large spoons and ladles more brute force was required, and cramping the rough spoon in a vice and using a gouge, preferably a bent one, was the most common method. Another effective tool for this purpose was the bowl adze, which could be used one-handed while manipulating the spoon with the other, thus eliminating the need for cramping.

Good bowl adzes were difficult to find. In most of those produced by local blacksmiths, the blade was too much at a right-angle to the handle, when it should have been bent back almost parallel to it in order to cut into the depth required in a large ladle. The bowl adze was a dangerous tool to use, and it was the last to be entrusted to the hands of a learner.

Most domestic spoons that have been unearthed from an early period appear to have a sharp shoulder at the point where the bowl joins the handle, and it is difficult to understand why this obviously bad design lasted so

Part-finished spoons drying out.

long. If any cracks were to occur during drying they would appear here, due to heavy-handed use of the axe. Dirt would also gather here over a period of time, and such a spoon is far less comfortable to use than one where the shoulders are shaped in a gentle flowing curve into the handle.

Once the bowl was hollowed out, the remainder of the rough spoon could be finished off using a wooden spokeshave and straight knives. The more waste that could be removed while the wood was still damp and easy to work the less hard work there would be when it came to the final finishing cuts.

Drying and boiling

Skilled carvers who are asked for advice often explain: 'never have to remove wood with a knife that you should have taken away with a spokeshave, and avoid using this tool to smooth away what should have been cut with the axe.' During the roughing-out stages, no attempt was made to obtain a smooth finish. At this stage the intention was only to remove as much waste as possible and to bring the spoon to as near its completed form as practicable.

Once the roughing out had been completed, the spoon was dried as quickly as possible to prevent any staining. During warm weather, a

John Davies, Aber-cuch, Pembrokeshire, carving domestic spoons.

sunny spot on an open windowsill would provide a warm circulation of air that could dry even the largest of ladles in a couple of days. On cold damp days in winter more heat was required, and small spoons would be left beside the stove or boiler overnight. Larger spoons were treated to a gentler heat for a little longer to avoid the risk of cracking, although if the wood had been carefully selected, and the axe-work kept under control, there would be little risk of a mishap.

Some makers boiled their spoons, either at this stage, or after completion, claiming that this raised the fibres of the wood, which could be cleaned off at the finishing stage. This eliminated roughness once the spoon began to be used. Some turners carried out much the same procedure for soup bowls, while others boiled the rough blanks at an early stage, which softened the fibres and made the wood easier to work.

Boiling would take place in a large iron cauldron in an outhouse (preferably not at the same time as the weekly wash or the making of pig swill). A few handfuls of salt were thrown in – this was believed to improve the taste of an otherwise bland timber.

Finishing

Once the partly-completed spoons were dry there was no immediate urgency to finish them, and often a large pile would accumulate before the work would commence. Finishing spoons was considered the easiest of tasks, something that could be done if the maker was a little under the weather – through illness perhaps, or from too much beer the previous night. Many spooncarvers preferred to keep old worn tools for finishing work, convinced that the thinness of the blades resulted in a finer finish. The amount of finishing work required would depend on the state of the spoon at its drying stage, and experience alone would decide just how much waste to leave to compensate for slight movement and to allow for 'pulling' into the final shape.

The first stage of finishing was to go over the entire spoon with a spokeshave, taking the finest of cuts, correcting any slight twists, and smoothing over the odd patch of rough grain. A plane with a finely set blade was the best tool for straightening the handles of cooking spoons and large ladles.

Traditional domestic spoons intended for everyday use were not glass-papered and certainly not polished until recent times. A good 'tooled' finish was considered sufficient – a fine finish would soon vanish once the spoons were dipped in hot water, which was the accepted method of sterilising domestic wood-ware. The practice of selling spoons with only a 'tooled' finish continued until the demise of the craft in the late 1930s, and the use of abrasive papers and polish has only been carried out in recent times.

With the exception of a few demonstrations at craft fairs, since the 1930s the only place where traditional spooncarving could be seen was at the Museum of Welsh Life, where it continued until the workshop was closed in 1999. At the time, the finished items were still suitable for domestic use, but most were bought as collectors' pieces. These customers became much more demanding when it came to finishing. A finer grade of abrasive paper was required, together with some form of polishing. The best proved to be a light application of cooking oil, or some of the various brands of polishing oils that had by then appeared on the market.

4. Design and method

Fragments of spoons excavated from the early Iron Age Glastonbury lake dwellings show the origin of the design for most Welsh domestic spoons up until the decline of the craft in the late 1930s. These excavations, which took place between 1892 and 1910, yielded a wide variety of fragments of wooden artefacts, and it was hoped that explorations at sites in Wales, like those at Llangors Lake, would result in further discoveries of spoons and domestic turnery, but this was not to be the case. Nevertheless, spoons and fragments of domestic items of wood from other European sites confirm that spoon design changed little during a period of over two thousand years.

Once they had familiarised themselves with a practical design, spooncarvers would retain it for a considerable period and, unlike potters and furniture-makers, were not influenced by changes in fashion and design. As they grew older they became even more reluctant to change their designs, passing them on to apprentices and kinfolk who in turn would pass them on to theirs. Although basic designs remained largely unchanged sometimes for a century or more, regional variations began to develop, but in contrast to other crafts, that of the spooncarver was among the least influenced by change elsewhere.

The regional variations found in Welsh domestic ware designs were very few and were mainly confined to eating spoons. These, unlike other kinds of spoons, were more likely to be the work of individual and part-time makers, who would be influenced by slight changes in design that they happened to come across.

Most of the variation was to be found in the handles. A broth spoon with a rounded handle, commonly known as the 'rat tail', was considered to be a

Examples of domestic spoons in sycamore

Pembrokeshire design, while a similar one with a flat handle was the favoured pattern for Carmarthenshire. There appears to be no regional design for neighbouring Ceredigion: craftsmen working in Ceredigion were happy with both designs and used either, depending on their proximity to the other two counties.

It is difficult to determine regional variation in other parts of Wales – there were no established woodturning centres in north Wales, for example. In Iorwerth Peate's book on Welsh rural craftsmen, *Y Crefftwr yng Nghymru*, which covers the period of the 1920s and earlier, a Caernarfonshire spoon maker describes the kind of spoon he made, which was known in the trade as the 'fish back', as it had a slight hollow in the face of the flat handle, and when laid on a level surface was expected to make contact at three points.

Traditional sycamore buttermilk spoon

The majority of domestic spoons were hand-carved throughout, without recourse to any mechanical device, but there were a few variations that were partly turned on a lathe. Not all part-time spoon makers had a water- or treadle-driven lathe, but a primitive pole lathe was quite adequate for most work. The practice of turning a whole spoon profile on a lathe and sawing down the middle to obtain one spoon from each side, which were later hollowed by hand, was well known to many production turners, but was completely alien to Welsh woodturning practice. Nor did Welsh carvers resort to complicated jigs and formers to complete a whole spoon on a lathe without the use of any traditional spooncarving tools. Such complicated devices have had a new lease of life following the increased interest in woodturning that has taken place during the past thirty to forty years, but they were never used by traditional Welsh turners and spoon makers.

The most common use of the lathe in spoonmaking was to turn the

25

handle, but in reality there was no justification for this, either on the grounds of speed or tasteful design. The mass-produced wooden spoons of today bear no resemblance to the beautiful, well-balanced and delicate products of the spooncarving era.

Many experts on domestic 'treen' (the term, derived from 'tree', is used to describe any small wooden object made for personal use) consider the work of 'British' carvers to be inferior to those on the continent, but it is now general opinion that this is incorrect. Spoons produced by Welsh carvers were certainly as good, if not better, than many of their continental counterparts.

Mounting a partly roughed-out spoon blank between the lathe centres and turning the handle was an easy enough task, but had the disadvantage that once the procedure had been completed it was no longer practical to return the piece to the lathe for finishing, unless a small waste piece had been retained at the front of the bowl.

Another object that required the use of a lathe was a bowl with an attached turned handle. This involved both spindle and face turning, which were dangerous procedures on any lathe whose speed could not be controlled. The use of a pole lathe, with its reciprocating action, would in theory allow the entire bowl to be turned right to the point where the handle joined the bowl, but it appears that most turners-cum-spoon-makers only used their lathes to complete the interior and top and bottom part of the bowl and the handle, and finished the remainder by hand.

A classic handled bowl made by the Welsh woodturner was one used for buttermilk. In order to obtain an overall length of about 12 inches (30 cm), a sweep of at least 16 inches (40 cm) above the lathe bed was required. Although a considerable sweep, this was not an uncommon height above the bed on traditional pole- and wheel-operated lathes. In some cases both handle and bowl were turned, but in the case of the traditional buttermilk ladle the handle, with a hook at the end, was shaped by hand. Another interesting feature seen on buttermilk ladles was the equal depths of the bowl and hook: this allowed the spoon to remain level and not tip when it had been filled and placed on a flat surface.

When it came to making salad servers from the mid-1900s, many carvers clung to the traditional designs, producing beautifully matching pairs of two eating spoons with fork prongs cut from one. Hard dense woods such as box and holly were favoured, but many were intended for decorative purposes only, often joined by a length of chain similar to the carved lovepoons.

Mixers were also popular in the 1950s and 1960s; easy to make, they were the ideal starting pieces for beginners, as they did not require the use of the dangerous hollowing knife. One particular design was claimed to be the 'traditional mixer', but as few of any great age have survived it is impossible to confirm if indeed this was the case.

Replicas of two domestic ladles: (top) English, with turned handle from the Pinto Collection; (bottom) An unusual ladle with a pouring lip from the Ceredigion Museum.

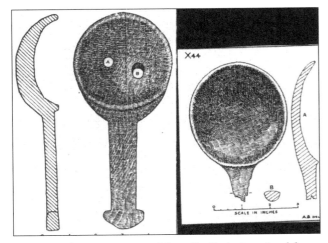

Domestic spoons recovered from the Early Iron Age lake dwellings at Glastonbury during excavations from 1892-1910.

5. Marketing

Wooden spoons in general, and eating spoons in particular, were not expected to have the same life expectancy as those made from metal. However well cared for they were, eating spoons would wear out at frequent enough intervals to ensure a steady demand from the makers, who sold their produce at local fairs and markets. Ladles, cooking spoons and other less frequently used items such as butter spoons would give some years of service, but eating spoons in daily use were considered to be ready for replacing about once a year.

The usual method of buying and selling all produce in rural Wales was through local fairs and markets, and wood-carvers, perhaps more than most craftsmen, had to take their produce to their customers. It was very seldom that a buyer would turn up on their doorstep.

Fairs were special events that took place only a few times a year, but markets were held weekly in most towns, and on a different day within an area of around thirty to forty miles. Going to market would involve an early start and a late return for those wishing to take advantage of a wide selling area. The amount of produce carried to markets by the various turners and spoon makers (who were usually one and the same), was in fact much larger than is generally thought: for example, William Rees of Henllan, one of the best known figures in the 1920s and 1930s, would take well over a hundred assorted spoons and ladles as well as a wide range of turned items to the markets of the three west Wales counties.

At the end of the day some unsold stock could be sold to local shops, presumably at retail price, but spoons were so cheap and the profit margin to the shopkeeper so low, it was hardly worth the effort of re-selling. Craftsmen who sold to retail outlets further away found the only loss of revenue was the cost of transporting their produce to the big cities. The price paid to the makers by the big city stores were about the same as those they themselves charged in their local markets. Both William Rees and the Davies Brothers did in fact supply some of the large London shops during the declining years of the trade in the 1930s, but this consisted mostly of turned bowls. Spoons were still confined to the home market.

It is therefore quite clear that spooncarving alone could not provide a living, and had to be supplemented by turned ware. The price of spoons in the mid 1930s were:

Broth spoons	1/6 (about 8p)
Cooking spoons	3/- (about 15p)
Ladles	6/- to 10/- (about 30p-50p)

A collection of traditional Welsh domestic spoons in holly

It should be realised these prices were for a dozen, and for bulk purchases, which suggests that a fair number of spoons were being sold to retailers and dealers in the markets as well as to individuals.

Attending a fair was a day of lost production, unless the maker had an assistant who could remain in the workshop. The indications are that even the smallest family concern did in fact manage to keep production going during their master's absence, and if all the tradesmen who are reputed to have attended several markets in a week actually did so it is difficult to see how they could have found time to produce. For most it was a six-day week and upward of ten hours a day to make ends meet. Survival depended on diversification, and a few acres of land and a range of production yielded far more than a few domestic utensils.

What carving work the recession of the 1930s had not yet put out of business, the Second World War finally killed off. By the late 1940s only a few part-time spoon makers remained, and most of them confined their work to special orders, exhibitions and competition items.

When the Welsh Folk Museum opened at Sain Ffagan near Cardiff in 1948, the authorities offered employment to W. R. (Bill) Evans, who was one of the few remaining rural woodturners at the time. He had learned his trade at the Aber-cuch workshops, which had included traditional domestic spooncarving. Apart from exhibiting the techniques of his craft, he was expected to teach apprentices, but most of these left early, having acquired few of the skills required.

The museum did not attempt to produce spoons or any other item on a commercial basis, but it was able to offer quality spoons for sale at a price that was a competitive alternative to the crude mass-produced factory spoons of the period. By the early 1950s they were being sold at the following prices:

Small eating spoons	2/6 (12p)
Cooking spoons	3/- (15p)
Ladles	5/- (25p)

This time the price was for single items. The apprentice's wage started at £3 a week, rising to £4 if he stuck it for two years. Working on the assumption that he could make a broth spoon in about an hour and a half, and worked a forty-four-hour week, one may calculate that he could just about produce enough to cover his salary.

By 1960 there were no other spoon makers left in Wales, but there was still a steady demand, many spoons being bought by foreign visitors as souvenirs. Occasionally elderly people who still ate their broth with a wooden spoon would make a purchase, although they would usually grumble at the price, which by then had risen to:

Broth spoons	8/- (40p)
Ladles	15/- (75p)

The author spooncarving at the Museum of Welsh Life, early 1980s

In the early 1970s the prices were 75p for a small spoon and £1.50 for a ladle, which was still well below a reasonable profit margin.

By this time the tourist boom was in full swing and a number of craft shops were opening up to cater to the demand for anything 'quaint' and Welsh. The revival in domestic spooncarving was weak: most craftsmen with the skill to make them concentrated instead on decorative lovepoons, but at around this time 'hippies' and those seeking a self-sufficient lifestyle were being attracted to rural Wales. Living off the land proved to be difficult, and spooncarving was among the many rural crafts that these

W. R. Evans making a spoon at the Welsh Folk Museum, 1959

newcomers to the countryside turned their hands to in an attempt to supplement their income.

Some took the work seriously and set up small workshops to produce all manner of domestic wood-ware, but when it came to making spoons in the traditional manner using only a few basic tools, many found it beyond their capabilities. With no knowledge of the craft, and often with limited woodworking skills, most of the attempts to make saleable spoons were little short of disastrous.

Before the present-day revival in craft fairs, all makers, whatever their trade, sold their produce through retail outlets, and had to endure a mark-up of a hundred percent or more. With a small eating spoon selling in these shops for around £2 each, making a spoon for £1 became even less economical than having to compete with factory-made spoons in the 1930s.

With most hand-carved domestic spoons now being bought as decorative rather than practical items, traditional sycamore has lost popularity to more colourful woods, which are also much more expensive to buy and take longer to work.

At the beginning of the twenty-first century, a well-made broth spoon, if it can be found, should sell for about £5. This is below minimum wage for over an hour's labour. While work could be speeded up with the use of a bandsaw instead of an axe for roughing out, for example, this could result not only in a weaker product but also carries greater risks to the maker. Skilled craftsmen used to work fast by nature and the old saying 'practice makes master' is true, but speed could also result in accidents, and many an elderly

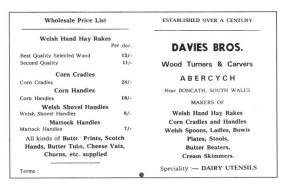

Wholesale Price List		ESTABLISHED OVER A CENTURY
Welsh Hand Hay Rakes	Per doz.	
Best Quality Selected Wood	13/-	**DAVIES BROS.**
Second Quality	11/-	Wood Turners & Carvers
Corn Cradles		A B E R C Y C H
Corn Cradles	24/-	Near BONCATH, SOUTH WALES
Corn Handles		MAKERS OF
Corn Handles	18/-	Welsh Hand Hay Rakes
Welsh Shovel Handles		Corn Cradles and Handles
Welsh Shovel Handles	8/-	Welsh Spoons, Ladles, Bowls
Mattock Handles		Plates, Stools,
Mattock Handles	7/-	Butter Beaters,
All kinds of Butte Prints, Scotch Hands, Butter Tubs, Cheese Vats, Churns, etc. supplied		Cream Skimmers.
Terms :		Speciality :— DAIRY UTENSILS

Trade Price List, Aber-cuch Workshops, 1935

craftsman gained the scars to prove it. The pressure of speed also resulted in a lowering of standards, but spooncarvers were no different from other craftsmen, and had to tread the narrow line between quality and quantity when it came to earning a living. Cutting corners and saving time by making the maximum use of machinery for the initial shaping should no longer be viewed as critically as it was a few decades ago. Most items of 'treen' that appear on the market are now judged by their final appearance: how that appearance is achieved is no longer as important as it was in the past.

Wholesale Price List		Wholesale Price List	
		Butter Beaters	
Wooden Spoons			Per doz.
	Per doz.	Butter Beaters, 8 in. turned in one piece	13/-
Small Pointed Hand-made Spoons	1/6	Butter Beaters, 9 in. turned in one piece	15/-
Ordinary Welsh Pat " "	1/9	**Cream Skimmers**	
Pickle and Pudding Spoons	3/- to 6/-	Cream Skimmers, 8 in.	7/-
Butter Scoops	3/- to 6/-	Cream Skimmers, 9 in.	8/-
Welsh Ladles		**Milk Plugs**	
Welsh Ladles	5/-, 6/-, 8/-, 10/-	Milk Plugs	2/6
Welsh Bowls		**Cream Stirrers**	
Welsh Bowls	3/-, 4/-, 5/4, 6/-	Cream Stirrers	6/-
Plates or Trenchers		**Welsh Rd. Stools**	
Plates or Trenchers	3/-, 4/-, 5/4, 6/-	Welsh Rd. Stools	12/-, 15/-, 18/-, 21/-
Handled Bowls		**Turned Cheese Vats**	
Handled Bowls	12/-	Made to Order.	

Trade Price List, Aber-cuch Workshops, 1935

*The author displaying the
different steps in carving a
traditional domestic spoon*

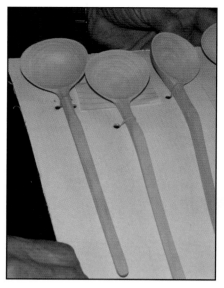

Traditional domestic spoons by Andrew Jones, a spooncarver from Lampeter

A rack of spoons by Andrew Jones

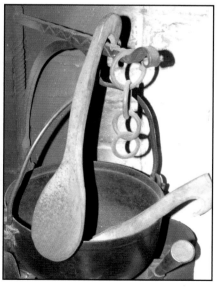

A traditional rack at the Museum of Welsh Slate, Llanberis

Traditional 'cawl' ladles by the fireplace, Museum of Welsh Slate, Llanberis

34

A selection of traditionally styled domestic spoons carved by the author

The author with his finished spoons in his workshop

Richard Downes, Swansea carving out the bowl of a lovespoon

Mike Bartlett working in a garden shed in Dwygyfylchi

Edwin Williams at his work-bench in Pontarddulais

Mike Davies carving a lovespoon at an exhibition

A selection of Mike Davies' lovespoons

Small lovespoons by Huw Jones

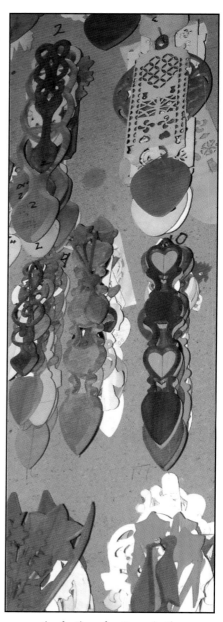

A lovespoon in a gallery

A selection of patterns in the
Pontarddulais workshop

38

A pattern marked out on wood in the Dwygyfylchi workshop

Skill and patience are needed while carving the ingenious patterns

A basket of lovespoons – work in process

Finished commissions

One of Siôn Llewellyn's lovespoons   *Attention to detail*

A variety of patterns in a craftsman's workshop

Panel handle, rectangular, with fretted wheel

On this stem, the outline of the heart has been cut and studded with pins

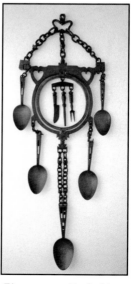

With tapering panel handle

Five spoons attached to a circular frame

A panel handle fretted with heart and geometrical devices

42

Leslie Williams, Capel Coch, Llanrwst with a stock of lovespoons ready for the market

An example of a 'double' spoon by Leslie

More examples of Siôn Llewellyn's patterns

Large spoon, carved from a broad flat board

Heart, circle and soul motifs on this lovespoon; carved in 1840

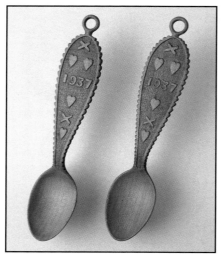

Pair of identical lovespoons by D. Lewis, Ffostrasol, Ceredigion, which won first prize at Llangeitho Eisteddfod, 1937

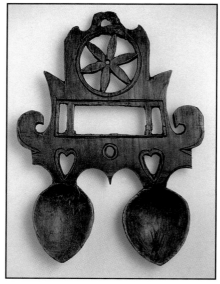

Panel handle lovespoon with two bowls

A finished commission by Mike Bartlett

Siôn Llewellyn exhibiting at the Royal Welsh Show, Llanelwedd

The craftsman's feat celebrated in a Cardiff craft shop

A model of a spooncarver in the shop's gallery

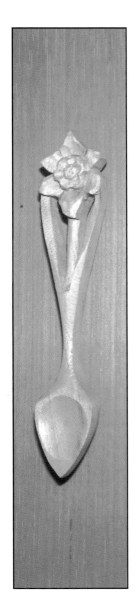

Examples of Edwin Williams' lovespoons

6. The present day

The craft of the domestic spooncarver is obsolete in Wales today, and few if any carvers are capable of producing spoons in the traditional manner. Attempts at a revival during the late 1980s were short lived, and the dwindling band of elderly spooncarvers who set up evening classes in parts of rural west Wales in the 1970s and 1980s to teach the skills met with little response.

Coming at a time of increased leisure activities, and an upsurge in all aspects of rural woodworking, together with the formation of numerous carving clubs and societies in many of the south Wales urban areas, it is difficult to understand why the craft was not revived. One would have expected that the increasing number of lovespoon carvers who mastered the basic techniques of whittling would have found the transformation both interesting and challenging.

There is no longer any financial reward to be gained from the production of high quality domestic spoons. For those who still prefer wooden cooking spoons to their plastic substitutes, the products of third world countries are available cheaply at specialist kitchen shops. Machine-made domestic spoons of a remarkably good quality are sold through a well-known Swedish retail outlet at a fraction of the price of hand-made items. There is also a limited demand for reproduction 'treen' from re-enactment groups, film companies and collectors, and this includes a demand for domestic spoons. What is in dispute is the price these bodies are prepared to pay for high quality hand-made reproductions.

The revival in rural crafts during the past two decades or so did result in a small niche market for hand-made domestic spoons made by a few woodworkers, most of whom live in rural areas. Many claimed to have invented a special finishing formula, which involved pickling the finished spoon in a secret solution and then heating it in a microwave oven. Others went to great lengths to perfect their technique, even to the extent of guaranteeing their products for many years to come. As many of them disappeared within a short space of time, the guarantees were not worth a great deal. Some of this work still finds its way into craft galleries, but its quality leaves much to be desired.

During the period of many years when I was directly involved in rural woodworking skills I met a number of these present-day carvers, and corresponded with others, and was most impressed by the quality of their work. Most of them had adapted traditional spoons to pleasant contemporary designs, using a variety of hard, close-grained and often

Contemporary variations of domestic spoons using colourful fruit woods.

colourful hardwoods. Their items were not cheap, but the prices reflected the skill, time and effort put into each individual piece.

Nowadays the only remnants of what was once a widespread craft in Wales are the occasional competition for 'cawl' spoons which may be found among the entries at rural agricultural shows. The appearance of the same exhibitors year after year confirms that younger competitors have no inclination to take up the challenge.

As the spoonmaking skills of the past declined and languished during the second half of the twentieth century, traditional carvers were much sought after to give demonstrations at shows and county fairs the length and breadth of Wales. Some, like Tim Wade, took the survival of the craft so seriously that he approached the few remaining experienced makers to learn the basic skills. This was unnecessary, as he was a competent woodworker who in later years went on to hone his skills to a high degree, and became one of the foremost authorities on rural woodworking. He also spent some time in central Europe researching country crafts, and returned with many innovative ideas.

As the century drew to a close and the attempts at a revival had mostly fallen on stony ground, the only place where the skills of domestic spooncarving remained was at specialist rural craft fairs. Enthusiasts came and went, some bringing with them their efforts at constructive criticism, others to watch, often in awe, as a spoon appeared as if by magic from a rough block of wood.

The only hope for a revival now is through the number of rural craft courses being organised during the summer months up and down the country, but there are numerous problems. Sharp tools are dangerous in inexperienced hands, and with the tightening up of existing Health and Safety regulations and the current compensation culture, the few remaining tutors are becoming increasingly reluctant to offer a course that carries even the slightest risk of injury.

Photographs and films of past spooncarvers at work are stored at museums and archives and, sadly, this craft, like so many others, can now usually only be viewed on a screen.

Spoons and ladles in hollywood using the bark as a decorative feature

Len Evans, Abercynffig, Glamorgan hollowing a soup ladle, 1971

Lovespoons

The custom of making small domestic and personal objects and decorating them with symbols of love, initials, names and dates was common in rural communities in Britain as well as much of Western Europe from the late Middle Ages to the end of the nineteenth century. Such objects came under the general term of 'love tokens', and were made from a wide range of materials such as paper, bone, glass and china as well as wood.

In some cases the basic artefact could be bought and decorated by the donor before it was passed on to a loved one: sailors would buy glass rolling pins and incise decorations on them during long voyages, along similar lines to those they would carve or incise on pieces of bone and walrus tusk. Small items of furniture acquired in readiness for married life could be decorated with names and dates and other forms of embellishment prior to a couple setting up home. Those who were not so competent with their hands could buy ready-made tokens, such as elaborate H-shaped combs and valentine cards, although the latter were confined to one day a year.

Most love tokens, however, were the sole work of the donor, and wood, being readily available and easy to work, became the main material that was used. Wooden love tokens are called 'treen', which covers all small objects intended for personal and domestic use that were made from 'the wood of a tree'. The term 'love token' covers a wide range of items, which varied from area to area and country to country, depending on local crafts and customs.

In parts of England where lace making was popular, for example, bobbins were made in large quantities and were always an acceptable gift among women. Knitting sheaths were also useful objects in areas where women supplemented the family income by knitting. 'Stay busks', lengths of wood that were used as stiffeners in the bodice of a dress, were often decorated with symbols of love and personal initials, and were also popular in parts of England, but the one type of love token that had no utilitarian purpose whatsoever was what has become known as the lovespoon.

A token of affection

The lovespoon functioned essentially as a message from a young man to a young woman. The man may well have been illiterate, was possibly tongue-tied or at least shy, and perhaps found it easier to convey his

A typical example of converting early domestic spoons into tokens of affection by adding a simple link, date and initials. The pair are from Pembrokeshire and carry the date 1761 and the initials G.I. on the back.

feelings by presenting the woman of his desires with a token that symbolised his affection for her. At a time when practical skills were an important consideration in a suitor, the maker's skill and ingenuity would have gone a long way to influence the strength of a girl's response to her suitor's devotion.

A few decorated spoons of this nature were made in parts of northern England, but the indications are that it was almost exclusively a Welsh custom. The claim that love tokens similar to the Welsh lovespoon were made in Scandinavia, notably in Norway, cannot be authenticated according to leading Norwegian folklorists, although there is a striking resemblance. Others that originated from the north of England and found their way into various collections may have been made as love tokens, but the numbers are far too small to indicate a tradition on the same scale as that in Wales. A few spoons do carry dates, but the majority do not, and dating these is virtually impossible, as the makers were not influenced in any way by fashions of their period. These examples are too recent for scientific dating techniques to be useful, and in any case this would only date the wood and not the time the object was made. Even dated specimens are not foolproof: copies of earlier spoons are known to have been made, complete with the original date. The original could later be lost or destroyed, leaving the replica as the sole survivor.

The origins of the lovespoon are vague and uncertain, largely on account of an almost complete lack of documentary evidence. Many other Welsh folk customs relating to courtship and marriage are well documented, but this custom, which was so unique to Wales, is largely absent from the record. As J. Rosenberg observes in *An Autumn in Wales*, well-known English travellers who published accounts of their journeys in Wales – writers such as Daniel Defoe, Thomas Pennant and, later, George Borrow, to name but a few – made no mention of the custom, which is considered to have been at its height at the time of their visits. Some had opportunities to witness courtship and marriage customs at first hand, and if the custom of carving decorative spoons was as widespread as we now assume it to have been, surely some of these observers would have seen young men whittling away at pieces of wood.

This lack of first-hand evidence led to widespread speculation among historians, writers, and collectors about the origins and background of the custom. It is impossible to determine how widespread the custom was, and although there is ample evidence that lovespoons were made throughout Wales from the middle of the seventeenth century until their decline towards the end of the nineteenth century, one may only speculate as to the number that were produced. Many would not have survived, and it would have been only a matter of time before some of the most delicate were destroyed.

Origins and meanings

The question most frequently discussed by researchers and by those interested in the custom is why young men in Wales should choose to give a spoon rather than a more practical object as a present. There was common belief among early collectors such as Owen Evan Thomas that some lovespoons may have been put to ritual use, but there has never been any evidence to support this theory. Those spoons that do bear signs of wear to the bowl were probably damaged when the spoon fell from its hanging place onto a hard surface, which resulted in the chipping of the delicate front. Even today lovespoons are still susceptible to this kind of damage. There are some who insist that the spoon had no symbolic significance at all, but was merely to confirm to the girl in question that her suitor was capable enough with his hands to make many of the items that were required to set up a home. This is sound enough in theory. However, most collectors of 'treen', including Ernest Pinto, settle for the same answer, and quote from *Trotters Distressed Seaman* of 1789, which observes of sailors: 'they are stowed spoonways, so closely locked in one another's arms that it is difficult to move.' While spoons of a similar size certainly do fit closely together, and this could be one reason for their symbolism in courtship, it must be remembered that only manufactured silver spoons fit this category, and it was only the gentry who would have been familiar with such objects. On the other hand, suggestions by some researchers that lovespoons are copies of elaborate silver spoons given by the gentry as christening and betrothal gifts must carry an element of truth, particularity when the shape of the bowl is considered. This is shallow and oval, and very different from the traditional Welsh 'cawl' spoon.

There are those who suggest that there was no symbolic 'spooning' connection, and that the custom, which was practised only among rural young men, was a gradual development of domestic spooncarving, which had been a widespread basic pastime, and also a necessity. As already discussed, although eating spoons were not in general use before the seventeenth century, rough wooden paddles for stirring and cooking would have been made by young men much earlier than this. We have no means of knowing how long spoonmaking was practiced before the decorating began, however. It must have been a gradual process, and as the custom gained popularity, spoons became increasingly decorative, until they reached a stage at which they were regarded more as tokens of affection than as practical objects.

Many original lovespoons do not display a high standard of workmanship compared to decorative spoons from other parts of Europe, but this is understandable when one bears in mind that they were not made by skilled craftsmen. The difficulty of discriminating between Welsh spoons and those from the continent has led to the supposition that any spoon of a crude and badly made nature must be of Welsh origin. This is unjustified. Unlike many other love tokens, which could be bought or commissioned, lovespoons were always solely the work of the donor, and not of a specialist, or, later, even of a part-time specialist, as was the case with domestic spoons.

The lovespoon eventually developed into an elaborate token of affection, an object of time-consuming attention on which the maker would lavish all the skill and patience at his command. As Jonathan Levi observes in *Treen for the table*, many early lovespoons started as initials, chip-carving decoration, or as simple symbols carved on ordinary domestic spoon handles, with the possible addition of a ring carved at the end.

It is not to difficult to conjure up a romantic image of early spoon carvers – rural lads whittling away in a stable loft during the long winter evenings, or sailors passing away the time during weeks at sea, or even prisoners serving sentences, who were known to while away the long hours carving chains. All of these had some time on their hands, and perhaps thought of a loved one far away; what they lacked in skill they made up for in patience.

The tools used by early lovespoon carvers would have been primitive, probably consisting of little more than a pocket knife, with perhaps an axe and a saw for the roughing out. The makers had neither plans nor technical knowledge, although they might have been influenced by someone else's efforts, and under the circumstances it is remarkable what they managed to produce. In many instances the end result was crude in the extreme, but there is no doubt that the time spent in decorating even a basic lovespoon was considerable, and such an object was regarded with pride by the recipient. If marriage did take place between donor and recipient, such a token would hang in a prominent place in the home, in much the same way that wedding photographs are treasured today.

The significance of accepting such a gift has always been vague: some speculate that a popular girl might receive several such tokens from suitors before making up her mind. There are many who are not convinced by this theory, largely on the grounds that the effort put into making the spoons was so great that the donor would have been fairly sure of a positive response before making the offer. An acceptance was certainly not a sign of betrothal, as has been believed, but more likely indicated that a certain understanding had been reached between the couple, and they would henceforth be seen together and regarded as sweethearts by the community.

Neither was the giving of a lovespoon, as has often been suggested, a formal declaration of a pending marriage, as such a formality was something that only took place among the middle and upper classes. In rural communities 'official' marriages were not that frequent until the end of the eighteenth century, and many did not bother to exchange vows at all, or at most went through an unofficial secular ceremony in a public house on a fair day. It must be remembered that until 1837 official marriage had to take place in church, and as for numerous reasons many people did not frequent churches, it was often the case that a couple simply set up home together.

It is interesting to note that the term 'spooning' became accepted in local vocabulary as an alternative for 'courting', and the word 'spooner' is still used among Welsh speakers in parts of south and west Wales when referring to a young woman's male companion. With unmarried cohabitation once again common, the term is now beginning to be used to describe a woman's male partner regardless of his or her age.

Surrounded as we are by cheap mass-produced material goods, it is very difficult to imagine today the importance that was given to the making and giving of such tokens of affection. Other kinds of tokens, including many unusual specimens, such as coins cut in two (one half for each partner to carry), various brooches, and a wide range of personal items are well documented in books on folk customs, but those tokens made by the donors themselves are in a category of their own, and of these lovespoons are the most numerous in Wales. The fact that so many

*Wooden knife and fork joined by chain –
a later variation of the lovespoon theme*

*Two lovespoons, one with a broad panel
handle, the other with a slotted handle*

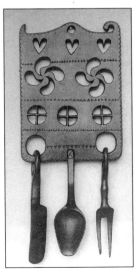

*Two spoons connected at the
top and mounted on a stand
– originally from Tenby*

*Lovespoon with slotted
chamber and fretted panel*

Broad panel lovespoon

have survived is clear evidence of the widespread practice of this custom by young men in rural areas, which is unique to Wales.

Three lovespoons with narrow panel handles

1. Decoration and design

Original lovespoons were made from wood, and no surviving examples in any other material have come to light. This is perhaps rather surprising, as a number of other love tokens were made from bone, the only other suitable raw material that could be carved into a spoon.

Every effort was made to carve the spoons out of a single piece of wood without any breaks or joins, and despite the obvious difficulties for the inexperienced carver, some remarkable work was achieved. This was particularly evident in the form of chains, links, and 'balls in cages', or lanterns, as some prefer to call them. There were a few exceptions to the 'one piece' rule that featured clever jointing, which, as the dirt of years built up on the surface, became impossible to detect, but the vast majority of original lovespoons were carved from a single solid block of wood.

Some makers would put size before quality, and spoons a yard long were not unknown. Large spoons were usually made by those who could not adapt to fine delicate work, and very crude examples are common. The quality of the work does not appear to have improved over time: the earliest dated specimen of 1677 indicates a far higher degree of skill than many spoons produced some two hundred years later.

The most popular choice of wood for the lovespoon, as for the domestic spoon, was sycamore, probably due to its wide availability, good carving qualities, and its use in domestic wood-ware. It is not known if it was used in its 'green' unseasoned condition, as was the practice for domestic spooncarving, but at least the initial rough shaping would have taken place while the wood was still wet, making it easier to carve with the simple tools that were available. In any case the time involved in carving many an intricate lovespoon was so long that the timber would have dried long before its completion.

Any attempt at carving intricate designs in wet wood would have had its problems: the danger of cracking would always have been present in the early stages, and thin panels would also have warped as the timber dried. Very few of the originals bear the marks of such damage, and it is reasonable to assume the maker would have been able to rectify minor mishaps as he proceeded, or be forced to start again if anything went seriously wrong. A few unfinished original spoons have survived, whose carver had perhaps lost his lady love, or perhaps he found the task too daunting, or some misfortune befell him.

Another popular choice of timber was fruit wood – apple in particular. According to tradition this wood was used because of its connection with Adam and Eve in the Garden of Eden, but there is no documentary evidence to support this. Harder than sycamore, apple was probably used for no other reason than its excellent working qualities and fine finish. Other woods were also used: foreign timbers, such as varieties of mahogany, could have been acquired by sailors or those with access to furniture-making materials. Years of patina and polish, to say nothing of dirt, together with the practice of hanging lovespoons on the chimney breast, and perhaps staining them at a later date make it almost impossible to identify the wood of many originals.

During the years of the revival, boxwood, holly and elder became favourite timbers. These hard, close-grained woods can be worked to a fine detail and can be finished to near perfection. Nowadays, commercial carvers use lime a great deal; it is one of the most popular carving woods, but the pale colour shows every blemish, and many resort to staining to hide the most obvious disfigurements. Other makers use a wide range of imported woods, more because of availability than suitability.

A similarity between the lovespoon and the functional domestic spoon, out of which it was a natural development and which, left as it was, gave little room for decoration, lies in the most noticeable feature of all original lovespoons: the fact that the bowl was left unadorned. Some were shaped to represent a rough heart, but on the whole they were almost identical to the crude domestic spoons that were made for daily use.

The first and most obvious way to provide an area for decoration was to enlarge the handle into a wide panel, often large in proportion to the bowl of the spoon. These panels varied in thickness and width. The thinnest were usually pierced through, and various patterns were cut with a thin-bladed knife. Thicker panels were sometimes chip-carved. This highly effective method of embellishing flat surfaces was often used on Tudor and Jacobean furniture, but most of such work carried out on lovespoons was crude, and involved little more than picking the surface: it did not penetrate to a sufficient depth to be considered genuine chip-carving.

The insertion of red or black wax into incised or slightly hollowed surfaces, either as a planned design or a border is to be found on some spoons. This method of decoration could either be a separate design or appear in conjunction with pierced or chip-carving surfaces. Most of the surviving specimens featuring wax decoration (and there are very few of them) are very crude, with one exception in the Museum of Welsh Life collection. This is almost certainly the work of a sailor. Regrettably one piece is missing.

A few examples feature a sunken panel into which a piece of glass was

An unusual 19th century spoon depicting a pair of spectacles

fitted; behind this was displayed either a lock of hair or part of a letter (photographs arrived much too late to be included). In many cases the glass has long since vanished, but the panel remains to testify to its original use.

Another easy method of decoration, but one that was very little used, was to burn in a design with a heated nail. The few remaining examples of the so-called 'poker work' are crude and bear no resemblance to the highly skilled pyrography used successfully by carvers today.

Although a few lovespoons carry dates, they are certainly in the minority, and these only indicate the year. This confirms that the early lovespoons were not given to commemorate a particular event, such as a wedding, and in any case for centuries dates had little significance in rural life (in some instances even the clergy were hard-pressed to remember the correct date to enter on church records).

Low relief carving, which is so popular with present-day spoon makers, is seldom found on early lovespoons. This type of decoration, which involves raising the design from the background by cutting around it to a shallow depth, requires at least a few basic carving tools, and their absence from the rural tool kit is the main reason why this effective method of embellishment was seldom used. The best most could do was a rough design incised on the surface.

It may well be that the few examples of spoons with low relief carving that are classified as lovespoons are in fact the 'spoon' part of a pair of salad servers. Any matching spoon and fork that are not joined together must be regarded with suspicion, and were probably never intended as love tokens.

The carving of initials was much more common than actual names, but those that are to be found are invariably the girl's name, with one exception: on a plain spoon in the Museum of Welsh Life collection the name JOHN has been pierced through the handle. Did the recipient have so many suitors that it was necessary for this one to identify himself?

The roughest, crudest and heaviest lovespoons that I am aware of are

A rare and superb example of captive cages spoon that has been ruined after being coated with a thick layer of paint

two that were based on a butter scales. They are quite unique, not only because they are free standing, but because they are very much on the borderline between what is considered a lovespoon and some other form of token.

A fascinating type of lovespoon which is guaranteed to attract attention is the 'ball and cage' variety. These are among the earliest lovespoons, proving that sophisticated spoons developed by the middle of the seventeenth century (if one dated 1667 can be proved to be genuine). These spoons feature a number of 'balls' running freely between pillars, normally in what is a square 'cage', but there are instances of octagonal ones, which demand a much higher degree of skill.

Normally they are found either as part of a length of chain, above the bowl and below a decorated panel, or as a feature in themselves. The number of balls vary from one or two to a dozen or more and, as one would expect, there are some original spoons with empty 'cages', their contents, if they ever had any, having fallen out over the years.

If more than two or three 'balls' were made in one length of timber it was common practice to separate them from each other by leaving a solid block in the 'cage'. This had the advantage of strengthening the pillars and preventing loose play, which would not only allow the 'balls' to drop out, but would leave the maker open to accusations that they were made separately and pushed in, rather than carved inside as they should have been.

The so-called 'balls in cages' are a well-known feature in folk art throughout the world, and they are not difficult to execute once the knack has been acquired. The nearer the balls are to a perfect sphere the better they look, but in most of the original lovespoons they fall far short of this perfection. The challenge, after all, was to get them running freely inside the pillars without falling out. Indeed in recent times, any carver who has managed to produce a near perfect sphere is often accused of having inserted it by some devious means.

Another feature along the same lines is what, for lack of a better description, one might call 'multiple cages'. Here 'cages' are carved within each other, a remarkable feat, and there are two such specimens in the collection of the Museum of Welsh Life. Regrettably, one of them was badly damaged by being painted at some time in the past.

The whittling of lengths of chain from one piece of wood without breaks in the links is common throughout the world, and on the whole the examples featured on Welsh lovespoons are of a high standard. In order to qualify as a lovespoon, however, something that represents a bowl has to be attached to one or both ends of the chain, and in some cases a variety of pivots and swivels were incorporated as well. The links of these chains were usually straight on the early spoons. The sophisticated twisted versions achieved by present-day specialist carvers appear to have been beyond the capabilities of most of the young suitors. In early spoons, links varied in number from three or four to a dozen or more. No doubt it was the case of carrying on whittling until all the wood was used up or a link was broken, at which point, in the absence of super glue, one could go no further.

Chains were not only confined to lovespoons. A few knitting sheaths carry them also, but they were hardly strong enough to be worn as personal adornment, although lengths of chain made of hard thorn-wood were used as girdles in France in the Middle Ages.

A well-known and much copied nineteenth century ball and chain spoon

Original lovespoons were not 'finished' in any way but left with the tool marks on the surface, although some may have been scraped with bone or some other sharp object. Those made for wedding gifts and, at a later date, as competition pieces were given the 'beauty treatment', and although there were often set rules that forbade polishing, the prize would invariably be awarded to the spoon with the best finish. Carvers had their own secret ways of achieving the desired finish. One popular method was to rub the spoon with the knuckle joint of an animal bone. It is sad to note that many fine original lovespoons were ruined during the Victorian period by being coated with a thick dark varnish to match the sombre mood when the queen was in mourning.

2. Symbols

The most contentious aspect of both original and contemporary lovespoons is the significance of the various symbols that appear on them. During the revival period of the last forty years, considerable speculation has arisen regarding the importance, or otherwise, of these symbols. This has become even more confusing with the appearance of dozens of new motifs that were never seen on the original spoons.

Present-day makers of lovespoons insist that all these motifs have symbolic meaning, and some go to great lengths to convince their customers by issuing leaflets with their purchases explaining their so-called 'language of love'. While there is no evidence whatsoever to support this interpretation, it is a common belief that young men who made the originals may have been shy and unable to express their feelings, and resorted to various symbols to get their message across.

Some carvers during the early revival period let it be known that every spoon they made 'told a story', which may have stirred the imagination of those with romantic inclinations, but only confused even further anyone attempting a serious study of the subject. There are, of course, many well-known symbols that are linked with love, courtship, and marriage to be found on lovespoons, some dating back hundreds of years, and not only confined to Britain but common throughout western Europe. The most prominent is the heart, and although not all lovespoons depict this symbol, there is no doubt it was in common use on all types of love tokens.

Hearts were carved singly or in pairs, and in some cases several were used to form a pattern. They were pierced through the panels, incised on the surface, or intertwined, and would vary in shape, size, and position. Some would be used as borders around initials or dates, and although it was uncommon to find links carved as hearts on original spoons, contemporary carvers have utilized this technique to good effect.

Another well-known original symbol is that of the 'comma' form. Some early collectors of lovespoons believed it was copied from Paisley shawls, which is quite possible as they were widely worn in Wales, but examples have appeared on spoons before these shawls became popular. Another suggestion is that it was the symbol for the soul in Egyptian mythology (the soul was said to leave the body through the nostril – hence the similarity of the symbol). This is one of the most difficult interpretations to accept: how such a symbol might have been transmitted is entirely unclear yet it still remains the most frequently quoted.

Diamonds were thought to represent wealth (though not necessarily

Typical nineteenth century lovespoons in the Museum of Welsh Life Collection

monetary wealth). The most likely reason for carving diamonds and other geometrical designs is surely the ease with which they could be executed, all being well within the modest skills of most young lovers.

Wheels in their various forms were considered to represent the 'wheel of life', and were often adapted from the well-known floral design marked out with a pair of dividers. Some were chip-carved, others pierced, and neither were easy to cut out successfully in any but the hardest of woods.

Celtic ribbon motifs are uncommon on original spoons and have only recently become popular, due to the upsurge of interest in all things Celtic. Another symbol much used by present-day carvers but never seen on any originals is the horseshoe, closely followed by wedding bells.

One of the most unusual motifs found on lovespoons, which has defied understanding, is the motif of knives and forks, which are invariably carved in three dimensions. There are a few examples of forks being made at the end of a length of chain rather than a spoon, but whether this was only a variation, or had some other significance is unknown. Most knives and forks appeared in pairs, usually on either side of the main spoon. One interesting speculation is that they symbolised the maker's wish for children, as they represented extra mouths to feed. This is something of a variation on the theory that 'captive balls' represented the desired number of children. Another more down to earth theory was that the maker who depicted a knife and fork on his spoon hoped to be fed – a modest expectation of married life in the past.

The methods used by the suitor to suggest the number of children the proposed marriage would bring have been a major source of interest to collectors and researchers alike, and there have been some disagreements.

An early nineteenth century lovespoon in fruit wood with a scratched outline of a house, tree and the initials 'H.W., 1822'

Ernest Pinto suggests that it was the number of links in a chain that represented the number of offspring, but this theory did not meet with widespread approval, on the grounds of the large number of links involved. Chains with well in excess of a dozen links were made, and although large families were common at the time, such a number might well have given the girl cause to reconsider her suitor.

The most popular theory, therefore, and the one most often repeated these days, is that it was the number of 'balls' in the cavities that represented future children. The number of balls varies from two to a dozen, and in terms of numbers is the more acceptable of the two theories. No doubt the less skilled carver would have found a few dropping out during his efforts, but on the whole it was easier to control their number than the number of links in a chain, because the usual method in chain carving was to make the spoon first, and then proceed with the links until all the wood was used up, or a broken one put an end to the work. It was therefore rather difficult for the inexperienced carver to determine ahead of time the number of links he could finish. (An interesting point, although not relevant in this case, is that chain carving is the only way a piece of wood can be made longer by cutting it.)

It is not difficult to imagine the connection that chains and links may have had with marriage, but the theory that they were only made by sailors is incorrect. The only spoons with chains or links that can be attributed exclusively to sailors are those with an anchor or some other seafaring symbol attached. Spoons decorated with inlaid red and black sealing wax are also attributed to the work of sailors.

Chain carving was a popular form of folk art in some of the eastern states of America, particularly Kentucky and Indiana, and they ranged from small delicate pieces to huge links several feet in length, as Simon Bronner documents in his book *Chain Carvers*. It is known that prisoners also carved chains, and what could be more symbolic for someone in such an unfortunate situation. Ernest Pinto notes a fine specimen that is said to be the work of a prisoner of war in Cardiff jail during the Napoleonic conflict. Another unusual spoon from this period which depicted a very accurate figure in the uniform of the Montgomeryshire Yeomanry was mentioned by Dorothy Wright in an article for *Embroidery* magazine in 1937. Regrettably its present whereabouts is unknown.

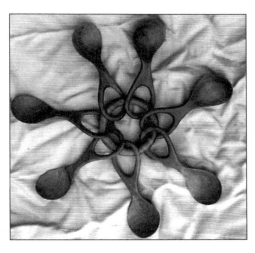

Lovespoon of the 'endless chain' technique in applewood made by the author and based on an original in the Pinto Collection said to have been made by a prisoner during the Napoleonic Wars.

Chip-carving is a well-known universal whittling technique, and need not necessarily have any connection with love tokens. It was an opportunity to show off individual skill, or to pass away long hours. Chip-carving has always been a popular method of decoration on all types of folk art, and is the ideal way to cover a large area of flat, plain surface. It is not easy to do well, and much of what appears on lovespoons is crude and not comparable to the fine work found on furniture in the Alpine countries. Even modern-day carvers shy away from attempting it unless they are highly skilled.

Claims that chip-carving has some religious significance have never been proven and it is generally accepted it was only used for decoration. With the exception of crosses, there are no religious symbols to be found on early lovespoons, which is rather surprising. Dorothy Wright also suggested that spoons with twelve links denote the Apostles, and three together the Holy Trinity, while the swivel was a symbol of matrimony. The speculation that lovespoons have a connection with ancient Catholic ceremonials is difficult to support. One particular spoon, which according to tradition came from a farmhouse near Dolgellau where it was greatly treasured, was known as the 'Sacred Spoon', and was said to have been rescued from nearby Cymer Abbey after the dissolution of the monasteries. Its design has no similarity to the typical lovespoon, but it was said that local young men based some of their efforts upon it. It was dated at the time to be from around 1500. Whether this was the one I was shown by its owner, who refused to discuss how and from where he obtained it, or whether I saw a later copy, I will not ever know.

A significant occasion could be an inspiration for the carving of a lovespoon, and the opening of the Menai Bridge in 1826 resulted in two spoons depicting it (and probably more). Another celebration was Queen Victoria's Jubilee in 1897 – several spoons appear to have been influenced by this occasion. One spoon, which depicts the crown, the royal arms, the word 'Jubilee' and an inserted picture of the queen, is said to have been made by an old man in Chester asylum. It was also said that he intended to give it to the queen, but this never occurred. The location of this spoon is also unknown.

Another challenging motif on spoons was a bunch of keys, together with padlocks and keyholes, which could represent imprisonment – either real imprisonment or symbolic imprisonment through marriage.

Double spoons are uncommon, and more than this number are rare. Pairs, where they occur, are found side by side at the bottom of a panel, or at both ends of a chain. They probably represent unity. Smaller spoons attached to the main panel are very rare, although present-day carvers are known to use this variant to denote children.

Some less common motifs that display the ingenuity of the maker are occasionally found. Among the most interesting are a pair of spectacles, a spoon carved in the form of a rib bone (a Biblical touch, surely), a pair of sugar tongs, and several spoons attached to a ring. One specimen carries the outline of a house crudely cut into the surface, possibly to inform the girl that the maker had a home ready, or the ability to build one. Young suitors carved what was within their ability, or whatever influenced them, which may or may not have had a connection to the mysterious world of love.

The name of the girl was seldom found carved on original spoons, but in a type which appears to originate in Caernarfonshire, a glass panel was inserted, and a scrap of paper bearing a name was inserted behind it. Coloured glass and pieces of mother of pearl were also used for inlaid decoration.

Initials were usually confined to two, and we have no way of knowing for certain if these were to represent both name and surname of the girl, or the Christian names of the couple concerned. On early spoons they were found incised on the back, but later became part of the carved decoration.

Miniature pairs of shoes carved in wood were among some of the many gifts given to married couples at their wedding, but surviving examples are rare. They are on the borderline of genuine love tokens unless they were the actual work of the bridegroom.

A great deal of superstition is often found associated with love tokens, although there is a Biblical connection with shoes, and silver ones are still used as wedding cake decorations. Tiny children's shoes have been found buried in foundations of houses and are probably a symbol of a new life.

At the height of their popularity as love tokens, decorated spoons were being made throughout Wales, and examples have been collected from every one of the old counties. Contrary to popular belief, there were no specific regional variations: the makers carved whatever patterns were within their capabilities, or whatever took their fancy. Most would work out their own designs, and a careful study of the few hundred remaining original specimens in public collections has failed to justify any claim that certain patterns were popular within a specific area. There are very few duplications of designs, but no doubt copies of originals were made as the custom fell into decline and spoons began to be produced as wedding gifts.

A few examples of lovespoons have filtered into public collections from stately homes, but none can be positively identified with well known gentry families, even in rural areas. Nor can any be associated with any notable Welsh personality. The closest such identification is a spoon in the collection of the Museum of Welsh Life, which has incised on the back, possibly at a later date, the words 'This spoon belonged to Ellis Wynne'. There is no way of proving if this was the legendary 'Sleeping Bard'.

It is most unusual to find the girl's address carved on a spoon, and to the best of my knowledge the only one in existence is a fine specimen in the Brecknock Museum dated 1843, which carries the following inscription: 'Mary Davies, Coed, Land Y Vailog Vach.' The use of the Anglicised version of Llandyfaelog Fach, a nearby hamlet, is curious.

3. The decline

Although lovespoons continued to be made until the end of the nineteenth century there was a gradual decline in their popularity as love tokens from about 1850. A number of factors influenced not only the giving of love tokens in general, but all aspects of folk customs relating to courtship and marriage, and these contributed to the decline. The Anglicising of the Welsh way of life, together with the repercussions from the publication of the infamous 'Blue Books' on the state of education in Wales in 1847, which poured scorn on its traditions and culture, were only partly to blame. Young men left the countryside to seek a living in the industrial towns, leaving behind them centuries of customs and traditions.

Much damage came from within, as the Nonconformist movement gained ground and attempted to stamp out all that was cheerful and light-hearted among the members of their congregations. By the middle of the century they had successfully eliminated the harmless custom of 'bundling', or courting in bed, which meant that young courting couples found it difficult to be alone together.

How much this restrictive attitude influenced the decline in lovespoon making as a courting custom is hard to say, but the custom was not entirely forgotten elsewhere, as immigrants pursued the promise of a better life in the 'New World'. In his novel *The Race of the Tiger,* which follows a Welsh family emigrating to America, Alexander Cordell describes a young man carving a lovespoon during the voyage. Cordell's work may have been fiction, but the custom did find its way across the Atlantic: there are some lovespoons of puportedly Welsh origin in Kentucky, and no doubt in other places where Welsh emigrants settled.

As a result of the decline in giving spoons as love tokens, there was a gradual shift away from the crude items made by the less skilled to finer, more precise carved spoons made by more skilful carvers. At first they were given as gifts to friends and relatives on the occasion of their wedding, but there is evidence that by the 1860s decorated spoons were being commissioned by others who did not have the skill to make their own.

For example, Romilly Allen reports in *Archaeologia Cambrensis* in 1905 that two finely made pierced and chip-carved spoons, similar but not identical, were made by Thomas Williams of Ystradgynlais as a wedding gift in 1867. Carved entirely with a pocket knife, they were still treasured family heirlooms forty five years later.

The making of lovespoons for third parties was well established by the

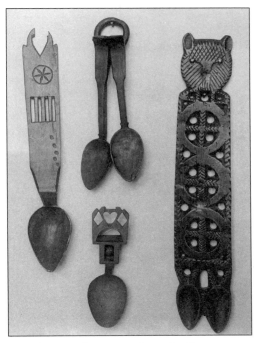

Three panel spoons and one double spoon

Knife and fork pendant on one spoon; 'Cymru am Byth' carved on the other

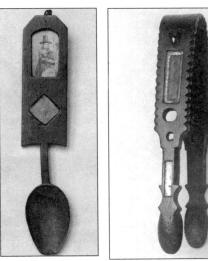

Panel spoon with inset portrait

Wooden sugar tongs

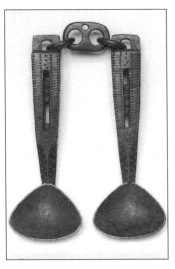

Two interlinked spoons from Pembrokeshire

71

1880s, and a knife and fork made during that period and now part of the Museum of Welsh Life Collection carry the following inscription on both the handles: 'Madam Sybil Margaret Thomas, born February 25 1857. Married 27 of June 1882.' Although not well made, they are unique in that they are the first to include a long inscription. However, they cannot be considered genuine lovespoons. They are, nevertheless, a clear indication of the change taking place in the making and giving of decorated spoons during the latter part of the nineteenth century.

Many of the finest spoons in various collections, although undated, can be attributed to this period, and indicate the early stages of the involvement of proficient, if not professional carvers. For the first time a suitor still wishing to follow the old custom of presenting a lovespoon to his beloved could approach someone better qualified than himself to undertake the work.

By the latter half of the century there were indications that this unique Welsh custom had virtually died out. The period saw the publication of a number of papers and journals, such as the *Cambrian Journal* and *Byegones*, that encouraged correspondence from its readers dealing with folk life and customs, but nowhere within their pages can be found any comments or queries on lovespoons.

The novelist Daniel Owen, who vividly portrayed rural and urban life in north-east Wales during the latter part of the eighteenth century, found no reason to make even the briefest reference to the making of lovespoons among the young. Neither were there any articles, letters or queries on the subject in local and national papers in Wales when they began to appear from the 1850s onwards. While some, like the *Cronicl* and later the *Tyst* and *Dydd* had a strong Nonconformist influence, there is no reason why such a harmless custom could not have received some attention if it still existed.

By the turn of the century it had become so obscure that it prompted Romilly Allen, a Fellow of the Society of Antiquarians, to submit an article to a well-known archaeological journal appealing for information. In the article he was able to include illustrations of a few spoons in private collections, but the response to his appeal was virtually nil.

Collectors in of the early twentieth century were able to acquire a number of spoons, which appear to have been reasonably plentiful in the 1920s and 1930s, but found little documentary information. After realising he could contribute less than two pages about their history in his book *Domestic Utensils of Wood*, Evan Evan Thomas wrote: 'It seems a very great pity that so little attention has been paid to the folk lore of the Welsh lovespoon, and the interesting customs and beliefs that must have centred

upon it.'

It appears that the custom vanished for ever, taking with it an important part of folk tradition, but it is possible that we have perhaps got it all wrong. Despite all the interest and publicity given to lovespoons during the last fifty years, it might be that the tradition of giving a lovespoon to the beloved was just an obscure rural custom of no great significance, and that the few hundred or so surviving originals are all that were ever made. One thing is certain: more lovespoons have been made in Wales during the last twenty-five years than in the previous two to three hundred. There in no disputing the fact that the interest in purchasing lovespoons as engagement and wedding gifts has peaked, but there is ample evidence that the popularity of carving them as a pastime remains, and their place as examples of twentieth century folk art is assured. Long may their chequered history and the challenge they provide in their making remain.

Two lovespoons made as a wedding gift by Thomas Williams of Ystradgynlais, Glamorgan, in 1857. Note that the extensive chip-carving and pierced work covers all the surface apart from the bowl. Illustration from some forty years later when they were still treasured family heirlooms.

4. Collections

Lovespoons began to become collectables at the beginning of the twentieth century and gathered pace rapidly during the next three decades. Ernest Pinto, who was to become the foremost private collector of 'treen', claims to have bought his first lovespoon in a London junk market when he was still a boy before the First World War. He paid 8/6 for it. During the years that followed the war, collecting wood bye-gones increased in popularity, with Pinto and Owen Evan Thomas becoming the best-known collectors.

Owen Evan Thomas was the son of a Neath chemist who was living in London by the mid-1920s and who, unlike Pinto, obtained much of his collection at auctions in and around south Wales. By the late 1920s he had built up a collection of some twelve hundred pieces of 'treen', which included around fifty lovespoons. The spoons were shown at an exhibition of antiques at Olympia in 1928, where they were much admired by the queen. At the same time Pinto was obtaining most of his collection from the London markets, which proved that a large number of lovespoons were already on the move from rural Wales to English dealers.

Some years before his book on the subject appeared, Owen Evan Thomas offered his collection to the nation in the mid-1920s for £10,000, but the offer was declined. The reason for the offer and its refusal were probably both financial: the owner needed the money, but the museums could not afford to buy the collection.

Having failed to sell his collection intact, Evan Thomas set about breaking it up and selling it at auctions and to a few private buyers during the early 1930s. It is surprising that Pinto did not acquire more of the collection than he did, but he told me in the 1960s that he also lacked the finance to make a bulk purchase. Most of the lovespoons in the Evan Thomas collection were sold as individual pieces, and most have not been seen since, apart from the odd one or two donated in resent years to regional museums.

Another well-known collector of 'treen' in Wales was Alan Whitehead of Plas Derwen in Abergavenny. His collection was mostly confined to love tokens, which he obtained locally through dealers. When it was loaned to the Museum of Welsh Life (at that time the Welsh Folk Museum) in 1953, it included about a dozen lovespoons, and when these were compared with the illustrations in the Evan Thomas book it became apparent that about half were from that collection. Whether they were bought directly from Evan Thomas or later through dealers has been impossible to ascertain.

Pinto's remarkable collection was offered for sale for the token sum of £25,000 in 1966, on condition that it would be displayed as near intact as possible. There were a number of interested parties, most of them local authorities, but there was a postal strike taking place at the time, and the collection went to Birmingham, which had the foresight to telephone in its offer. Although Pinto's collection included a number of foreign carved spoons, there were around thirty which could be genuine Welsh lovespoons.

The most regrettable aspect of all collections, both national and private, is the lack of information about the provenance of individual spoons. Dealers and auctioneers made little attempt to record where or how they acquired them. The one exception was an auction held by J. Kyrle Fletcher of Bond Street in June 1936. The firm had a branch at Newport, and it is reasonable to assume that most of the fifty or so lovespoons in the auction were obtained by them. In the catalogue, which contains some illustrations, a detailed account was given of the location where they were obtained, along with other relevant information. Had other dealers at the time been more meticulous in their recording it would have made the work of present day researchers considerably easier.

A damaged spoon with the missing links replaced by wire

The catalogue contained an estimate of the price each spoon would fetch; the highest estimate was £12 for the best spoon, with the remainder upwards of £2. This price was well over a week's wages in the mid-1930s, and it is therefore clear that even in the depression years, lovespoons were still commanding high prices and were good investments.

The most recent auction of lovespoons took place at Sotheby's in London in 1999 when over thirty spoons went under the hammer. The catalogue does not give any details of where individual spoons were obtained but the indications are that most,

Lovespoon, one part missing, with incised glass panel and inlaid wax decoration and nautical designs

75

if not all were from a private collection that had not appeared in public for many years. The estimate for the finest specimen by far (a superb 'endless chain' Celtic ribbon and three spoons, rather optimistically dated as early nineteenth century, when it was probably much later) carried a price of £3,000. Another two – large, crude, pierced specimens in beech of some 27 inches in length – were given estimates of £3,500. Even as far as lovespoons are concerned, it appears that 'size matters'.

There have been numerous claims that the making and presenting of carved spoons to loved ones also occurred in Brittany, but so far research only indicates that small miniature spoons were worn by men in their hats on special occasions. A collection at the former Musée National des Arts et Traditions Populaires in Paris may include some spoons of Breton origin (the museum collection is now part of the Musée des Civilisations de l'Europe et de la Méditerranée, which opens in Marseille in 2008).

The national collection at the Museum of Welsh Life numbers just over two hundred spoons, and small regional museums, notably Brecon, have acquired around a dozen. Not all can be considered 'genuine' older spoons: about ten in the national collection are from the twentieth century, or 'suspect' in some other way.

The number of lovespoons in private collections is impossible to determine. Given their current value, owners are naturally reticent about revealing both their whereabouts and the number of spoons in their collection. Auctions of lovespoons have taken place from time to time since the revived interest in the custom, with prices of some very plain specimens now running into hundreds of pounds.

Some years ago two damaged lovespoons in poor condition from a private museum in Ceredigion were sold for £200 each, and in a much-publicised event on television at the end of 1994 a charming but by no means remarkable spoon was sold by telephone auction for over £300. It is inevitable that a few fakes will now begin to appear in antique shops, much as they did when the collecting mania began around eighty years ago, but most are badly made and easily detectable to the expert eye.

Bearing in mind the secrecy that surrounds collections, it is pure speculation as to the number of originals that have survived. Excluding twentieth century specimens, it is unlikely that many more than around five hundred have survived from the previous two centuries, and even this estimate may be optimistic. In years to come it will become harder to estimate the real number, as the natural aging process of 'treen' makes it impossible to date accurately.

The number of spoons on view to the public are increasing, as museums, aware of their popularity, recover them from the depths of their storerooms. While they cannot compare for technical quality with the work of today's specialist carvers, they should be seen and valued for what they are: the forerunners of what has proved to be one of the most popular rural crafts of recent years.

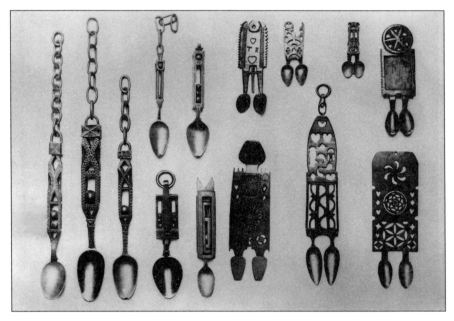

A collection of lovespoons at the Museum of Welsh Life, Sain Ffagan

5. The revival

An upsurge of interest during the early 1950s, not only in lovespoon carving but in many other aspects of rural crafts, resulted in exhibitions being held in some of the large cities. Working in conjunction with the Rural Industries Bureau, a body that was set up to promote other rural crafts as well, large department stores such as David Morgan of Cardiff sponsored week-long craft exhibitions and demonstrations. Skilled rural craftsmen, many of whom were the last of their kind, were relocated from parts of rural Wales and tempted with a week's free board and lodgings in the capital city, and were brought to display their skills to an often bemused audience far from an area where some had lived all their lives.

Many were appearing in public for the first time and were uncomfortable trying to work behind the makeshift stalls that were set up to vaguely resemble their rural workshops. Others from predominantly Welsh-speaking areas found their command of English somewhat lacking, which made it difficult for them to communicate and explain their techniques. Some brought along wives for moral support, and very often it was the women who did most of the talking while the men huddled away self-consciously over a basket, a stick or a spoon. One spoon-carver from Pontarddulais attending an exhibition spent the entire time whittling away in a corner while his wife tried to explain to the onlookers what he was making.

One of the most noticeable factors of these early craft displays was the age of the participants: all were middle-aged or older, and some were quite elderly. The main purpose of the Rural Industries Bureau was to bring employment to rural areas by capitalising on the skilled labour already there, but there was no definite policy for safeguarding some of the rapidly disappearing crafts of the countryside that for decades had not been commercially viable, as it was felt they faced an uncertain future in the new rural economy.

Most, if not all of the lovespoon carvers who were enticed to these demonstrations by the Rural Industries Bureau, and later by the Welsh Tourist Board, were amateurs who had no intention of offering their work for sale, even assuming a market could have been found for it, which, in the early 1950s, was most unlikely.

The tourist boom of the 1960s was still a long way away and the only market for lovespoons was the occasional engagement or wedding gift, very much along the same lines as it had been towards the end of the nineteenth century. It is noticeable that very few of the *domestic* spoon carvers who remained (who at the time could be counted on the fingers of

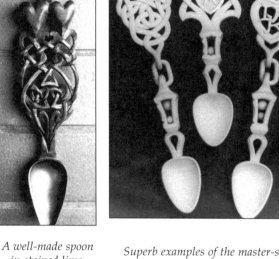

A well-made spoon in stained lime, made for the retail market by Peter Coupland

Superb examples of the master-spooncarver's craft, including contemporary variations on the Celtic ribbon design and tantalising captive balls in a tapered cage. Made by Alun Davies of Abercynon.

one hand) showed an interest in transferring their skills to the more ornate lovespoons. For example, Ieuan Evans of Llandysul, who since the 1920s had won many prizes for his domestic spoons and ladles at local competitions, showed no inclination to start adding extra decoration to his work and passing them off as lovespoons.

The only one of this dwindling group who began to capitalise on the renewed interest in lovespoons was W. R. Evans. Bill, as he was known to almost everyone, had been employed at the Welsh Folk Museum as a woodturner since 1949, and was a competent, though by no means brilliant spoon carver. By the mid-1950s he was producing a range of two or three simple but attractive lovespoons, which would take him around two hours to make. Being in the ideal place to contact the buying public he soon found himself with regular orders. The initial price he charged was £1, which was raised to £1.5.0 as demand began to exceed supply.

A few miles away at Swansea, Brinley Roberts of Morriston was

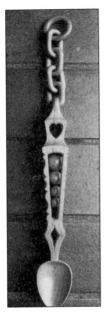
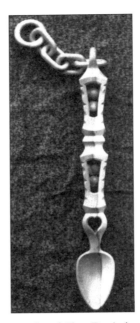

Another two excellent examples of Alun Davies' lovespoons

(above and opposite) Variations on the ball and cage technique using various jigs and formers to assist in the shaping. Made by David Gwilym Jones, Port Talbot.

venturing into lovespoon carving with no experience and for a very different reason. Having been forced through failing health to give up his career as an aircraft engineer, he was in need of light work that would keep him occupied, yet bring in some financial reward. He had a flair for the work and in a few years became firmly established as probably the first full-time professional lovespoon carver.

Concentrating almost entirely on low relief carving, he soon became widely known, receiving much promotion through the Welsh Tourist Board, who frequently used him as a demonstrator at their events. Among his early commissions was a fine spoon made for Ernest Pinto, the collector of wooden bygones, as a gift to his wife Eva. With some orders coming in to produce 'wedding spoons', Brinley was also fortunate to capitalise on the growing practice of 'Twinning' that was sweeping the country at the time. It was becoming almost obligatory for all cities and large towns to be 'twinned' with another similar place on the continent. Although it was often said this was just an excuse for councillors to obtain free trips abroad, it provided Brinley with numerous orders, as it was customary to exchange gifts on such occasions. Some enterprising person

thought the Welsh custom of lovespoons could be utilised to good effect, and the age of the presentation spoon was born. These had no resemblance to the traditional lovespoon, depicting as they did such motifs as daffodils, dragons and the heraldic coats of arms of towns and cities.

Much of the revived interest in lovespoon carving appears to have taken place in south and west Wales, and Len Evans at Abercynffig in Glamorgan had a much higher aspiration. One of the few carvers who had moved up from domestic spoons and ladles with attached rings, Len set about with great enthusiasm to make a lovespoon for the Queen Mother. Why this particular lady was chosen to receive such a favour he never fully explained, and it is perhaps surprising that it was accepted, as the royal family showed no great inclination to be showered with gifts of rural crafts. Nevertheless, it was accepted, and it gained the maker instant accolade. From then on Len became something of a celebrity, and was much in demand as a speaker at Women's Institute meetings and Church Hall gatherings. He always took along his knives and 'twca cam', the traditional hollowing tool, to give a short demonstration, and as a result there was much running around looking for a dust pan and brush at the end of the lecture.

When members of the public came into contact with the spooncarvers of the period they were under the impression that the skills being demonstrated had taken years of patience and practice to master. However, while the old adage 'practice makes perfect' was fundamentally true, there were those who went straight to the top with very little experience.

Such a man was Goronwy Pugh, who hit the headlines when he took first prize at the Caerphilly Eisteddfod in 1950, and again at Cardiff ten years later. Although like him a Meirionnydd man, I did not track him down until the early 1980s when I was invited to his remote hill farm, Rhiwogo, in the mountains above Tal-y-Llyn. There he told me the story of his almost overnight success, which made him one of the foremost lovespoon carvers of the early revival period.

Goronwy had always been something of a whittler, spending the long winter months making walking sticks, tool handles, and any other object of wood that took his fancy. When his attention was drawn to a lovespoon competition at the 'National' he had no idea what a lovespoon looked like, let alone how to attempt to make one. At first he showed little interest, but word got around, and eventually he was challenged that he could not make a lovespoon.

He had no idea how to begin, but someone supplied him with a photograph of an original chain spoon which, it later emerged, had come from the Evan Thomas collection. Having never carved a chain before, he had to discover the technique himself, and knowing from experience that hard close-grained wood was required, he sought out some box wood that he had obtained some time previously from Plasrhiwsaeson at Llanbrynmair.

Like most spooncarvers Goronwy kept no record of the time he spent on his masterpiece, and there was doubt in his mind when he had finished whether it was good enough to be entered. A steady trickle of friends and neighbours came to admire his handiwork, nodded their approval, and generally agreed that he had at least fulfilled the challenge and produced a lovespoon. Whether he would win against those 'experts from the south' was another matter.

Win he did of course, and handsomely too, and the spooncarving habit was well and truly caught. For the next ten years, much of his spare time was spent on spooncarving, and by 1960, when he was awarded first prize in the National, he had built up a superb collection of ball and chain specimens.

What became of his masterpieces after his death is uncertain, but one must hope that they will be handed down in the family. His wife had the last word and summed up his impressive work by saying: 'I cannot understand why someone with hands as big and clumsy as Goronwy can make something as delicate and beautiful.'

Fate was less kind to the spoons of another fine carver of the period, Dan Theophylus of Rhandiwmwyn in Carmarthenshire. He lived alone on a farm, and after his death many spoons were found on a dung heap, too late to be rescued.

Most of the lovespoons available during the 1950s were obtained directly from the makers, as there was a growing reluctance among them to supply the increasing number of craft outlets. It was claimed then, much as it is now, that the mark-up of the majority of retail outlets was too high. Most shops increased the sum they paid to the makers by up to a hundred percent. With so few spoons available, as their popularity increased the few well-established shops were able to sell all they received within a short time. Later on the mark-up became even higher, as is the norm when supply exceeds demand. In those early days it caused a certain amount of bad feeling between maker and seller.

Until the early 1960s the standard of work finding its way into the retail outlets was reasonably high, but a change was about to take place. Christos

Spoons and salad servers made by Ieuan Evans, Llandysul, late 1950s

Levardi, an immigrant from eastern Europe, set up a business which he cheerfully admitted was aimed at the bottom rung of the craft market ladder. Having furnished a workshop in the upper storey of a ramshackle building in a Bridgend back street, he hired a couple of local lads to do roughing out, and in a short space of time was flooding the market with cheap souvenirs. The age of the mass-produced lovespoon had arrived.

The 1960s saw a gradual expansion of commercial lovespoon carving, and by the end of the decade a number of talented craftsmen were able to earn a modest living at it. A few considered that it had sufficiently lucrative a prospect to give up employment and a regular salary. Among them was Charles Jones of Cricieth. He was to become perhaps the first established professional lovespoon maker in north Wales.

Having the skills to produce an acceptable product was only a small part of the enterprise, however. Finding a market was something very different. Charles took a risk and rented a shop just off the main street in Cricieth, a popular seaside town, and relied mostly on the summer visitors for his sales until he became firmly established with enough orders. As he used the premises as both a workshop and a shop, he was soon confronted by the problem of keeping dust away from the display.

He resorted to hanging large sheets of polythene from the roof to separate his work area from the sales counter, and every time a visitor opened the door these billowed like the sails of a square rigger running before a stiff breeze. The effect was not lost on many a quick-witted admirer who could not resist connecting the transparent shrouds with the designs on the spoons, for Charles' work had a pronounced nautical feel.

It goes without saying that however expert the maker has become at roughing out, lovespoon carving is a time-consuming occupation, and the tendency has always been to cut corners. As the finishing took as long as the carving on many of the better-quality spoons, many carvers had to work long hours to make ends meet. Some were heard to complain bitterly that when they had no alternative to channelling their work through retail outlets, their rate was as low as a pound an hour.

It was not unreasonable, therefore, for them to enlist the assistance of a wife, if she was considered to have little more on her hands than household routine. I recall meeting a carver who had just started a business in a small town, who introduced the attractive woman by his side as 'the sanding and finishing department'. He said his business was showing signs of taking off, thanks to her efforts. Her once well-manicured hands were red and raw and she had traces of dark stain under the fingernails, but this was a small price to pay for a revival.

Broad panel spoon, 'Preasant to Miss Annie Walters 1889'

A selection of lovespoons from the collection at the Museum of Welsh Life

84

6. Competitions

The strong response to the lovespoon competition at the 1950 National Eisteddfod, when most other rural craft sections could barely attract one competitor, confirmed that it was by no means the obscure craft that had initially been imagined, and this Eisteddfod was important to the upsurge of interest in and revival of lovespoon making. But local competitions in the field of rural crafts had been taking place for generations, and once the lovespoon began to decline in popularity as a genuine donor-made token of affection, it was only a matter of time before they would be seen at local competitions alongside baskets and bowls, tool handles and walking sticks, and anything else that tested the skills of the rural craftsman.

As far as I can ascertain, the first time a spooncarving competition took place at the National Eisteddfod was in 1899, when a prize of ten shillings (50p) was offered for three spoons. The rules stipulated that they had to be made 'by a labourer', but why there was a restriction to this particular class of person is unclear. Perhaps it was intended to prevent skilled spooncarvers from entering. In all probability these would have been domestic spoons, and a similar competition was set again in 1903 and 1909, although on these occasions there were no restrictions on who could enter.

There is no mention of any further spooncarving competitions at the National until the 1920s, by which time there was a general decline in all branches of rural crafts. Even the elderly appeared to have lost interest, and it was well into the 1930s before lovespoons began to appear again at local shows and eisteddfodau.

One of the most inspired lovespoons to have survived from this period is probably the one made by D. Lewis of Ffostrasol for the Llangeithio Eisteddfod in 1937. Not only was it a spoon of exceptional quality, but the design was also most innovative, breaking away completely from the traditional single or double spoon with a decorated panel. Here the maker carved out of sycamore a large heart held upright by a cleverly fitted pivot, with two small spoons attached to the main body by wooden hooks. It thoroughly deserved first prize.

This brief revival in the 1930s was quickly shattered by the Second World War, and there was little in the form of competition work again until the National Eisteddfod was held at Caerffili in 1950. Iorwerth Peate, the head of the newly formed Welsh Folk Museum (later renamed the Museum of Welsh Life) was elected Eisteddfod President, and it was due to his influence that a number of rural craft competitions were held.

It is often said that competitions bring out the worst in people, and there is ample evidence over the years that both local and national events have created a great deal of bad feeling, not only among literary competitors but among craftsmen as well.

Adjudicators have always come in for criticism, but there are still those who are prepared to place themselves in such an intolerable position. However, there has never been a shortage of critics, particularly in the craft world, who enjoy passing comments on the work of others. When they are of a constructive nature they can be of great benefit to the inexperienced craftsman, but very often they are petty and ill-founded. To make matters worse, there are too many 'experts' in craft circles, each one with his own whims and tastes, and it is therefore not surprising that lovespoon competitions during the revival period proved to be disappointing from the point of view of both competitors and adjudicators. Nevertheless, the 1950 Eisteddfod was an exception. In other craft categories the response was poor, with only one entry in many of them, but fourteen lovespoon carvers competed, a surprisingly large number that suggested the craft was far more widespread than had been imagined.

The adjudicator of the lovespoon section was D. J. Davies, a member of the museum staff and an ideal candidate for the role. Although not a practicing lovespoon carver himself, he was a talented rural craftsman with a wide range of knowledge. D. J. Davies remarked to me that the standards were reasonably high – but the entry by Goronwy Pugh, a hill farmer from Tal-y-Llyn in Meirionnydd was well above everyone else, and he was duly awarded the one-guinea (£1.10) prize. His entry was the only one to be displayed at the Arts and Crafts exhibition and there was therefore no means of discovering who the other thirteen entrants were.

Goronwy Pugh's fine chain spoon may have been the first of its kind to be displayed at a National Eisteddfod, but a chain twelve feet in length was made as far back as 1885 for the Aberdare Eisteddfod. It is not possible to say if it had a spoon attached: at that size it was beyond the realms of lovespoon carving in any case. The maker used the very appropriate pseudonym of 'Patience'.

That Eisteddfod was unique in the generosity of its prizes in the arts and crafts section. A sum of £3 was on offer for the best walking stick, when over fifty years later £1 was the average prize money. The victor in this section was 'a poor man living on Denbigh moors', who hoped someone would buy the stick, which was for sale for a pound.

After the Caerffili Eisteddfod, no further lovespoon competitions took place at the National level until 1960, but in 1958 the Arts and Crafts Committee asked for entries for a general craft display in a range of different materials. This was repeated through the 1960s, giving individual craftsmen and women (who were by then widening their craft range to include woodwork) the opportunity to submit work for display without entering a specific competition.

More restrictions began to appear towards the end of the decade. At one competition, the number of items that could be entered was restricted to three. Sadly, there was no response from the growing number of spoon carvers. The only one displayed at Newtown in 1965 was a fine double spoon by Goronwy Pugh.

Lovespoon by D. Lewis, Ffostrasol, prizewinner at Llangeitho Eisteddfod, 1937

Perhaps many of the lovespoon makers were daunted by having to enter their work under the general category of 'woodwork', but there is no doubt that at this time an important opportunity was lost to put the lovespoon well and truly on the National exhibition agenda.

At the Cardiff Eisteddfod of 1960, perhaps remembered better for the walkout of prominent Nationalists during the queen's visit than for its craft display, Goronwy Pugh again took first prize, but this time he was up against much stiffer opposition. All eight entries were displayed, which included three by Jack Barnet, a very talented Carmarthenshire carver. His entries of delicate ball and chain spoons in boxwood, elder and sycamore were awarded second and third prize. He thoroughly deserved a financial reward, but the entire prize money of £5 went to the winner. This low sum reflected the low value that was put on craft competitions at the Eisteddfod. Only two of the entrants were prepared to sell their work, asking £4 and £6 for well-made pieces. In those days new lovespoons did not command high prices.

No further lovespoon competitions took place until 1976 and 1977, but

Mike Davies, lovespoon carver, exhibiting his craft at the Museum of Welsh Life

Vivian Phillips, working on a lovespoon

there appears to have been only a very poor response, and the next did not take place until 1981, when the Eisteddfod was held at Machynlleth. Here Goronwy Pugh was asked to adjudicate on his own ground. The number of entries was again low (fewer than ten) but there appeared a wide variation of style and technique. Both first and second prizes went to Emyr Hughes, a Llangollen man at that time teaching in London. His two entries of larger-than-usual balls in cavities with chains in sycamore were well made, and he deserved to be honoured, but there was concern among some of the other entrants about awarding him the second prize as well.

The publicity gained at the Machynlleth Eisteddfod should have proved an incentive for an annual display of high quality lovespoons but it was not to be. During the years that followed there was ample opportunity for spooncarvers to enter some of the broad-based competitions, under such headings as 'an item suitable for sale in a souvenir shop', or 'any item made of wood'. There was hardly any response to these, but at the Lampeter Eisteddfod a dedicated lovespoon competition was held, and here for the first time restrictions on design and type crept in. This particular competition asked for 'two spoons connected by a chain with initials'. Setting a competition with specific requirements was often a deliberate policy by the Arts and Crafts Committee, as it helped to prevent previously – made items from being entered. This was a common practice in local competitions, in which the same items could be entered year after year. In this instance it was counter-productive, as the best lovespoon makers simply did not have the time or the inclination for a one-off piece.

As a result of yet another poor showing, at a time when some very talented spooncarvers were in evidence throughout Wales, I contacted the leading carvers to try and discover why they were reluctant to compete at the National which, together with the Royal Agricultural Show, was still regarded as the most prestigious event in the Welsh calendar.

The reasons that emerged were varied and astonishing. Prize money was no incentive; indeed, what most wanted was an opportunity to display their work at the National events without having to enter into competitions. There was an almost unanimous objection to competing against each other, some saying they were against it on principle, others complaining of inconsistent adjudication, although this was a cause of concern for everyone. What was more astonishing was the general opinion that the honour of winning was far outweighed by the disgrace of losing. One leading professional was adamant that it would do his reputation and business more harm if he entered and failed to win than it would do good if he had the honour of taking first prize.

There was also the feeling that quality exhibition spoons were out of circulation for far too long. They were expected to be in the hands of the Arts and Crafts Committee by April and assuming, they were accepted, could not be reclaimed until the end of August. During this time they could have been displayed at other events, including the Royal Welsh Show in July, bringing in much needed publicity to their makers.

The National Eisteddfod Crafts Committee was made aware of these feelings, and it was suggested they should re-introduce the open crafts displays of the 1960s. Far from improving, matters got worse, culminating with the Ebbw Vale Eisteddfod in 1990. Here, after several years' absence, there was again a lovespoon competition, but to the amazement of all those interested, the committee had insisted that the words 'Eisteddfod Genedlaethol 1990' be carved on all entries. They also stated that 'a new approach to this traditional craft' was expected and called for design and working drawings to be submitted. With most spooncarvers working spontaneously using only rough sketches as guidelines, this highly technical approach, more in keeping with furniture-making, must have proved an obstacle to many a talented carver who would otherwise have entered.

It was argued that the 'new approach' required would open the door to some innovative modern work, but in contradiction, the requirement to carve the lettering of the complete name was not compatible with the fine pierced carving being practiced by several of the leading carvers.

As it stood, the name demanded was far too long to be included on a fine small lovespoon and could only be fitted on a large specimen of the carved panel variety, which severely restricted the design options that were available. Most of those who entered went to great lengths to shorten the name. One choice was carving 'Bryn Bach', the name of the location where the Eisteddfod was being held.

It caused a mixture of surprise, disappointment and fury when the Arts and Craft exhibition opened to reveal that all entries without the proper wording were considered not to have met the required rules, and had therefore been removed from the competition; to make matters worse they had also been banned from the display.

A strong representation was made to the Arts and Crafts Committee on behalf of those entrants who did not have their work exhibited, particularly as there was ample space available. It was pointed out that to most entrants the actual prize money was of no importance, but that many competitors had spent considerable time on their entries, and they all deserved to be displayed. It was also pointed out that a lovespoon displaying such lettering had no commercial value to the maker after the event.

Shortly afterwards the Eisteddfod changed its rules, and there was a definite bias towards fine arts at the expense of traditional crafts. No further individual competitions were held, and instead craft-workers were and still are invited to submit photographs of their work. On the strength of these a short list is drawn up for the Craft Gold Medal. A superb chain spoon was entered by Nansy Hemmings when the National Eisteddfod took place at Aberystwyth, and many were of the opinion that it should have won the coveted award, but there remained a bias among the Arts and Crafts hierarchy against lovespoon carvers.

The work of the leading lovespoon carvers has now risen to nearer pure art form than ever before, and there is no reason why one of them should not be awarded the prestigious Craft Gold Medal, as their skills are comparable to those of the ceramicists, weavers and jewellers.

What was needed at this time was a Welsh Craft guild similar to the flourishing English county guilds, but it was not forthcoming, which was a great shame for up-and-coming spooncarvers who were struggling to be recognised in gallery circles.

While lovespoon competitions within Wales appear to have foundered, interest has increased at national woodworking shows held in England, and some progress was made when Mike Davies, one of the leading spooncarvers, was asked to be among the judges. In the few events where a competition has been held, there has been a high standard of work, but it is debatable whether many of the entries could really be considered lovespoons in the traditional sense of the word.

For the time being, at least, competitive lovespoon carv-ing appears to be on the wane in Wales, even at the local level. Bearing in mind the animosity it has caused over the years, perhaps it is just as well.

A collection of Vivian Phillips' lovespoons

7. Publications and Publicity

Media interest in lovespoon carvers during the revival years took some time to materialise, and coverage was usually confined to a photograph of a smiling worker holding one of his creations aloft, surrounded by tools and half-finished spoons, with a few lines of caption underneath. As the number of carvers increased, the interest became more widespread, and articles began to appear in local newspapers and in magazines covering aspects of rural life. Most were superficial, confining their text to the maker's location, sometimes with a few other remarks about how the carver had found himself making what was still regarded as something of a curiosity.

No concerted effort was made by feature writers to delve into the background of the custom, and when news coverage was low it was common practice among editors of local papers in Cardiff and the south Wales valleys to send out a junior reporter and cameraman with instructions to 'go and find a lovespoon carver'.

The first breakthrough on television came in the late 1960s when I was asked to make a reproduction of a well-known and much-photographed original lovespoon which was to be featured in a Welsh-language series on folk customs and rural life called 'Lloffa' [Gleaning]. The first series of the programme ran for several weeks, and the credits ran with the spoon revolving as a backdrop. It generated much interest.

At about this time writers began to consider lovespoons and their makers worthy of inclusion in books on Wales. Robin Page travelled the length and breadth of the UK in 1970 and published his experiences under the title *Journeys into Britain*. He only spent a short time in Wales, during which he spared a few hours to visit a hill farm near Rhandirmwyn in Carmarthenshire, where he talked to Dan Theophylus. Dan was of the old school of spooncarvers, who had brought his skills to the attention of the wider pubic by attending craft displays in Cardiff and Swansea during the early years of the revival. He lived alone, and was a shy man, ill at ease with strangers, and it took Robin several hours of quiet persuasion before he was shown Dan's collection of lovespoons and was supplied with the information he required.

Spooncarvers who took up the craft during those early years of revival found it difficult to obtain written material explaining the complex techniques of ball and chain whittling. Dedicated amateurs who had mastered the complexities were often reticent when it came to revealing so-called trade secrets to carvers who were setting out to make financial gains.

If verbal advice was difficult to obtain, books on the subject were even more of a problem. Illustrations of original lovespoons from well-known collections could be consulted in the two books on 'treen' by Ernest Pinto and Owen Evan Thomas. Indeed Pinto had published an updated volume of over four hundred pages of his collection in 1969, which as well as illustrating most of the lovespoons, provided important information on their background. Potential carvers found themselves doing the rounds of museums, often unsuccessfully, as lovespoons in museum collections were hidden away in a dark corner of a store room, not having seen the light of day for many years.

When it came to technical information there was only one book that covered the entire field: an American publication entitled *Whittling and Woodcarving* by E. J. Tangerman. Published in 1936, it was long out of print, and a paperback version did not appear in Britain until 1962, when it immediately became the 'bible' on the subject. It provided detailed sketches and

A broad panel lovespoon embodying horses and the initials 'MJJ'

accounts of all aspects of carving that would be required even by the most ambitious spooncarver.

The Story of the Welsh Spoon was one of the first books to fill the gap and provide illustrations of original lovespoons; it was published in 1973 by the 'Celtic Educational Services of Swansea', but the photographs of some of the carving techniques were of very poor quality. The book included a number of colour plates of lovespoons in the collection of the Museum of Welsh Life. Before it appeared, it was anticipated that the text would contain a detailed history of the lovespoon, but only a few pages were allocated to background and had little to offer; the text was of little historical value and contained many whimsical and inaccurate statements.

Although *The Story of the Lovespoon* remained in print for some years, it left much to be desired. Over the years a number of small booklets appeared, mostly for the benefit of the growing tourist trade. All were fanciful and some downright misleading, with such titles as *A Spoonful of Love* and *The Lore of the Lovespoon.*

Retail outlets began to supply leaflets explaining the meaning of the many new symbols that were appearing on lovespoons, which added even further to the confusion that already existed, as most of them came from the imaginative minds of their makers and had no connection with the original motifs.

A tea towel was printed that featured a dozen different designs, each of which was attributed to the old Welsh counties. This caused even more of a problem for the makers, when customers ordered a particular 'county design' that did not exist. Unlike domestic spoons, whose different patterns could indeed be attributed to some counties, no such attributions were possible with lovespoons. Those depicted on the towel may have been obtained from a particular county, but they certainly were not representative of it.

As the interest in lovespoons grew, so too did publicity, which left historians and researchers battling against a tide of misinformation about origins and symbols. Lovespoons made from brass began to appear, and Rhiannon Evans, the well known jeweller, began to market an attractive range in the form of necklaces and brooches. Miniature lovespoons became very popular, either as personal adornment or as key fobs, and one company published a range of greetings cards that had a miniature spoon attached.

One of the greatest difficulties that spooncarvers faced, particularly those who were working in a semi-professional capacity, was the problem of getting their work exhibited. Craft galleries appeared to cater for all aspects of craft apart from woodwork in general and lovespoons in particular. I recall contacting several galleries to enquire if they were prepared to stage an exhibition of the work of some of the foremost carvers, but was told by most that they did not consider lovespoons to be worth the effort.

It was therefore left to individual makers to seek out likely display areas, and some very unusual venues showed a willingness to assist. One sympathetic person was the manager of a Cardiff Building Society, and for a couple of years the Society's windows were used to display a variety of crafts which changed regularly. It was here that many up-and-coming carvers had their first opportunity to bring their skills to the attention of the public. The favour ceased abruptly when the manager moved on, and the new manager decided the window space would be put to better use advertising the Society's interest rates.

By the 1980s lovespoon carvers were so well established that it was only those who produced the unusual who attracted the media. A carver who exchanged his carving tools for a chainsaw and out of a fallen tree produced what was claimed to be the biggest lovespoon ever made gained instant publicity. This was closely followed by the 'smallest', which was made out of a matchstick. Both these spoons found a permanent home in a Cardiff craft shop, where they were the centre of attraction for years.

Lovespoon, based on an original, made by the author for the Welsh Language Television programme, Lloffa, *in the late 1960s.*

Bibliography

Allen Romilly, *Archaeology Cambrensis* (1905).

'Carved Wooden Spoons', *Archaeology Cambrensis* (1901).

Bronner, Simon. *Chain Carvers* (University of Kentucky Press, 1985).

Davies, Mike. *The Welsh Love Spoon* (Private publication, 1991).

Evan Thomas, O. *Domestic Utensils of Wood* (E.P. Publishing, 1973).

Hendall, Ralph. *Love Spoons* (Private publication).

Levi, Jonathan. *Treen for the Table* (Woodbridge, 1998).

Pinto, Ernest. *Treen* (Bell and Son Ltd, 1968).

Owen, Trevor. *Welsh Folk Customs* (1959).

Rosenberg, J. *An Autumn in Wales*, trans. W. Linnard (1985).

Stevens, Catrin. *Welsh Courting Customs* (1993).

Wright, Dorothy. M. 'Traditional Love Spoons' in *Embroidery Magazine* (1937).

Page, Robin. *Journeys into Britain* (1970).

Williams, Edwin. *The Love Spoon* (Private publication).

Trotter's *Distressed Seamen* (1789).

Tangerman, E. J. *Whittling and Woodcarving* (1962).

The Story of the Welsh Spoon (Celtic Educational Services of Swansea).

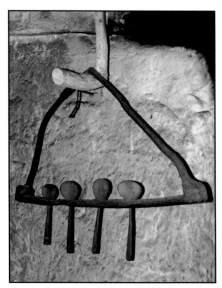

MUSEUM OF WELSH LIFE
St Fagans, Cardiff, CF5 6XB.
Tel: 02920 573500
website: www.nmgw.ac.uk

An extensive and attractive collection of traditional spoons are displayed in the gallery of the Museum of Welsh Life. During special festival days, wood carvers and spoonmakers display their craft at the museum.

ORIEL MÔN SIOP Y PENTAN SIOP Y GLODDFA
Llangefni Caerfyrddin Blaenau Ffestiniog

and many shops and galleries throughot Wales – exhibitions and lovespoons for sale.

BRECON MUSEUM
Brecon.

A collection of over twenty traditional spoons.

CEREDIGION MUSEUM
Coliseum, Terrace Road, Aberystwyth, Ceredigion.
Tel: 01970 633088

A collection of traditional spoons and carving tools.

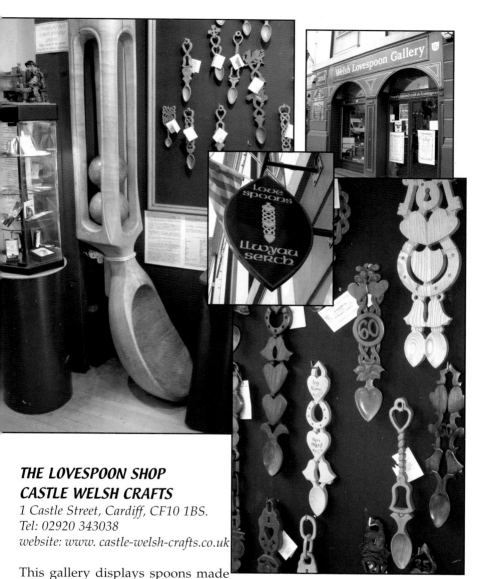

THE LOVESPOON SHOP
CASTLE WELSH CRAFTS
1 Castle Street, Cardiff, CF10 1BS.
Tel: 02920 343038
website: www.castle-welsh-crafts.co.uk

This gallery displays spoons made by some of the master craftsmen of Wales and the shop also offers overseas shipping. Interesting attractions here are 'the world's largest lovespoon' and 'the world's smallest lovespoon'. Directly opposite Cardiff Castle entrance, it also sells a very extensive range of traditional Welsh crafts, gifts and mementos.

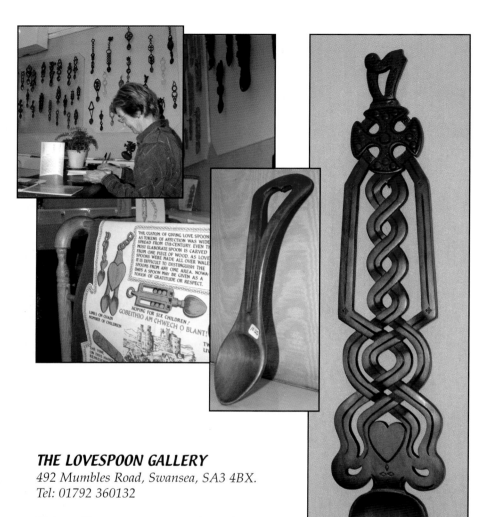

THE LOVESPOON GALLERY

492 Mumbles Road, Swansea, SA3 4BX.
Tel: 01792 360132

This gallery is tcommitted to displaying and selling high quality lovespoons. The collection has been selected by Patricia Price, the owner, a recognised authority on the Welsh lovespoon. A postal service is offered and over ninety designs can be chosen from if a special commission is needed.

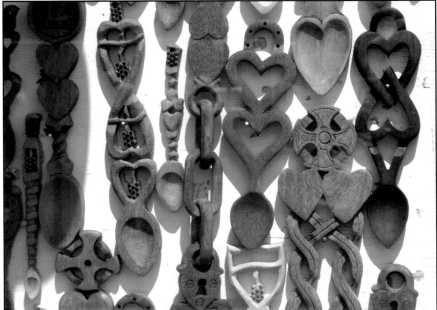

THE WELSH LOVESPOONS CENTRE

Corner Cabin, 22 Market Street, Llangollen, Denbighshire, LL20 8PS.
Tel: 01978 860187
e-mail: info@lovespoons.info
website: www.lovespoons.info

Displays a selection of hand-carved lovespoons and also has an on-line shop on their website.

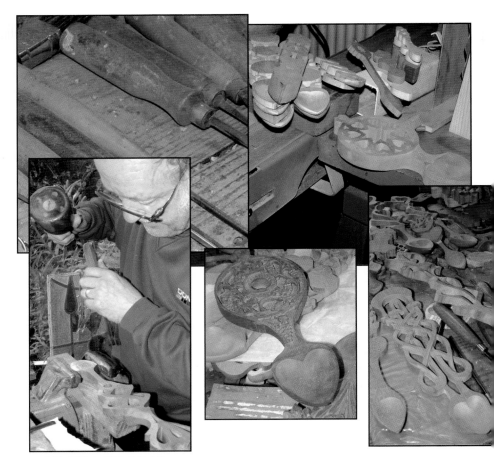

EDWIN WILLIAMS

121 St Teilo Street, Pontarddulais, Swansea, SA4 1RA.
Tel: 01792 882723
e-mail: sales@wewilliams.co.uk

Edwin started carving with a penknife at a very early age. Later he went to art college to study sculpture, working in numerous materials. He went on to work as a woodcarver in one of the top furniture makers in London whilst continuing with his sculpture, exhibiting at some of the top art galleries, before opening his own workshop at Pontarddulais, from where he runs his business with the help of his wife, Olivia and his sons, Odin and Thor. There is a gallery at their workshop, and they also produce a catalogue and offer a world-wide postal service.

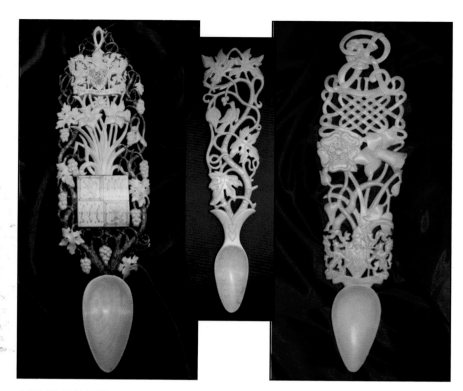

MIKE DAVIES

211 Ffordd y Dyffryn, Saron, Carmarthenshire, SA18 3TN.
Tel: 01269 597626
e-mail: mdavies@lovespoons.fsnet.co.uk
website: www.mikedavieswelshlovespoons.com

Born in Swansea, Mike Davies taught himself to carve wood after attending an art and design course. He got interested in lovespoons and studied the collection at the Museum of Welsh Life, St Fagans. He has now been carving them for over forty years, concentrating on three different kinds of spoons – traditional designs, more 'Celtic' designs and modern, original designs inspired by the shape, grain and colour of the wood. Mike has received commissions and has exhibited throughout Europe. He still carves in his workshop in Carmarthenshire, publishes a catalogue of his designs and exhibits annually at the Royal Welsh Show at Builth Wells.

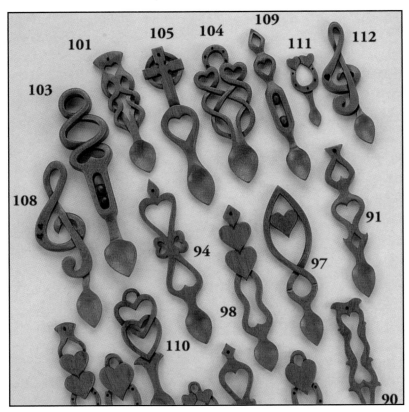

PAUL CURTIS

Distributed by Cadwyn
Dolwerdd, Llanfihangel, Pencader, Carmarthenshire, SA39 9JU.
Tel: 01559 384378
Fax: 01559 384194
e-mail: info@cadwyn.com
website: www.cadwyn.com/llwyau or www.welsh-lovespoons.co.uk

Paul Curtis is a native of the southern valleys of Wales and discovered his love and talent for woodcarving when he was very young. When he was sisteen, a friend took him to meet Gwyndaf Breese, the author of this book. The author taught him how to carve lovespoons and today Paul's lovespoons are much soughtafter all over the world, distributed by Cadwyn – a co-operative company which promotes Welsh craft industries.

ELWYN HUGHES LOVESPOONS
(Mike and Avril Bartlett)
Glyn Dŵr, Chestnut Avenue, Ffordd yr Hen Felin, Dwygyfylchi, Penmaenmawr,
Conwy, LL34 6TL.
Tel and Fax: 01492 622293
Workshop: 01492 623030

This company was established by Elwyn Hughes of Dyffryn Nantlle who
opened a craft shop at Craig-y-don, Llandudno in 1975. He had visited
many farmhouses and collected traditional lovespoon designs. He started
carving spoons for his own outlet and gradually found himself producing
hundreds for wholesaling, exporting and personal commissions. Mike
Bartlett, a local engineer, came to be his apprentice in 1988 and when
Elwyn retired, he and his wife took over the business and the workshop
at the bottom of the garden. The company publishes a colour brochure
and offers a postal service.

RICHARD DOWNES

26 Lôn Coed Brân, Swansea, SA2 0YQ.
Tel: 01792 205359
e-mail: richarddownes@onetel.com

Richard Downes is a full-time carver and spoon maker. Born and bred in Swansea, he spent time as a cabinet maker before studying carving and design at the City and Guilds of London Arts School. After gaining experience as a furniture carver and antiques restorer, he turned to carving Welsh lovespoons and started his own business in 1997. He uses hundreds of different designs and combinations and receives special commission work. He offers a postal service and some of his designs are displayed on his colour leaflet.

SIÔN LLEWELLYN
6 Gwendoline Street, Nantymoch, Cardiff, CF32 7PN.
Tel: 01656 841904

Siôn was inspired to start carving when his sister received a lovespoon from her boyfriend when he was only twelve years old. He was well instructed by Len Evans, Abercynffig, a spoincarver, and Myrddin Madog, a harp-maker. Siôn won the Student of the Year at Bridgend College and the main craft prize at the National Eisteddfod, Caernarfon, 1979 for a harp he designed and built. He set up his own lovespoon carving company in 1997 and now exports all over the world. He exhibits at the National Eisteddfod and the Royal Welsh Show, Builth Wells.

DAVID WESTERN

3274 Albion Road, Victoria BC, Canada, V8Z 3TY.
Tel: 250 386-2379
e-mail: dhwestern@shaw.ca/lovespoons@shaw.ca
website: www.davidwesternlovespoons.com

David Western was born in Cardiff. He graduated in English at the University of British Columbia, then made a career change and qualified in cabinet-making and advanced furniture design at the London College of Furniture. He settled in Victoria, British Columbia where he opened a cabinet-making shop.

A casual interest in Welsh lovespoons gradually blossomed into a passion, and hobby-level carvings eventually evolved into professional works of art. David now sells his lovespoons worldwide and is extremely proud to continue the Welsh lovespoon tradition in Canada.

PAGEANT WOOD PRODUCTS
(Leslie Williams)
Capel Coch, Scotland Street, Llanrwst, Conwy, LL26 0AL.
Tel and Fax: 01492 641190
website: www.faze3.co.uk

Leslie Williams followed his father, Tegwyn, in the craft of spoonmaking. A small chapel in the market town of Llanrwst was adapted as a workshop and the company now produces a variety of spoons, including the 'double' wedding spoons. The workshop also produces wooden plaques with Courtney Davies' carved Celtic designs. An annual catalogue is published and a postal service is offered.

٢

The
Customer
Challenge

*The inside story of a
remarkable transformation
in customer service*

TOM JOHNSON

WITH MARK JAKEMAN

London · Hong Kong · Johannesburg
Melbourne · Singapore · Washington DC

PITMAN PUBLISHING
128 Long Acre, London WC2E 9AN
Tel: +44 (0)171 447 2000
Fax: +44 (0)171 240 5771

A Division of Pearson Professional Limited

First published in Great Britain 1997

ISBN 0 273 626337

British Library Cataloguing in Publication Data
A CIP catalogue record for this book can be obtained from the British Library.

10 9 8 7 6 5 4 3 2 1

Typeset by Pantek Arts, Maidstone, Kent
Printed and bound in Great Britain by Biddles Ltd Guildford and King's Lynn

The Publishers' policy is to use paper manufactured from sustainable forests.

About the Authors

Tom Johnson has been with BT since the mid 1960s. He has lived through the transformation of this once lumbering Civil Service department to the BT of today which is playing such a major role in shaping the future of the telecommunications industry.

Writing this account of BT's Customer Challenge came about because of the interest in the story and in particular from Tom's front line view of customer service. He has been heavily involved in running and shaping BT's operations since privatisation in the thick of increasing competition for the business customer market. As General Manager of BT's City of London District he was  part of the team that achieved a turnaround in BT's service reputation in the early 1990s. Prior to that he held a number of senior general management jobs in London through the "difficult years" when BT's service was far from perfect following privatisation.

He became an operational director in BT in 1992 and established BT's sales and marketing activities for the small and medium business market. Since 1994 he has been Director of Business Customer Service which he combines with responsibility for all BT's commercial dealings with government.

Tom is seen as the service champion in BT and is passionate about developing customer service as a professionalism – using technology to give information and power to people at the front line.

Mark Jakeman has been with BT since the late 70s and has worked in a number of different roles including computing, sales, marketing and latterly customer service. His main focus currently is managing a series of programmes to improve customer satisfaction for business customers.

This book is dedicated to all BT people past and present. There are no better people to work with; there is no better company to work for. The future is ours for the taking.

Contents

Introduction

In 1997 BT stands at a watershed. Our recently announced plans to merge with MCI, when realised, will take us into a whole new era and complete our transformation from a UK-focused company into a truly global player. With this event dominating the telecommunications world it is hard to remember what things were like ten years ago, and how far we've come since then. If you go back even further, say fifteen years to before BT was privatised, the landscape is unrecognisable. We had barely even heard of customers; we didn't have them – we had subscribers.

With privatisation and the beginning of competition, we had to learn a whole new way of working. We had to turn BT from a lumbering bureaucratic organisation run for the Treasury's benefit, into a competitive modern business designed to put customers first.

It takes a long time to transform an organisation the size of BT (we employed over a quarter of a million people back in the mid '80s – twice the number we have today). We started with a huge amount of expertise in certain fields such as network technology, but with virtually none in customer service. We made a lot of mistakes along the way, but we also scored a lot of successes. We certainly learnt an enormous amount about how to end up with satisfied customers. And we did all this in an environment of fast-moving technology, global competition and ever increasing customer expectations. This book is the story of how we made that transformation.

I wanted to write this book for three main reasons. First, it is a fascinating story, and if it isn't written down it will be forgotten. That would be a great shame because we were pioneers in the privatisation process and in the deregulating world of telecommunications. Most of what we achieved was learnt as we went along – there were few parallels. In today's BT there are things that we do so instinctively that we have almost forgotten how we arrived at them. But it is important to remember the route we came by in case we need to apply the same lessons in future. By the same token, other organisations may well be facing some of the changes, threats and challenges that we have come through. I hope this book will help them to learn something from our experience.

Secondly, I wanted to record BT's customer service revolution as a tribute to the people who were a part of it. Customer service is all about people; they are the key to success. Some of them were directors and managers; most of them were service receptionists, operators, engineers and others in the front line. This story is about how we all learnt a whole new approach to our jobs in order to turn BT into a formidable force in world telecommunications.

The third reason for this book is to remind us all just how much we are capable of. We still make mistakes – everyone does – but the mistakes are becoming smaller, and we're growing faster and better at finding the solutions. In a changing industry we will always face new challenges. It is how we deal with those challenges – whether we can apply the lessons we've learnt so painfully – that in the end will make the difference between success and failure.

Although this book is written with the co-operation of many of my colleagues it is, in the end, a personal view. Against the background of such a huge subject some points will inevitably be missed and others barely touched on. I've tried to capture the most important elements as I see them in a way that everyone will be able to understand.

The last thing that BT must ever do is to be complacent – the challenges of our industry just won't allow that. But looking back at how far we've come in the last few years, looking at the sheer hard work and determination that got us through, should convince everyone that top quality customer service is an achievable goal. I hope that if anyone starts to doubt their ability to get there this book will help to restore their faith in themselves and in their people.

Tom Johnson

When you're at the bottom the only way is up

O rganisations often go through difficult times, and this was certainly the case for BT in the early 1980s. Some of our problems were caused by our history as a public-sector organisation:

- *We were still treating our customers as if they all shared the same needs.*

- *We had no commercial culture or structure.*

- *We knew nothing about competitive pricing.*

- *We had huge backlogs of work; the company was still working to old pre-privatisation systems and timescales.*

- *Managers spent virtually all of their time managing problems rather than people, and looking after today rather than planning for tomorrow.*

However, we had one company characteristic that helped us through the difficult times: our public-service inheritance meant that people were wonderful at coping in a crisis.

Dissatisfied customers and engineers in the firing line

In the early to mid '80s, BT customers didn't get the kind of treatment they do today. Some of them were reasonably satisfied, but a lot of them were not. BT wasn't organised to cope when things started to go wrong, so far too many customers were treated badly and left very frustrated.

> There are BT engineers who can even remember having customers threaten them with baseball bats. One customer, driven to desperation over BT's failure to repair a fault, rang one of our managers to say that he was going to hold hostage the BT engineer who had called but who could not fix his problem. The customer only released the engineer when the repair was completed.

It was when privatisation was on the agenda that the company really started to come alive. We knew that we faced a huge challenge, although at the time none of us could foresee just how much we would have to do. Even in those days BT always had successes as well as failures, but in the early '80s, when things went wrong, they went seriously wrong.

'There are BT engineers who can even remember having customers threaten them with baseball bats.'

> The King's Cross telephone exchange was due to be modernised, but this was running several months behind schedule. As a result, the old exchange was overloaded and large numbers of calls never got through.

3

An unfortunate BT customer had just started up a business and was connected to the King's Cross Exchange. He found that he couldn't make outgoing calls, and couldn't receive calls. He complained, but there was nothing we could do until the new exchange started operation. So the customer struggled on in frustration. Eventually, we switched the exchange over – and made a hash of it. A thousand customers lost all service and this customer was one of them. After months of problems, he still couldn't communicate with his customers, and it was our fault. In the end he wrote to us saying, 'You've killed my business; I've had to close down.'

Why was the service so bad?

It wasn't the case that BT staff didn't care about service and its effect on customers. You will still find BT people who were working on the King's Cross exchange at that time who feel dreadful about putting that customer out of business. So why were things so bad? To answer that question we need to go back a little into BT's history, and to look at the whole culture of the organisation.

Until privatisation in 1984, anyone who worked for BT was a public servant. Only 15 years before that, the Post Office had been a government department (it didn't become a nationalised industry until 1969).

In the 1950s and '60s it could be really difficult for an ordinary member of the public to get a phone. Waiting lists often ran into months, and there was a general perception that phone calls were an expensive luxury. People associated government departments such as the Post Office with bureaucracy and inefficiency – that was certainly how the media saw them.

The Leeds evening paper mounted a vitriolic attack on the Post Office when phone charges went up. This despite the fact that the paper's own cover price went up the following week, by a far greater percentage. The paper saw its own price increase as a justified response to rising costs.

Meeting the organisation's, not the customer's, needs

In those days, the level of service was set entirely according to what was convenient for the organisation – never mind the customers. It was reckoned to be good if a new telephone line could be provided in under a fortnight; between a fortnight and a month was acceptable. A customer was only considered to be on a waiting list if providing the service took more than a month.

Under investment

Years of under investment meant that the standard of equipment was outdated, and that it was poorly maintained. Customer (or, rather, 'subscriber') records were all manual, which made the overall system very difficult to administer. The only recourse people had when things went wrong was to complain via their MP. There was no such thing as OFTEL (the telephone regulator). Problems were usually rectified once an MP passed on a complaint, but, understandably, the press and public objected to the fact that an MP had to complain before anything was done.

'...there were thousands of people waiting for a first telephone line, it simply wasn't fair to give somebody else a second line.'

A civil service approach

The civil service approach to business was, essentially, non-existent. The civil service isn't about commercial business, it is about public service. This has huge potential benefits in a commercial company, but it also has enormous drawbacks. The old public-service BT was allocated a certain amount of money every year, by the government, to run the best telephone service it could on that budget. There had never been any concept of customer choice, and BT was supposed to supply the same service throughout the land. It would have been wrong to give one customer better service than another. For example, it could be extremely difficult for anyone to get a second telephone line put in – if there were thousands of people waiting for a first telephone line, it simply wasn't fair to give somebody else a second line.

Customer choice is essential. See Chapter 3

Privatisation
....

By the early '80s, the aim was to install new lines within a fortnight, and to repair faults by the end of the day after they were reported. However, we only expected to achieve this target 85 per cent of the time. So a 'success' of on average 85 per cent could conceal some really dis- astrous horror stories.

There was a strong climate of dissatisfaction among politicians and business leaders, particularly since most of them were based in London, where service was consistently worse than in the rest of the country. People were beginning to get used to having more choice in other areas of life, and so they wanted choice when it came to their telephones, too. All of this came to a head when a series of strikes hit the company.

'...£1 billion worth of bills were not sent out.'

The most damaging of these strikes was probably the one by the CPSA (Civil and Public Services Association), which crippled the billing system. As a result, £1 billion worth of bills were not sent out. There was a growing mood that politically it was timely to introduce the disciplines of the private sector into nationalised industries. Privatisation was put forward by government as a means to introduce competition and a commercial outlook as well as allowing the government to realise the value of the organisation's assets. BT became the first of the many privatisations in the 1980s and the spotlight was on us.

After privatisation, BT still held onto its civil service attitude: the attitude after all came from the people, and the people hadn't changed. There was no clear company strategy for helping people through the enormous changes that lay ahead. And BT's internal departments did not function in the usual way for a commercial company:

- The **marketing department** was not the driving force for change. It was very secondary to the discipline of engineering. There simply wasn't the need to market aggressively when the company was a monopoly.
- The **sales department** was simply there to take orders.
- The **finance department** kept the books. Revenue was never related to the cost of the service.

It had never been necessary to price competitively, either – that would have been a waste of money in a public-sector organisation.

After privatisation, the company recruited marketing, sales and finance people, but it took a long time to instil the culture of selling, marketing, competitive pricing and so on in a company that had never dealt with it before.

Facing up to competition

For a year or two after privatisation the company struggled on, in the wake of a very well publicised flotation but with all the service problems still there. Then competition began to appear.

In the early years it took the form of a breed of companies who offered new telephones and switchboards. They made us wake up to the need to expand our portfolio. However, the heartland of BT – the network – didn't really face competition until the middle to late '80s, when Mercury got into its stride.

Most people had realised that competition was going to happen, of course, but the arrival of Mercury suddenly made it seem real and immediate. We now had to compete for the very life blood of our company: telephone calls. Our first efforts at competition focused on mimicking the price reductions Mercury was bringing to the market place. Price was all-important and service was very much in second place.

This focus on price brought tremendous pressure to reduce costs and took us to the very edge of a vicious cycle of being unable to invest for the future because of the cost. While Mercury was starting out with a lot of new state-of-the-art equipment, much of BT's was badly in need of upgrading. A debate raged within the company as to how we should respond. Technology and price were seen as the factors that would give a competitive edge; customer service was not the driving force.

'BT was organised to make life easier for BT, and not for the customer.'

The organisation was still structured for its own convenience: BT was organised to make life easier for BT and not for the customer. For example, a customer who wished to query paying a bill because their service was faulty and hadn't been repaired, would find that the billing department and the repair department just didn't communicate. It was difficult to find the right person to talk to in the first place, and almost impossible to get any single department to take responsibility for resolving the problem.

Chapter 2 explains how BT was restructured at the end of the 1980s

Solving today's problems left no time for planning the future

So by the mid 1980s the pressures piled up. The organisation was trying to run commercially, but under a civil service structure and with civil service attitudes. The technology needed upgrading, but costs had to be kept down. Backlogs of work began to accumulate and outdated equipment generated additional faults that modern technology would have prevented. Meanwhile, there was an increasing demand for telephones lines and more modern equipment. Unlike many of the other privatised nationalised industries, BT was operating in a potentially growing market place, but even when the market is expanding, if the necessary resources aren't available, it can be hard to feel positive.

'BT staff were embarrassed to admit that they worked for BT'

On a day-to-day level, the huge and growing pressure meant that managers and staff were running to keep still – or even to go backwards. Managers were preoccupied with solving today's problems, and had no time to think about tomorrow. They certainly didn't have time to 'manage' their people in the true sense of the word. The success of a manager was largely measured by their ability to deal with today's problems.

We did clear the backlogs eventually. See Chapter 5

There was one more important reason why things became so bad: the psychological factor. Customers' complaints grew so great that BT staff were embarrassed to admit that they worked for BT, our engineers had a hard time and anti-BT jokes became commonplace. After a while, this kind of thing embeds itself in the corporate psyche and is tremendously dispiriting for everyone. This contrasted strongly with the perception that we now faced big new competitors who were fit and able.

Staff morale is a key issue. Chapters 4 and 6 explain how we dealt with this problem

We had to face the fact that we were in serious trouble unless we responded fast and *wanted* to respond. But at the time it seemed that no one knew how to do it. What were the priorities? What did customers want? Were the competition really so much better? We all felt battered and bruised, and for a time the light at the end of the tunnel went out.

Organisations must constantly change to keep ahead.

BT hadn't done anything specific to reach such a low point. In fact, doing nothing was the problem. The company simply failed to recognise the full extent of the need for change after privatisation.

How bad did it get?

We have already described some of the worst examples of what could go wrong in the early days, but even the everyday complaints and problems were, by today's standards, quite unacceptable. In many of our districts (the local geographic BT organisation at the time) the complaints departments were expanding – a sure sign that things weren't right. We were spending a fortune on putting right mistakes that should never have been made in the first place.

> A company in Sussex, which employed about 40 or 50 people, wanted to upgrade to a bigger telephone system. We sold them one. Unfortunately, we sold them one they didn't want and that didn't meet their basic requirements. To make matters worse, it didn't work properly. When the company complained, instead of accepting the obvious drawbacks, we started to argue with them. We tinkered with the system to try to put various elements of it right, but the problem dragged on and on because nobody took responsibility for it.
>
> After about a week it was clear that we had sold the company a product that simply wasn't fit for their purposes, and wasn't reliable. After about six months we finally did what we should have

done right at the beginning: we gave them a new system. By then we had spent a fortune, our engineers were exasperated and the customer – despite the fact that they were eventually compensated – had developed an understandable horror of dealing with BT.

Between 1984 and 1987 OFTEL allowed BT to raise prices quite quickly in order to fund its programme of capital investment. This caused a certain disquiet among the public and the media, especially in areas where service was poor. Service in London were still consistently worse than in the rest of the country largely because of previous under investment and it was here that customers were most demanding. It was obvious to everyone that substantial improvements were essential.

The City of London was a catastrophic place to be delivering such a poor service. City dealers can make millions of pounds in just a phone call or two, so the telephone is their lifeline. In the 1980s it took a hundred days (or more) to provide a 'private circuit' (a dedicated phone line between two points) for a business house that enables dealers to talk to one another. Customers were getting extremely angry with us. They would frequently order two circuits on the assumption that they might at least get one of them within a hundred days.

Chapter 3 explains how we got lead times down

We had run out of capacity for exchange lines in the City, so customers could not have any extra lines. Some small businesses and residential customers had no phone service at all.

In a new development at Wapping we found ourselves unable to provide *any* service. Some customers had to wait six months for a line. BT had to make decisions such as whether to give a big business a couple of lines to get them up and running, or to give a line each to two smaller businesses. There was no system for prioritising, so BT staff had to keep making individual judgements about who should have a phone and who shouldn't.

Payphones were one of the first things we tackled. See Chapter 2

One of the most notorious failures was our public payphones. The service was dreadful. Most phones were dirty and many were vandalised. Fewer than one in five payphones worked at any time. And to most of our customers the payphones on every street in the land were our showroom!

Managers simply didn't have enough day-to-day control of their departments. In well run companies then (and in BT now) managers look at performance figures on a real-time basis, so that they are always right on top of any fluctuations that need fast action. In the 1980s BT management would often see just a monthly summary two weeks after the end of the month! So by the time they were in a position to identify the problem, they were already weeks behind in implementing a solution.

1987: BT's *annus horribilis*

1987 was the worst year in BT's history. The public had undoubtedly seen the privatisation three years before as a success – everything about it was upbeat and caught the public imagination. People had begun to have high expectations of a privatised telephone service. 1987 saw these expectations dashed. Throughout the year the company moved smoothly from one disaster to the next.

'...the company moved smoothly from one disaster to the next.'

Bad weather

It started right at the beginning of the year with the toughest January weather for fifty years. The old network was terribly susceptible to bad weather and suffered a huge number of weather-related faults that required repair. We lacked the spirit of co-operation we have today, where engineers will move from department to department, or from one part of the country to another, to help each other out. Each geographical district coped with its problems alone.

The strike

Before all the faults were fixed the second problem struck: trouble with the unions. We had spent all winter negotiating changes in working practices designed to provide for more efficient and lower cost operation. Finally, one Monday in early March, we seemed to have agreed a deal. Two days later a union meeting resulted in the rejection of the agreement, and by Friday we were into industrial action.

The result was that 116,000 engineers were out on strike for a month. Managers continued to work, so they ran the network. We survived surprisingly well, but the installations and repairs that would normally have been done didn't happen, including those remaining from the bad weather in January.

Surprisingly, the strike led to one glimmer of good news for BT. Although the public and the media hated us, they definitely did not want to see the situation made worse by a strike. It soon became clear that the unions had very little public support and BT was given credit for standing up to them. We took little comfort from this (in the end there is never a winner in this type of industrial dispute), but it was some consolation to feel that our efforts to put the company on the right track had received some recognition.

A backlog of faults

When the strike was finally over, the aftermath caused another problem: the engineers said that they couldn't clear the backlog of repairs and installations unless they worked overtime. Management responded by saying that the company wouldn't pay for overtime to cover the costs of the strike. Without the overtime they asked for, the engineers couldn't clear the backlog of work.

And with that public support dwindled with the inevitable delays to phones being installed or faults being repaired. In July a report in the press stated that BT was the most hated public-service company in the country. All through that summer and autumn press coverage worsened.

Autumn saw the 'Big Bang' (deregulation of the Stock Market) in the City. The demand from dealers for more telecom-munications services was huge. At the same time we were introducing new technology to the network and exchanges serv-ing the City, and this didn't go well at the first few sites. We got into more and more trouble with our City customers, and built up even worse backlogs.

The first nine months of the year had brought relations with our staff and the public to an all-time low. We had struggled with installation and repair backlogs. In October a natural disas-ter, completely beyond our control, made the situation even worse: the 1987 hurricane hit the South East of the country. It blew down a large proportion of our overhead wires in the South, South East and East network, an area that covered the most heavily populated part of the country.

It's an ill wind...

Surprisingly, the hurricane proved to be a turning point. The installation of an important new exchange illustrates how this crisis brought out the best in everyone.

In the week in which the government was floating the last of its shares in BP, generating calls from thousands of people wanting to buy them, BT planned to switch over BP's exchange to a more modern one. BP's chairman called Sir Michael Bett

(Managing Director of BT (UK) at the time) to ask him to delay the switchover – he couldn't risk anything going wrong with BP's phones that week. Mike told him that it would cost a fortune to change a plan of that complexity, and BT could only do so if BP footed the bill. BP's response was that they wouldn't dream of paying, but would sue BT if anything went wrong.

Crisis brings out the best in people.

So the switchover had to go well. It was scheduled for 7 o'clock in the morning. Just a few hours before it was due, the hurricane hit London. Mike Bett can remember getting up at 2 o'clock in the morning to shut the windows, registering what was going on outside, saying to himself, 'Well, that's my job gone.'

Meanwhile, unbeknown to him, the engineers were so keen to make the BP switchover perfect that they had all spent the whole night at the exchange. Undeterred by the hurricane which Mike had assumed would prevent them even getting to work – they performed the changeover so smoothly that BP couldn't detect any difference in service.

One of the advantages of the civil service mentality is that public servants cope wonderfully in a crisis. That's what they're there for: to serve the public. The hurricane was a catalyst that turned things around, because BT people have never lost their public-service attitude. Engineers were drafted into the South East from as far as Northern Ireland and Scotland. They worked all hours, and their work was very obvious to the public. People could see them putting up poles and digging up underground ducts that had been damaged by tree roots.

'Engineers...worked all hours, and their work was very obvious to the public.'

Slowly, the press reporting changed. BT was seen to be working hard to give people back their telephones; we were even seen as doing better than other public services. Finally, the last month of 1987 saw us edging back in the public's good books again, after our worst year ever.

How did we realise we had to do something?

One of the most unexpected discoveries of the strike in early 1987 was that removing staff actually caused a reduction in the number of faults on the exchanges. In other words, it turned out that a lot of faults were generated as we fixed other faults. This isn't to say that our engineers were to blame – it was largely the fault of the equipment. But it did demonstrate that upgrading the equipment would lead to considerable cost savings, because there would be far fewer faults to repair – and the customers would be happier.

Looking back, 1987 was a huge turning point:

- **There is a limit to how bad you can get without noticing.** We began to get a clear message from our customers: they didn't believe that BT took them seriously or understood what they wanted; they did believe that BT offered a very poor service (in everything, from answering the phone to the time it took to install new lines and repair faults). Complaints from customers were amplified by the media. We were the whipping boys for a lot of the popular press. You can't avoid seeing messages like that.

- **Our backlogs didn't result just from technology or resource problems, but from poor service.** We began to see that fixing something badly the first time was generating extra costs in having to go back and fix it again, costing the company money and causing the customer frustration. To clear the backlogs we had to

Poor service standards can generate backlogs.

improve customer service, and to do that we needed to rethink our approach to quality and our whole management style.

Chapter 2 describes how we established a top-quality management programme

● **New technology forced us to realise that service had to be improved.** Technology could bring huge benefits, but it also created difficulties for staff, because they needed more and better training to learn the new systems. We began to see that, for new technology to bring all the benefits it promised for our customers, we needed to change our whole attitude to customer service.

Improved technology demands improved customer service quality.

Why did we change?

The organisation felt huge pain, which in itself need not necessarily create momentum for change, but for BT there was the reality of the market place that became almost a survival issue. And it was that which made BT really focus on competition. Why was that?

Competition

The driving force behind was competition. It took a while for the reality of competition to hit home. BT had always been a monopoly, but by the mid 1980s it was clear that we were going to lose business if we didn't respond to the threat. As our service and our reputation grew worse we started to lose customers. We knew that we could not compete as the cheapest telecommunications supplier; instead we were going to have to be the best. We also had to ensure that customers realised that we were the best.

When you can't be the cheapest, be the best.

A focus on service, not hardware

We found ourselves becoming increasingly a service provider, rather than a hardware supplier. Liberalisation and changes in technology meant that our share of the market for installing and repairing phones and switchboards was shrinking. We moved from a market where customers were not *allowed* to attach an extra phone to their line, to one in which we provided a socket so that they could plug just what they wanted: fax machines, answerphones and so on. We even sold a do-it-yourself wiring kit – at the time a real 'mindset' change for our engineers.

We had to evolve into a service company, using the power of the network to generate business rather than relying on the supply of equipment. New technology gave rise to new services and applications that could replace the declining business, but our competitors could also offer these. In the same way in which supermarkets now advertise their service features (more open checkouts for shorter queues, etc.) because they cannot claim that their canned beans are better than anyone else's, BT had to make *service* the main market differentiator.

> *'We had to convince our business customers that we could use our technology to help them to run their businesses better.'*

The BT network gave us a head start, but to take advantage of the power of the network, BT had to become an expert service company. Our business customers were seeing that telecommunications could help them to run their businesses better and we had to prove that this was our real value – to help them exploit the technology. We have done this to considerable effect: our business customers now recognise their telecommunications capability as a means of generating revenue, and, indeed, improving *their* customer service.

By the end of 1987 our response to the hurricane, and the public recognition of how well we had done, gave us a sense of winning at last. The priorities at the top of the organisation shifted to tackling the enormous job of transforming our customer service. Although we had already started to recognise the need for this shift, it was the boost in morale, combined with the fervent desire never to go through another year like 1987, that proved to be the turning point. We knew that we faced an enormous job, but no one quite realised how huge the task would be.

The key lessons for business in this chapter are:

.....

Every organisation faces change but few have had to recover from such difficult times.

.....

The problems were inherited – under-investment, civil service style, poor service.

.....

It was the nadir of 1987 that tells the story of just how bad things could get...

.....

Privatisation and competition catalysed the organisation and the following chapters tell the story of the turn-around.

.....

The first step: listening to customers

If we were to put the nadir of 1987 behind us, there were four key issues to tackle:

- *We had to find a good starting point: something that would be a symbolic step change for both BT customers and staff.*

- *We needed to develop an organisational structure that suited the customer and that also had the flexibility to adapt as customer demands changed. Our current structure by geographic region failed on both counts.*

- *We desperately needed to use management approaches to unify the company and dynamise our people.*

- *We had to change the way we judged our customers – so far we had acknowledged their contribution to our profit, but hadn't begun to look at customer satisfaction.*

Where to start?

Once we had made the decision to concentrate on improving our customer service it was really a question of where to begin. The organisation had over a quarter of a million people, servicing virtually all the telecommunications needs – business and private – for an entire nation. It supplied equipment, installed it, repaired it, upgraded it, and gave advice and information on telecommunications. It was divided into 27 geographic districts, each of which operated, in many ways, as discrete organisations. We were going to overhaul our customer service. Where would *you* start? To answer this question, we had to work out the criteria for defining a good starting point.

> **Identifying the criteria for a good solution is a first step towards finding one.**

Our first criterion was to begin on a part of our service that was really crying out for improvement; we didn't want to just fiddle around about the edges. Unfortunately this did not narrow the field as much as it should have.

The next criterion was slightly more helpful: everyone had to recognise that we were making changes. We needed to make a public statement. Customers had to see that BT was capable of giving a really good service, and the staff needed a morale boost, so we had to choose something that would make a real impact.

There was one final criterion, which was based on practical considerations. We had to start with a service that was fairly self-contained. Most of what goes on in BT is interwoven and interdependent. We needed to find a service that we could define and get our arms round.

So we were looking for an aspect of our operations that:

- was truly awful
- everyone would notice the improvements in
- we could really focus efforts on.

These pointed to one of our biggest problem areas of all: public payphones.

The payphone revolution

The payphone service was certainly in need of an overhaul. Part of the trouble with it was that we'd bought an unreliable product in the first place. Each phone had an average of 30 faults a year, and they were dirty and poorly maintained. The company was losing a lot of money on them. If we had been operating on purely commercial terms we could have closed them down altogether, but since we were *obliged* to offer the service we left the phones there, metaphorically and literally gathering dust.

> '*Across the country, a staggering average of only 17% of payphones was working at any time.*'

Each of the 27 districts in the UK was responsible for its own payphones. They were losing money, they were complicated to fix and nobody liked working on them, so they were always put to the back of the work queues. Across the country, a staggering average of only 17% of payphones was working at any time. They had virtually become a national symbol of BT's poor service, and as such they were the obvious place to start the campaign of customer service.

> '*Mike Bett... went on national television and announced that by a certain date we would have 90% of our payphones working at all times.*'

A public commitment to change

The Managing Director, Mike Bett, decided to be brave (at the time some said foolhardy). He went on national television and announced that by a certain date we would have 90% of our payphones working at all times. He then set a handful of top people to work out how we were going to meet this commitment.

Forming a separate payphone business

The first step was to separate the payphone operations from the district organisation and to create a national payphone business. We designed and ordered new phone boxes to replace the traditional red ones, and employed contractors to go round every day to keep the boxes clean. We selected good engineers to get the service right, turning payphones repairs into a prestige assignment.

It was a huge job. BT operate 128,000 payphones in every corner of the UK. They are often a lifeline for communities. Despite a rise in the use of mobile phones, payphones are still in demand in the countryside and cities alike.

The payphone engineers and their managers were inspired by the challenge of turning round the service. They knew they would share in the credit if we met our goal, and this gave them a pride in what they did. They worked overtime at weekends, and holidays were often deferred. They succeeded in getting 90% of the payphones working ahead of the target date – and they kept them working at that level. (Today, over 95% of payphones work at any given time.)

Public appreciation for our efforts

The strategy proved successful. We had genuinely improved the service, and for the first time our payphones were actually making a profit. The public and the press appreciated the change. Although some people criticised us for getting rid of the old phone boxes, there was recognition that the new phone box design showed more concern for the customer (they were easier to get into and easier to use). We also gave ourselves a huge morale boost.

> Spending money to improve service can cause a previously loss-making product or service to become profitable.

One corollary to the payphone success a few years later was that a BT manager Patricia Vaz became UK Business Woman of the Year – in 1994 – and, apart from her personal achievement of rising through the organisation, she was also recognised for her part in heading the payphone turnaround story. It was quite a prize for BT to have a manager so publicly acclaimed.

So we realised that if we put our minds to it we could provide good customer service. We'd done it with payphones; now we had to do it with the rest of the organisation.

Building a customer service framework

We fixed the payphones successfully, but they were a self-contained part of the business. It didn't follow that we could extend the same treatment to the entire BT organisation in such a piecemeal fashion. Not only were very few parts of the organisation so self-contained, but it would also be impossible to improve the service to the customer without overhauling the whole structure that supported it. The company wasn't equipped to give customers what they wanted; BT had never been designed with the customer in mind, so we needed to redesign the whole organisation.

'In our fast moving industry neither we nor our customers really knew what they were going to want next year, let alone any further into the future.'

Our first task was to lay the foundations on which to build a top customer service operation. In our fast moving industry neither we nor our customers really knew what they are going to want next year, let alone any further into the future. It was clear that the speed of change was such that we had to construct an organisation that would be flexible enough to cope with changing customer demand.

Successful organisations are structured for the customers' benefit, and are flexible enough to change with customer needs.

The re-design came in two major stages: the first was the introduction of Total Quality Management (TQM) throughout the company; the second was a fundamental change to the structure of the organisation away from one based on geography to one based on customer segmentation. This structural change was called 'Project Sovereign'.

The quality imperative

BT had to find a mechanism to start the changes, and TQM really did change the way we behaved. The driving force behind Total Quality was the Chairman, Sir Iain Vallance, who saw that without a new approach to customers and the way we did business a privatised BT would simply repeat the mistakes of the old public corporation. TQM offered a comprehensive approach, although much of the standard TQM style had to be adapted to the particular requirement of BT. Sir Iain has never regretted this 'DIY approach': 'it may have taken longer and there were mistakes and false starts. But it's important that you do it. It must get into the bloodstream.'

'TQM offered the essential comprehensive approach'

TQM was relatively new to the UK back in the mid 1980s and regarded as a bit of a fad, but it was designed to deal with three key issues:

- **Investment on its own would not solve problems – the whole culture needed to change.** TQM, which had proved so successful in Japan and the United States, worked because it focused on a continuous improvement approach as a way of bringing about competitive advantage.

- **BT was operating with a huge mixture of management styles.** These arose from the different districts and also because we had recruited a lot of new people from a wide variety of backgrounds. We hadn't any choice about recruiting new blood because we needed people who were experienced in finance, marketing and sales and they were appointed into each of the 27 independent districts. The influx of new people had benefits – it gave the company a broader outlook – but it caused some consistency problems. TQM was a way of moving towards a consistent approach – a common, shared view of the company and its operations.

- **Service quality was going to be crucial to BT's future.** We could save ourselves a fortune if we made fewer mistakes in the first place. Our backlogs were being caused by poor service, and the new technology was going to put more and more pressure on us to improve the quality of our service.

TQM is a means to an end, not an end in itself. It was important not to view it as a kind of panacea to be followed for its own sake. What it provided was a robust method for tackling the issues facing us. We introduced the TQM programme in the mid 1980s under the banner of 'Meeting Customer Requirements', because that was where we wanted the focus to be. There was bound to be a resistance of the 'just another management fad' reaction, and the real challenge was overcoming this so that everyone saw TQM as the best way to achieve the goal we were all aiming for: good customer service. We needed a shared concept of quality throughout the business: not just engineering quality, but a thorough do-it-properly, get-it-right-first-time approach. We wanted the sort of quality that didn't just mean getting rid of crackles on the phone lines, but a more intangible sense of 'quality' that would permeate everything we did.

> To make change happen everyone has to share the goal.

Overcoming scepticism

To begin with, many people were sceptical about TQM, including, it must be said, some senior managers. They thought it was just a passing fashion. It was therefore important to make sure that TQM lasted, and that it became an integral part of the corporate culture. We managed this in two ways:

- **The TQM programme was cascaded from the top down.** However, everybody saw that it needed to reach the roots of the organisation. *All* our managers went through a three-day workshop on how to handle situations differently, getting a new focus on customers, using new management techniques and so on. This was something completely new for our people; all across BT managers were learning to talk a new language.

> TQM works when it permeates the *whole* organisation.

- **Every manager had to have a quality improvement project, even if it was only to solve a small problem.** Once they had solved one problem they started on another. This approach was designed to ensure that the TQM initiative didn't fizzle out somewhere around the middle managers. We made sure that TQM flowed into every corner of BT. With the number of managers we had in the company we had soon solved a lot of problems! We kept going with the programme until it became obvious to everyone that it really was working, and often it was the very simplest techniques that people remembered. For example, Pareto analysis

> *'don't eat the elephant al at once'*

bases its approach on a view that in any situation 80% of the problems are caused by 20% of the activity. Fix that 20% and you've made a huge step forward. Phrases such as 'concentrate on the vital few rather than the useful many' became common in the organisation, and were turned into guidelines for action.

We didn't try to apply TQM overnight to everything we did. We recognised that it had to be tailored to meet the company's requirements. We concentrated on small parts of the operations. We used the phrase: 'don't eat the elephant all at once' to convey the idea that we should break down large tasks into smaller ones. Small successes helped to build confidence.

Don't be frightened of the size of TQM. Use it in a way that works for your organisation.

As people became more confident they became more prepared to take ownership of problems that they saw in their organisation and to be responsible for fixing them. Instead of saying 'it's not my fault' or 'it's not my problem' people began to have the confidence to solve problems that had been frustrating them for years.

The Quality Management System

In the mid 1980s no one in BT had a job description. There were no team meetings, no upward feedback, no one-to-ones (the regular sessions every employee has with their direct manager). Today we take all these things for granted. TQM is about management, but once the principles were very well understood we used these to overhaul the basic rules that governed how our managers worked. These new rules established the basis of good practice. They were (and are now) called the Quality Management System (QMS). A lot of effort has gone into getting people to understand that the QMS belongs to them, and must be viewed as a tool for helping them to do their job better. If it is not achieving this then something is wrong and it needs to be changed. There is never a reason for anyone to say 'I only do this because the rules say I must'. Anything they do must be done because it gets the job done properly.

Meeting customer requirements

TQM is very much about customer requirements. This was the first time that such focus really became explicit in the organisation.

In order to ensure that quality really got into the bloodstream of BT, we decided to test ourselves against the requirements of independent quality bodies such as the British Standards Institute. During the early '90s different parts of BT applied for and received the appropriate quality certification – usually the BS5750 standard.

There was a real sense of achievement and the real message that BT was a 'quality company' was touching everyone in the organisation . . . there was obviously much more to do, but this was huge progress for an organisation the size of BT. This process culminated with our entire UK operation achieving ISO9000 registration in 1994. It is important to note the motivation behind all this: it was not just a paper chase to get fancy certificates but a desire to reach the high standards the accreditation demanded. We wanted to reach these standards so that we could offer a better level of service to our customers.

Making TQM work

If this all sounds easy, it wasn't. Changing the culture of an organisation as big as BT is a long, slow and often painful process. BT had always been inward looking. Suddenly we were asking everyone to look outwards, at the customer – to make the customer's life easier, even if it made things more complicated for us. In November 1990 Sir Iain Vallance personally rewrote the company values to convey the key messages in as short a statement as

Don't expect instant change in a large organisation.

possible (just 23 words). These values told our customers and our people exactly what we stood for. They are still relevant.

- **We put our customers first.**
- **We are professional.**
- **We respect each other.**
- **We work as one team.**
- **We are committed to continuous improvement.**

These words, and the tremendous commitment they represent, have had an enormous impact on BT. At the time they gave all our people a yardstick by which to judge the worth of what they were doing – and they have lasted.

The BT Values, and the disciplines of the TQM Programme, represented a clear break with the old pre-privatised BT. Privatisation was not on its own enough to drive the changes we now needed. Our response to competition had to draw its strength from another source. TQM, and the commitment of the Board to make the BT Values a reality, provided the new start we needed.

Conveying the threat of competition

The company was asking its people to change the whole way they felt about customers, their jobs and themselves. In many cases they really didn't like this. One of the reasons that people were resistant to change was that they didn't appreciate how large a threat competition was going to be. With hindsight, we hadn't prepared them for the arrival of competition.

Right at the start of privatisation, staff were very aware of competition and what it might do to their jobs. But when Mercury actually arrived on the scene in the mid 1980s nothing much appeared to happen. We went through a 'phoney war' and, after a while, most of the front-line people began to feel that the competition wasn't any real threat. How wrong they were!

Perhaps we should have been more blunt and spelt out the problems that competition would bring and why, but it's difficult when it is theory and not reality. Inevitably, things took time to 'hot up' and we couldn't really capture hearts and minds with the result that the unions didn't see the need to adapt to competition in the way that they have today.

Once competition began to bite, the unions' attitude changed. By the early '90s they started using phrases such as 'competitive environment', which they had never had to do before. They started to see for themselves the damage that competition could do if we didn't respond. They saw customers start to desert BT for Mercury.

Putting theory into practice

This realisation that we *did* have to improve our customer service to counter the threat of competition started in London, because that was where Mercury first attacked BT, and in particular the lucrative telecomms markets of the City of London. Slowly the realisation spread across the country. Everyone was eager to solve some of the problems in their own patch. This is where all the work we had put into TQM came into its own. Suddenly all those workshops talking about problem-solving techniques had a point. People could reach into their intellectual 'toolkit' and, talking the same language as their colleagues, find a method by which they could start to get a grip on the issues facing them.

All sorts of techniques were used – Pareto, Forcefield Analysis, Herring Bone diagrams – and, to hold the whole thing

> *'...problem solving can only really be achieved through a continuous improvement approach...'*

together so they could understand where they were in the process, the now famous (in BT at least) 'problem-solving wheel'.

TQM enabled people to understand that problem solving can only really be achieved through a continuous improvement approach. And of course it was difficult to define what excellent service looked like – everyone was starting from a whole range of viewpoints and experience. Moving them forward and, more importantly, getting them to drive the changes themselves, would take time. At the basic level it started by getting people dealing with customers professionally and to recognising what that really means, then gradually working them towards *delighting* the customers.

At the end of the '80s, good customer service in BT meant removing any cause for complaint; now it means giving extra value every time. For an organisation of our size it has taken about ten years for the application of total quality to filter through to the point where today it is in the bloodstream. But from soon after its inception we had got through to people one of the most central concepts: that it is the customer who pays our wages.

BT became so committed to quality as the cornerstone of our business approach that we became a founder member of the European Foundation for Quality Management (EFQM). The European Quality Award self-assessment model is now an integral part of the company's strategic planning and management system. Organisations and awards such as these can help to keep the focus on quality. As well as joining the EFQM or the BFQ (the British equivalent), there is nothing to stop individual companies establishing their own quality awards to give everyone something to aim for. In 1996 BT was runner-up in the

Keep enthusiasm alive by joining some of the quality management organisations and entering for awards.

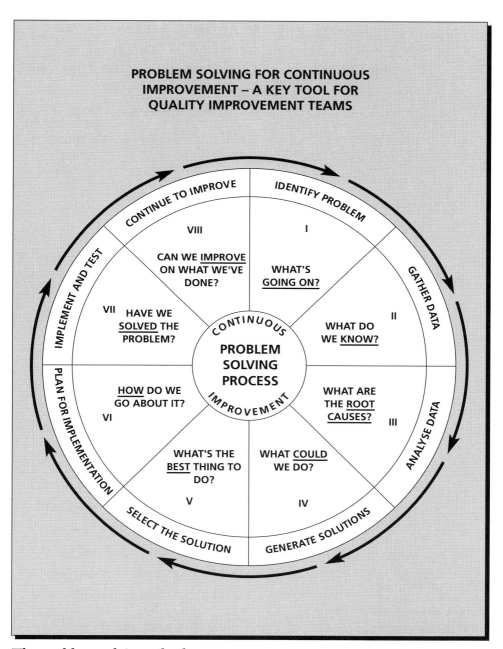

The problem-solving wheel

overall EQA awards. It was the biggest EQA assessment ever undertaken (BT had more sites than some entrants had people). It is now generally felt that BT displays the characteristics of 'systemic quality' – a state that is reached when the whole is greater than the sum of the parts. Although no part of the organisation is perfect, overall the parts work together to produce a result far better than an examination of each constituent part on its own would indicate.

Project Sovereign: creating a customer-driven structure

Once you start to make changes, you often find that you have to instigate more changes to make the original ones effective. That is what happened to us. Having set off on the road to total quality, we realised that we were in a completely unsuitable vehicle. On the one hand we were saying that we wanted to be customer driven, and to define our service standards by what the customer wanted; on the other hand we were running an organisation that was structured with anyone but the customer in mind.

The basic problem with the structure was that BT was – and always had been – organised into geographical regions. By the end of the '80s there were 27 districts, some divided even further into customer service areas. Each district had a general manager, and they were very powerful figures in the organisation. Each ran their own organization in their own way. Standards of customer service varied widely from district to district. There was a limited spirit of co-operation because, among other things, each wanted their own performance to be the best. Like it or not, districts competed against each other to be 'top dog'.

Think carefully about how you measure performance. Put measures in place that will reinforce the customer service you want to achieve.

For customers running, say, a small local business, this arrangement worked. They dealt with their local BT office. Each time they needed anything done BT would respond, do the work and send the bill. But for larger organisations, or even small ones that happened to have offices in different BT districts, the situation was complicated and frustrating.

A customer who wanted BT to put in a private line between two offices in different districts had to phone district A to ask them to run a line through to their office in district B. District A would be happy to do this, because they would get the money for the work. But district B, who would not get any money on this job, could think of plenty of things they would rather be doing than connecting up their end of the line for nothing, customers ended up waiting for the line to be connected and would finally chase the job up. They would then find that neither district wanted to take responsibility, and that it could be almost impossible to get them to communicate effectively with each other.

Now imagine a national high street bank with thousands of offices all round the country, or a national rent-a-car company, or a supermarket chain. The process of getting a private network put in, or even getting faults repaired, could be a nightmare.

Looking at ourselves from the customer's viewpoint

The crucial point, as TQM showed us, was the way the customer saw us. Customers weren't interested in being divided up into geographies. They saw BT as a single national organisation, and that meant BT had to *be* a single, national organisation. Any subdivision of the organisation into sections had to be by function, not by geography, because that was how the customers wanted it. Customers were happy to phone a different number to report a fault from the number they dialled to order a new phone, but they didn't see why they should deal with a completely different bit of BT just because they moved half a mile down the road.

These customer demands were increasingly being championed by the sales and marketing sections of the organisation who were taking a far more dominant role. They complained about the poor level of service they were forced to offer. There were complaints from our product managers about inadequate facilities and service standards for their products.

Private circuits as the example above showed were particularly bad. The problems could only be solved by organisational change. This means creating a self-contained private circuit organisation to avoid the geographic management problems – the same solution that worked for the payphone problem.

'...everyone came to work in April 1991 to a very different organisation...'

But we recognised that individual product solutions were not going to be a cure – we needed to reorganise the whole company.

And so we did. It was a complete restructure, and a year after announcing that the changes were planned, everyone came to work in April 1991 to a very different organisation. For many of the front-line staff there was relatively little difference to their day-to-day work, but for managers and – more importantly – to the customers there was a vast difference. The restructuring was known as Project Sovereign to reflect the idea that 'the customer is king'. In short, the organisation was designed with the customer at the top, customer-facing divisions segmented between residential, UK business and our growing global customers and all the rest of the organisation 'in support' of these customer-facing units.

At the same time as changing the structure of the organisation, we took out several layers of management. In some districts there had been as many as 13 layers. Now there were to be no more than six levels below the board of directors. This had huge advantages in pushing customer service to the fore. It is always the individuals with vision who generate change; now that there were far fewer layers of management, and the organisation was split into smaller groups, it was much easier for these people to move ideas up and down the management chain and to get real momentum into our service improvement drive.

> **Value people with vision. They are the ones who generate change.**

BT had always had people who were really passionate about customer service, but the level of service between districts had varied enormously. We simply didn't have the processes to make the organisation work seamlessly for our customers. Naturally the customers found this frustrating. After the districts were abolished, the apostles of customer service were far better placed to spread the word. The company began to focus on creating a consistent level of customer service everywhere, and on making sure that BT managed service for its customers, instead of the customers having to manage BT's service for themselves. It was a time when the importance of telecommunications for people's businesses was growing very fast, and this made establishing a national customer service standard even more important.

A common thread that emerged from this real focus on the customer was that we could characterise good service in four relatively simple statements and we developed these as our priorities:

- **Listening.** Good service starts with listening to the customer's needs, being knowledgeable about the possible solutions and being able to recommend the best solution for each customer.
- **Placing an order.** It must be easy for the customer to place an order once they have decided to accept the recommended product or service.

- **Prompt delivery.** The product or service must be available when the customer needs it, and it must arrive when it has been promised.

- **Helping the customer with any problems after the product or service has been delivered.** Any faults or difficulties must be dealt with swiftly and consistently.

It was also becoming clear that our future lay not only in our ability to supply good service and products, but also in our ability to market and sell them. The aim of Project Sovereign was to create a structure that would enable us to deliver high quality telecommunications services across the whole of the UK, to standards that satisfied the customers. Once we had achieved this, the trick would be to market this capability effectively. Supplying the right products, and delivering the best service was, therefore, the foundation upon which all our future ambitions would be built. We had no choice but to get it right.

Coping with change

With any huge change there are disadvantages. One of the problems we faced was that many of the staff found it difficult to cope. It wasn't that their jobs had necessarily changed greatly, but their sense of belonging had. Before Project Sovereign they had belonged to a district. Although they had technically been employees of a national company, they felt as though they belonged locally. Now, suddenly, they belonged to an organisation that was enormous by comparison, and that took some getting used to.

The other drawback with the restructuring was that it didn't necessarily help customers who were small or middle size companies and who didn't cross any district boundaries. They missed the local touch. Many of our staff dealt with these types of people all the time and so couldn't see the huge benefits for the majority of our customers. These staff wondered why, for example, we had separated our business customers and residential customers into different organisations. Although necessary from a marketing and sales viewpoint, in terms of the end product of customer service, at an operational level this wasn't ideal, and individuals were very conscious of the fact.

There were also interesting changes in the different BT groups that had each grown up with a different culture. For example, the sales people had started out in the early '80s almost as lepers – we'd always managed without a sales force before, and they didn't sit easily with the civil service culture. Now these people were really coming into their own, and being recognised as an important and necessary part of BT.

A different change was taking place among the customer service people. The customer service function had tended to be populated by staff who were viewed as being very reactive and thick-skinned enough to handle all our problems! We had to change this by making customer service be seen as successful, with a sense of excitement to really get things done. Gradually, BT people across the board started to recognise the importance of customer service. And having started to create a culture of focusing on the customer, we now had a foundation on which to begin to build a world class service.

KEY LESSONS CHAPTER 2

The key lessons for restructuring to focus on customers are:
.....

Find a good starting point. It should be something that badly needs doing, that customers will really notice and appreciate, and that will boost morale by making people recognise that they are capable of giving good service.
.....

Define your own company style. If a lot of managers have come from outside, they need a strong corporate approach that they can become part of. Total quality needs to be a part of this approach if the company is going to put customer service excellence high on the agenda.
.....

The way managers' performances are assessed must take into account the service they are giving to their customers.
.....

Measuring our performance

W*e needed to measure how good our customer service was.*

- *It isn't enough just to measure performance; we needed to find the right things to measure.*

- *We had to work out how to find out what mattered to our customers.*

- *We had to learn to use customer satisfaction to drive our service operation, instead of using our internal measures.*

We used to measure our performance in terms of how well individual departments worked. The organisation simply didn't reflect what our customers wanted. We had a lot of different internal measures; in fact we had just too many! We measured how long it took us to repair faults, how long it took us to install lines and networks, and so on. We measured everything we could think of, but we discovered that this wasn't actually telling us what we wanted to know.

The importance of accurate measurement

Here is an example of the kind of flaw the system contained.

> In our management of payphones, we measured how long they were out of order. At least, we *thought* that was what we were measuring. In fact, we didn't start counting a fault until a customer reported it. Most customers didn't bother to report faulty phones, they just found another one to use. It could be days before we found out that a phone wasn't working, and it could go wrong again half an hour after we'd fixed it. None of that was visible to us.

Another illustration shows how this applied at a more general level.

> One of our managers working in the customer service department in the City of London remembers being updated regularly by his staff on how many outstanding faults there were in the service for the City as a whole. Shortly after he started the job, he visited one of his customers, who claimed to have more faults on their service alone than he had been told there were in the entire City.

The manager returned to his office and asked how this could happen. He was told that the huge number of faults that were unaccounted for in the figures were all EFAs. He asked them to explain this term, and was told it meant 'excluded from analysis'.

In fact you could exclude just about anything from analysis if you wanted to. Our operator service people used to measure how quickly they answered calls. If it looked as if the score was going to slip too low, any manager could just 'busy out' the calls – in other words change the switchboard to the engaged signal for anyone trying to ring in – and the score would go up. In this way they only measured the response time for calls that got through, not the ones that never made it.

'...you managed the figures to keep your bosses off your back, so that you could get on with the job.'

It wasn't that the managers were deliberately trying to be dishonest. This approach had been there since civil service days: you managed the figures to keep your bosses off your back, so that you could get on with the job.

One of the worst areas was faults on private circuits. (A private circuit is where a business has its own link between two locations.) It was tempting to concentrate efforts on fixing the faults that made statistics look good, rather than to meet the customers' requirements. That meant the most recently reported faults were favoured so as to get a 'clear' in the target time. Hence the tough ones accumulated in a backlog! No one wanted to own up to the scale of the backlog and to see their figures drop as a result and we had to resort to clearing the faults once and for all by declaring an amnesty for a week, during which the managers could rectify as many faults as possible without having to enter them on their performance figures.

Make sure that your measures of managers' performance don't actually prevent you from achieving good customer service.

Measuring customer satisfaction

We were measuring everything that we thought could help us to improve our performance. We had so many statistics it was hard to decipher them all. Somehow the customers didn't seem to appreciate how difficult it all was! Our figures – even allowing for the EFAs – were telling us that we were doing well, but our customers were telling us that we weren't.

Once we launched the TQM programme, and made the other changes that put customer service high on the agenda, it became clear that if we weren't satisfying the customer, we must be doing something wrong. We decided that we'd better measure what the customers actually thought of our performance, to see whether this fitted in with what we thought. So back in the 1980s we launched a programme called 'Telcare' to survey customers to measure their satisfaction levels. Not surprisingly we found that these results didn't align with our internal measures. Our own statistics told us, for example, that most repairs were being done on time, and yet the customers were saying that they weren't satisfied. One of the measurements had to be wrong, surely?

> **If the customer isn't satisfied, you must be doing something wrong.**

Telcare wasn't as successful as it might have been: there was always the suspicion that if the figures came out so apparently at odds with the facts as we knew them this meant that we were doing something wrong with the sampling. And indeed back then there were imperfections, but we persisted and encouraged everyone to reason openly with colleagues that if BT was genuinely interested in satisfying the customer, the customer satisfaction measures were the ones that mattered. If our own measures didn't fit, they needed changing.

> *'If you measure the wrong things, things will go wrong.'*

This led us to one of the great truths about measuring performance: if you measure the wrong things, things will go wrong. This is not as obvious as it seems until the customer experience is the driving force. Here are two examples of how this affected our statistics in terms of, firstly, new installations and, secondly, repairing faults.

> We used to measure the time it took to provide a private circuit. The longer the time extended beyond the date we agreed to install it, the less satisfied the customer was. The customer satisfaction figures tallied with our installation time figures. However, this was far from the case with our repair services: we couldn't correlate the time it took to make a repair with the customer satisfaction. Why not? The answer was very simple, once we recognised it. It was because the time factor was only a part of what makes up customer satisfaction.

We used to think that the important thing was to drive up the speed of our repairs continuously. We now know that this on its own simply isn't true. For some customers certain circuits are so critical that they want them fixed in five minutes, but many customers don't mind waiting until tomorrow. They're much more concerned about other things, for example:

- Did we arrive at a convenient time?
- Did we barge into a meeting to get at the equipment to fix it?
- Did we give feedback on how the repair was going?

Beware of making assumptions about what matters to customers.

These things can be far more crucial to customers than the speed of the repair, but we weren't measuring them.

We were making assumptions about what satisfied the customer, and our assumptions were often wrong. Now we had to find out what customers actually cared about and measure that – easier said than done.

There were certain areas where speed was clearly important to our customers.

> Speeding up our repair times was important and we achieved a real step change, largely as a result of a Friday afternoon visit to a customer service office in Fife, about ten years ago, by Mike Armitage, who was then our assistant MD. He was on a routine visit to meet the people in the service office, and he got chatting to a receptionist who had just taken a call reporting a fault. Mike asked when the fault would be fixed, and the receptionist was pleased to be able to tell him that it would meet the target and be done by the next Tuesday evening.
>
> It suddenly struck Mike that if his wife was offered this standard of repair for the washing machine she would find it totally unacceptable – and yet this was what we were offering our customers. What's more, BT people thought they were doing a *good* job by meeting this target. It was simply the wrong target.
>
> A few days later the subject of service standards was being discussed at a strategy conference. Remembering what had happened in Fife, Mike wrote on the flip charts that the targets we would aim for would be five working hours for repairing business customers' faults, and nine hours for residential lines. These figures were based on what Mike's instincts told him would be acceptable. The vast majority of customers would accept this as a significant improvement, and Mike's experience told him that with hard work we could achieve it.

The operational directors threw up their hands in horror, but the marketing and sales people were grateful! After making the decision, Mike discovered that some basic research had already been done into the repair times customers wanted, and Mike's instinctive figures were very close to what the customers had said. Maybe it would have been better to have had the research available when the decision was made if we had known about it, but the point was that the heroic leap forward was made by passionate self-belief, rather than deep analysis.

Getting customer feedback

We introduced Telcare in the mid 1980s, and was in some ways ahead of its time with all the other problems we then faced.

Gradually we have introduced a wide range of customer satisfaction sampling and we use complaints positively rather than as a reactive function. When you look and see what people are complaining about, it tells you where to turn your attention first.

The first issues to address are those that customers complain about.

Analysing complaints is an important first step, but it is only a first step. Customers complain about things they feel really strongly about. There are plenty of other minor gripes that don't make the complaints statistics, but that will stop customers from telling you that they are really satisfied with your performance.

Chapter 8 describes in depth how we handle complaints

We began to survey customers in detail, using two methods:

- We left **survey cards** with large customers after a repair or an installation.
- We started running **telephone questionnaires** with customers who had recently had dealings with us.

We have honed these two approaches over the years and we now have standard survey cards and a quantitative telephone questionnaire. An example of the survey card that is left with customers after a repair to a big switchboard is shown opposite. We ask customers to rate us on a scale of 1 (very poor) to 10 (excellent). We analyse these figures and classify customers as very satisfied if they score us 9 or 10, and satisfied if they score us 7 or above.

Repair Specific Card

1. Was it easy to report your fault?   Marking 1–10

2. Was this a recurrence of the same fault within the last
three months?   Yes/No

3. How well did BT keep you informed of the progress
of your fault(s)?   Marking 1–10

4. In relation to the engineers' visit what was your
assessment of the following:
   a. Did the engineer arrive at the
   appointed time?   Yes/No/No appointment made
   b. Did he/she show their identity card?   Yes/No
   c. Did the engineer act in a professional/business
   like manner?   Yes/No
   d. Did the engineer advise you once the fault
   had been rectified?   Yes/No
   e. Did the engineer offer you a test to show that the fault
   had been rectified?   Yes/No

5. Did the engineer offer to discuss any other BT telecomms
requirements or queries which you might have had?   Yes/No

6. If you answered 'Yes' to question No. 5, did the engineer
cover these satisfactorily?   Yes/No

7. How satisfied were you overall with the
engineer's performance?   Marking 1–10

8. How satisfied were you with BT's overall service?   Marking 1–10

9. Following your recent experiences in
connection with the work that BT have
carried out, did this   1 improve your opinion of BT
                                   2 make it worse
                                   3 make no difference

Note: On the questions with a 1–10 marking, 1 is very poor and 10 is excellent.

*The survey card BT uses for customers who have had
equipment repaired*

Our aim is to achieve as many very satisfied customers as possible in each service we offer.

Our telephone questionnaires survey 11,000 customers a month; all of these are people who have had recent transactions with BT. The total list of questions runs to well over 100, but no customer is asked all of them – only those that are relevant to them. The interview takes around ten to 20 minutes, so it's fairly thorough. There's a case for reducing this time so as not to take up too much of the customer's time, and that's something we are working on. Clearly we want to be sure that we don't drop questions that we need to know the answers to.

> **Don't expect your customers to spend too long answering survey questions.**

In the past few years we have also been carrying out an annual, in-depth survey with our biggest customers. We arrange an interview with them, which can take up to an hour; it is almost an appraisal interview. These customers are usually happy to give up the time because their telecommunications are vital to them, and they want us to understand exactly what they need from us.

It takes a lot of time, effort and money to design workable and robust customer surveys. Two types of questions need to be included:

- **Questions that provide 'hard' measures.** For example, 'How long did the repair take?', or 'Did the engineer arrive on time?'. These are tangible measures.

- **Questions that provide 'soft' measures.** For example, 'Was the engineer polite?'. These are less tangible. Soft measures are extremely important because it is the personal touch that so often makes all the difference to how a customer responds to the way a job is done.

And of course it is the so-called 'soft' measures that are often the most difficult to get right.

We never stopped keeping internal measures – we have close on 100 key performance measures across our services to businesses. These are becoming more useful because we have found that, as we became cleverer at measuring customer satisfaction, we have been able to correlate internal measures with customer measures in much more detail. This makes life far easier for our people – we can explain why we want them to do certain things in a certain way.

> The more accurate your measurement of customer satisfaction becomes, the more useful internal measures can be.

It makes a difference to our customers whether or not they actually see our engineer on site making a repair. It is perfectly possible for our engineers to wander in, not speak to anyone, head straight for the telecomms room, fix the fault and leave. The customer has their fault repaired, so what's the problem?

The fact is that customers don't like it. They want to see the engineer – it gives them reassurance. To some of our people, this makes perfect sense but to others the point of the exercise is to fix the fault. Nowadays we can show them the figures that demonstrate that showing their face to the customer can make the difference between an eight out of ten customer satisfaction score and a ten out of ten. This not only gets the point across to the engineers, but makes them far more willing to introduce themselves to the customer.

We can back this up even further, because we now know that customers who regularly score us highly on customer satisfaction have an increasing level of spending with us, while those who tend to score us low have a decreasing spending level. Our engineers recognise the significance of this. Now that we can tell them what kind of behaviour will push up the satisfaction ratings, they want to hear it.

Raising the stakes

We have been measuring and targeting improvements in customer satisfaction for several years. We have learnt that the real gains do not come from simply satisfying customers – we have to *delight* them to make a real impact on how loyal they are to BT. This is common sense. All of us expect good service these days, but when we get the real personal touch we know it. So today our targets are set on driving up our 9 and 10 out of 10 scores – and that is a tremendous challenge that demands real determination.

'We have learnt that the real gains do not come from simply satisfying customers – we have to delight them to make a real impact on how loyal they are to BT.'

The following story of how we learned from our experience with providing the infrastructure for the National Lottery gives a flavour of what this has meant for us.

Delight, not just satisfaction

The work involved in setting up outlets for the National Lottery led to another watershed in our approach to service delivery targets. We decided to deliver when the customer wanted and change our previous 'standard lead times'. We had long been aware that customers were far from happy with our speed of providing private circuits and the challenge of the lottery work made us take another 'heroic step'.

When BT took on the contract for the Lottery it meant delivering around 25,000 private circuits in just a few months to most of the outlets that sold tickets – and a doubling of our normal workload. We had to look at how we could improve our lead times, or we weren't going to get through the work on top of our other orders. Lead times were 20 days or ten days, depending on the type of circuit. That didn't mean *within* 20 days or ten days. It meant exactly 20 days, or exactly ten days, measured from the day the circuit was ordered. We discovered that the only objection to delivering fast was the potential cost if every circuit had to be delivered very quickly.

From a logistical point of view, we could in fact change our processes and deliver in five days, eight days, nineteen days, or whenever the customer wanted it! So we went for it and managed to deliver almost all the National Lottery circuits in time, despite the fact that, at the peak, we were delivering more than double the usual number of circuits a week. We realised that we had never before needed to ask the bold questions about our capability – questions which, when answered, showed just how well we could perform. Once we knew what we were able to do we decided to start asking customers when *they* would like their circuits delivered, and measuring whether or not we met these target dates – the ones the customers themselves set.

There was a nervousness that customers would all say they wanted their circuit tomorrow, and that was one thing we really couldn't have coped with. When we introduced the new arrangements we weren't sure how the customers would react. We'd never asked them when they wanted delivery before, so we had no idea what their response would be. We didn't think that everyone *would* want their circuits tomorrow, but our fear was that a substantial number would want them within five days. Orders under five days could only be processed manually, so we couldn't afford too many of them.

What happened? It turned out that the vast majority of our customers plan well ahead and in fact average lead times have actually increased – but only because our customers choose it that way. Customer satisfaction levels have also shot up. Now they correlate with internal measures, because we are measuring whether we meet the customer's target date.

It took a while for the satisfaction ratings to go up because we mostly sell private circuits to customers who deal with us regularly and, to begin with, they didn't believe that we could deliver when they wanted us to. They knew what our standard lead times were and, when we asked them to give us a delivery date, they would say 'twenty days' or 'ten days' because they thought that was what they were going to get anyway. Some of them would ask for delivery in less than five days because they thought we would probably be late, but as their trust grew the number of circuits required in less than five days went down, and the number required in over 20 days went up.

A lot of businesses in this sort of situation charge customers a premium for fast delivery, but we were keen to avoid that. When a company says, 'If you want it in four days we'll have to charge you a premium.', the customer replies, 'Oh well, I'll have it in five then...' and it ends up in a dialogue. The customer isn't truly satisfied and, after all, if we can gain and the customers gain why charge more? We have made cost savings in the long term, even though that wasn't the motivation for the change. We get very few complaints to deal with now, so there is none of the extra work and management time that those involve. The circuits overall aren't costing any more to install than they did before.

> **If you charge a premium for fast delivery you aren't really satisfying your customer.**

Understanding customer feedback

We found that, although measuring customer satisfaction generated enormous improvements, it also created difficulties of its own which we had to adapt to.

Subjective scoring

First of all, the only effective way we have of measuring customer satisfaction is subjective. It has to be, because satisfaction itself is subjective. We are constantly aiming for the highest possible 'very satisfied' scores: 9 or above out of 10. We will never achieve these from everyone, and that isn't necessarily a reflection of our performance. At school some teachers regularly give excellent work an 'A+', and others never give above a 'B+', even if they think the work is excellent. Many customers feel on principle that they wouldn't give a company more than, say, 8 out of 10 in case they became complacent.

> **Customer satisfaction is a subjective measurement.**

One customer consistently gave us 7 out of 10 all through a telephone survey, and then stated at the end that he was very satisfied with BT and couldn't think of any negative comments. The manager who was talking to him asked how come, if he was so satisfied, he only gave us a score of 7. He replied: 'I'd only give life eight out of ten.'

Choosing customer-focused measures

The opposite side of this coin is that it is still possible to give ourselves unrepresentatively high scores if we ask our customers to rate us only for areas we know we are really good at. Even with external customer measures, instead of the old internal measures, it is still possible to measure the wrong things. We have to be sure we're asking the customers about the things they care about.

To begin with, the key issues for our customers were fairly clear, but the better our service became, the harder it was to know what

'One of the potential pitfalls of customer satisfaction surveys is that we ultimately control them because we set the questions.'

to measure next. In our drive for continuous improvement, we know that there is always room to improve, but it becomes harder to locate this. One of the potential pitfalls of customer satisfaction surveys is that we ultimately control them because we set the questions. We had to find a way round this, or we would always be one step behind the customer. We wouldn't know what the latest issues were until after the customers had become dissatisfied and started to complain.

We now have several techniques for getting the customers to set the questions for us:

- **Telecomms user groups.** These groups, made up of companies for whom telecomms are important, give regular feedback on what the important issues are for their members, and we can build these into surveys of customer satisfaction.

- **Asking customers what they would like to measure us on.** We ask a variety of customers, but especially our large ones. This can have drawbacks because customers themselves don't always know what they want until you show it to them. So, as well as inviting open suggestions, we sometimes guide them towards options. For example, customers may be happy with a certain standard of service because they think that it is the best they can get. If we tell them that the technology now exists to do it faster or better, they may raise their expectations. Customers didn't start, for example, telling us that they wanted itemised billing until they discovered that it was possible. Then they became dissatisfied with bills that weren't itemised.

Try asking customers to set their own survey topics.

- **Asking customers of new products and services how they want to measure us on them.** We sit down with the first few customers and ask them in detail what information they are going to want from us and how often, and what aspects of the service they are most concerned about and want to measure us on.

- **Bespoke measuring standards for individual customers.** We are now creating an even more bespoke service for many of our customers, by letting them each set their own standards to measure us against. This has drawn our attention to the fact that, if you let the customers set the questions, your score will go down. This is because they are bound to choose to measure your performance in the areas they are most concerned about. As soon as you start to improve, they will move on to new areas, so we have had to learn to adjust to the drop in customer satisfaction scores which, ironically, comes out of giving customers what they want – the opportunity to set the agenda themselves.

> Asking customers to set measurement standards will make your score go down. They will choose the issues they are most dissatisfied with.

It took us several years to get from purely internal measures to a proper understanding of external customer satisfaction measurements. It would have been difficult to go through the process any faster because, in order to understand it, it is necessary to monitor every stage. Once it is clear that the right customer satisfaction measurements are in place, some internal measures can be abandoned. They should be there only to help you to understand the process, and some of them may have served their purpose. We have now learnt never to lose sight of the fact that the only measurement that matters is what the customer thinks. Just as beauty is in the eye of the beholder, so quality is in the mind of the customer.

KEY LESSONS CHAPTER 3

Measuring performance is not as simple as it sounds. The rules that apply to any organisation that wants to measure what it does in order to improve customer service are:

.....

If you measure the wrong things, things will go wrong.

.....

If internal and customer measures don't correlate, listen to the customer measures – they're the ones that matter.

.....

If you want to know where you're going wrong, look at what customers are complaining about.

.....

If you don't know what your customers want, ask them.

.....

Make sure your customers are assessing you on the things that matter to them.

.....

Get the customers to choose their own survey topics.

.....

Aim for customer delight, not just satisfaction.

.....

4

Changing the style

As we discovered more about what our customers wanted, we needed to change internal attitudes and the internal organisation to meet those requirements. There were five key areas to address:

- *Our structure was very hierarchical, with layer upon layer of management.*

- *Relationships between managers and their people (they weren't thought of as teams back then) were very formal.*

- *Promotion was by seniority rather than merit.*

- *Anyone using their initiative was generally seen to be exceeding their authority.*

- *The use of technology needed to be as efficient as the service we wanted to provide for customers.*

It became clear very early on in our transformation from lumbering bureaucracy to customer-driven commercial business, that we would have to change internally as well as externally. It isn't possible to run a company on old fashioned lines and expect to have an up-to-date image with customers. This is especially true in a fast moving, high technology market such as telecommunications.

See Chapter 2 for a description of Project Sovereign.

As we saw in Chapter 2, Project Sovereign was about reorganising the company onto a more commercial, customer-oriented footing, but there were other internal changes that had to happen alongside this. It wasn't enough simply to restructure:

- **Our whole style had to change.** We still worked in much the same way as we had done for decades. We were convinced that changing the way we did business would influence our relationship with customers in the long term – and we were right.

- **We had to make our own internal processes and technology match the service we wanted to deliver to customers.** Each day we handled tens of thousands of transactions – covering new orders, faults and enquiries in every area of the business. Co-ordinating the work of our people and all the projects they are working on isn't easy. After we had restructured we had to ensure that processes between different sections of the organisation worked effectively, and that we had the systems capability to match.

The 'old ways'

BT had always been a very hierarchical organisation. There were 13 layers of management. Managers from about the second or third level didn't spend much time with their people. In the late '60s or early '70s, if a second-line manager visited a group of engineers everyone would almost stand to attention.

> '*In the late '60s or early '70s, if a second-line manager visited a group of engineers everyone would almost stand to attention.*'

People rose up the organisation by virtue of being the most senior person for the post that had become available. It was rare for anyone to be really senior before reaching a certain age. Bright young people couldn't get promoted as fast as they deserved.

The manager's role was to feed information up and down the line. The more junior managers had little in the way of real authority, so decisions had to go several layers up the system to be authorised, and then fed back through the layers to be implemented. Senior managers were there to tell people what to do, not because they were the experts, but simply because they were senior.

Junior managers and front-line people weren't able to take decisions of any significance. The rule was: if you haven't specifically been told to do something, don't do it.

A few years ago a customer rang a senior manager whom she had got to know fairly well over the years. BT engineers had been out two or three times to fix a fault, but without success because the phone needed replacing and they were not authorised to take her a new phone. The manager got onto the engineers and instructed them to take her a phone, which they duly did. The customer called back and said 'Thanks for sorting it out so fast. But there's just one thing . . . could I have a battery for the phone?'

Believe it or not, if one of our engineers needed an ordinary battery and did not have one with them for some reason, they had to go back to the BT stores. This usually meant driving quite some distance, possibly in heavy traffic, standing in a queue, getting the battery, and then driving all the way back to the customer. They could easily be gone two hours – a quarter of their working day gone, just to fetch a battery. Why couldn't they go out to the nearest newsagent, buy a battery out of petty cash and be back in five minutes? Because we did not trust our people enough.

This whole approach was very difficult for our front-line staff, who were in the firing line when the customer got angry about the phone not being fixed and yet, if they used their initiative, they could be disciplined by their boss! There was no recognition of the fact that people at all levels were responsible and brought different skills and experience to a problem.

> If you have employed the right people, you ought to be able to trust them.

Some positive culture changes

TQM made a big difference, even if it wasn't totally obvious at the time. We introduced TQM at every level in the organisation and began to move decisions down the managerial line. We encouraged people to take their own decisions, and, as time went on, these decisions moved further and further down, until the engineers were even allowed to buy batteries themselves!

We introduced team meetings, and insisted that senior managers should go to these meetings at every level in their organisation. To begin with this didn't work as well as it might have. When senior managers turned up at team meetings people often clammed up and felt uncomfortable. But slowly the style changed.

'We encouraged people to take their own decisions...'

- **Managers learnt to encourage their teams to talk about the issues that were bothering them.** More importantly, they encouraged them to find answers. The whole management chain became far more focused on what was felt and said by the front-line people.

- **Managers walked the job more.** This meant that when they went to team meetings they were more likely to recognise the team and more likely to understand the issues that they wanted to discuss. They were faced with fewer surprises!

You must have good communication between managers and their teams.

- **Senior managers went out with engineers to learn about the everyday problems they faced.**

Most importantly, we started to measure our people's views in a systematic way in the form of regular surveys. We asked them what they thought about their job and objectives, their training and development, benefits and working conditions, their managers, customers and the company. These wide ranging surveys are now annual, voluntary and cover everyone. They have turned out to be one of our most important channels for upward communication. Anyone who fills out the survey form remains anonymous, and any manager with eight or more people who complete the survey is given a report so that they can see how their own people feel about their job, the organisation as a whole and their bosses.

Employee surveys are a good way to find out how people feel.

This survey is known as CARE (Communications and Attitude Research for Employees). CARE asks employees to state whether they agree, disagree or are neutral about a series of statements. A sample CARE survey is shown on page 67.

Assessing progress

The CARE survey is extremely detailed, and we have devised a number of index scores compiled from answers to key questions. These are used to compare results across the company.

1. Overall, my job stimulates me.
2. I have sufficient freedom to be able to achieve my objectives.
3. The amount of work I have to do is about right.
4. My quality of life at home is not unreasonably affected by my work at BT.
5. My job allows me to use my skills.
6. My last APR (annual performance review) helped me to concentrate on improving my performance.
7. My performance is reviewed sufficiently frequently for my needs.
8. I am satisfied that the development and training I have received helps me to develop my career.
9. In comparison with similar jobs in other companies, I feel my pay is about right.
10. I am satisfied with my total benefits package (this includes Sharesave, Annual Leave, and any other non pay item).
11. Compared to others in the organisation my rewards are fair.
12. I receive recognition for doing my job well.
13. There is a good sense of teamwork in my team.
14. I get help and support from my manager when I need it.
15. I am thanked by my manager for a job well done.
16. I am kept well informed about what is going on in the company.
17. Rules and procedures do not prevent me from meeting customer requirements.
18. I have the necessary equipment to do my job effectively.
19. I have a safe working environment.
20. I am satisfied with my accommodation at work.
21. There is a good sense of co-operation between people in different parts of BT.
22. I like the kind of work I do.
23. I know clearly how my work contributes to the success of BT.
24. I am satisfied with the support I receive from my line manager on my personal development.
25. I have a Development Plan which has been agreed with my manager.
26. My Development Plan is being put into place.

A sample CARE survey

27. I feel able to challenge my manager.
28. My manager's manager visits my workplace or team meeting and talks with me/us.
29. Senior managers follow through on commitments they have made to BT people.
30. BT genuinely cares about its people.
31. The way people in BT are promoted in BT is fair.
32. I feel proud to work for BT.
33. I am committed to helping BT achieve its mission.

A sample CARE survey Continued

There is no doubt that surveys like this can be tough for the management team, but they at least show a real commitment to finding out how people feel. Our results were affected by a number of difficult 'downsizing' years, but have shown a steady and heartening improvement. Perhaps it is not the scores that are as important as the way in which CARE has given a focus to our managers to do the right things by their people.

'...the jobs had become more interesting: there were long hours, but there was a real buzz about the place.'

CARE is regarded now as 'business as usual' – a tool for improving the way things work. As time has gone on more people than ever have said that they do see changes happening for the benefit of our customers, our company and ourselves, both within their teams and across the company, as a result of CARE.

A new management style

By the early 1990s BT was changing 'from the inside out'. Technology was moving fast; we were rapidly building one of the best network infrastructures anywhere in the world; we had restructured the company with a focus on customers; we had some real successes under our belt. It was an exciting time.

A short while before it had been hard for some managers to fill their days. Now, suddenly, managers were working extremely long hours. Pushing decisions down the managerial line was essential to get closer to the customer and also because of the sheer pressures of work. In most cases at least the jobs had become more interesting: there were long hours, but there was a real buzz about the place.

Learning to respect each other

It is easy to talk about culture change, but it has been a reality in BT. There is still much more to do, but we are now facing the key requirement of moving the trust, authority and responsibility to front-line people.

We keep our team sizes down to about 15 or 20 people, depending on the job, so that the first-line manager can know them all individually, and find time for regular one-to-one sessions with them. Terms such as 'one-to-one' can sound a bit formal, but it is vital in a large organisation that every individual feels involved and well managed. That feeling depends on the relationship with the person they see as their immediate boss. These one-to-ones are two-way. Both people come with an agenda, and they discuss the things that each of them wants to talk about, from work problems to personal development.

We also try to show our appreciation. If a customer comments on good service we say 'well done!'. If we get a criticism from a customer we pass that back too, but we don't haul the person up and give them the third degree. Instead, we talk through with them what went wrong, and why, and we give our people credit for wanting to do a good job and to learn from mistakes.

Show appreciation to your people and give them credit for doing a good job.

As we have moved the authority to make decisions down the line, people have learnt to trust that we will back them up in their decisions. Where we used to say 'if you haven't been instructed, don't do it!', we now say 'you can do it unless you've been told specifically that you can't'.

If any of our managers has difficulty delegating authority – and some people do find it harder than others – the CARE reports pick this up.

Our communications have become far more honest. For example, management conferences usually try to involve everyone, not just the managers, in understanding what needs to be done. For a recent conference a group of engineers were asked to make a video saying what they thought the company was doing wrong. They went on video saying, 'This is good . . . but this bit's hopeless . . .' – something they'd never have dared do a few years ago.

Pride in the company

Ten years ago working for BT was tough because of all the knocks we were taking. Changing how people feel about the organisation is not achieved overnight, and in many ways can only be a reflection of how we are seen by our customers.

Today BT people are generally highly motivated because customers are at the core of all we do. When this happens people become more productive. They really care about customers because there is some point in doing so. When staff can't help the customer, because the system does not allow it, it is frustrating for them to get emotionally involved. Once people are in a position to do something for customers and have a chance to feel useful and appreciated, they will allow themselves to care more.

> People care more about customers if they are in a position to help them.

Everyone gets frustrated with customers from time to time, as they do in any organisation, but nowadays you won't hear anyone in BT suggest that customers should be anything other than top priority. It would not be realistic to think that BT people believe that everything is rosy – of course they don't – but it is interesting that criticisms are almost invariably about practices that might short-change the customer. Ten years ago not only would there have been many more negative comments, but relatively few of them would have had anything to do with customers.

'Our engineers are now proud to be ambassadors for BT.'

Our engineers are now proud to be ambassadors for BT. They are often the only BT person that the customer ever meets in the flesh. They care about presenting the right image, because if the customer appreciates them we will take notice and give them the recognition they deserve for it. Now if something goes wrong they can put it right, instead of being powerless when faced with a customer who is very angry.

> We recently had a phone call from a farmer. He rang to say that one of our engineers had backed a BT van into one of his vehicles, and smashed the light. The manager assumed the farmer was ringing to complain, but in fact he had called to say how impressed he was because there was no one around and the engineer could have driven off. Instead he had waited until he could report the damage to the farmer. Our engineers now understand that we will give them credit for being good ambassadors – as we did in that instance – because that farmer will now be a more loyal customer than ever.

No doubt these sorts of upbeat stories can be countered by anecdotes of where they still aren't right but the real point is to visibly reinforce the positive things that happen – and we do!

Using technology to change how we work

One of our major challenges had been to keep our technology up to date, especially with all the organisational changes that took place. For a service organisation the smart use of systems is a prerequisite for success. This is especially so for us in BT because we need to be a showplace for our wares.

It didn't seem like that in the 1980s, when each of our geographic offices was a stand-alone community. Often they just had individual phone lines coming in, which we couldn't even switch between offices! Great for a phone company!

'When we put CSS in, it was the biggest system in the world outside the Pentagon.'

We also had the problem that all our customer records were local and we used to keep them all manually. They slowly evolved into computer-based systems, but as separate geographically based ones. So by the mid '80s we computerised them and in such a way that we could link all our databases and get at any of the information from anywhere in the country. This Customer Service System (CSS) enabled us to get at records, amend them, check up on queues of work and so on. CSS was huge. When we put it in, it was the biggest system in the world outside the Pentagon. It took an enormous amount of effort to computerise all the records, and then to keep the manual system running while we trained everyone on the new terminals. But it worked and enabled us to do things we'd never been able to do before: we could get at all our repair records, all our sales records, and all our billing records.

CSS as we first used it now seems archaic. We have been changing and upgrading it ever since. It remains as an information warehouse, and we have many other systems fed from it. It is all too easy now to look back and underestimate the impact its introduction had at the time. If you're in a jumbo jet it is easy to be smug about a steam engine. Before CSS we were still in the age of the horse and cart.

CSS was a huge technological stride forward for BT both physically and emotionally. Physically it involved building new computer centres, installing thousands of new terminals and hundreds of miles of cables, re-organising departments to work with the new processes and finally converting from many old systems to a single huge new one. Emotionally it may have been an even bigger leap. We were finally facing up to the need for radical technology change – it was the first real step towards a new sort of company. Although we didn't know it at the time, the success of CSS was to give us the confidence to contemplate the even bigger change of Project Sovereign, and it provided a bedrock information system upon which this change could be based. Since then we have managed to work smarter using all sorts of technology. This makes us more effective and more cost efficient, and gives our customers better service.

See Chapter 2 for a description of Project Sovereign

The greatest impact is at the 'front end' of our operations in the offices where we take orders, faults and handle billing enquiries. BT offers such a wide portfolio of products and services, and the need to give our people up-to-date screen-based information is vital. Our systems today – all built up from CSS – have vast stores of information and tracking capability to ensure that every customer gets individual treatment when they contact us.

Our challenge is to provide our customers with 'one-stop shopping' and 'single points of contact'. We have moved a long way to reach today's state-of-the-art technology with highly skilled people driving their systems. These people are backed up by technical experts, whose job is to make their knowledge and information available on line where appropriate.

We now fix faults and provide many services remotely, without any need for an engineer to visit. This trend will continue, and we are seeing an increasing need for people to change their skills as these technologies continue to develop, not least our traditional 'engineers' who work out and about on customers' premises.

Working 'in the field'

Today field engineers work in constant contact with their offices by using mobile phones and receiving voice mail messages from their colleagues. They are equipped with laptop computers, which use radio to deliver work and which also give them technical information that previously was all on paper. Their toolboxes are becoming communication hubs, not just screwdrivers and soldering irons.

'...engineers are very independent, with far less time spent in the office.'

> The use of laptop computers also equips our engineers to do so much more than just traditional engineering. Now they use the laptop and show the customer any products they think they might be interested in. We will soon be able to get videos running on these laptops. But the machine is the easy part. The real challenge is changing the way we work.

We have only just begun to tap the full potential for making the engineer's jobs easier, more efficient and more customer friendly. We rely a great deal on the engineers to tell us what information they want to make it all happen.

Technology can make people feel isolated. Think carefully about how to get the most from it *and* to keep people interacting.

There is also the way this technology changes how people 'feel' about their role. Field engineers are very independent and they enjoy being with customers but they now rarely need to visit BT locations. Keeping a sense of involvement – being in a team – is important, and we're getting round this potential problem by changing the first-line manager's role. These managers no longer have desks. Their job is out and about with their people. Managers are there to help and must be seen to help – 'coaching' and 'counselling' – and keeping their teams in touch, informed and involved.

Not long ago managers spent 70 or 80 per cent of their time in the office dealing with paperwork. Now our managers have a car, a laptop, a cellphone and so on, and they're spending 70 or 80 per cent of their time with their people and their customers.

We're also encouraging managers to run team-building events. They will take the team out for an evening ten pin bowling, say, or on any other activity of the team's choice. It is very important not to let the technology displace the personal side of the job. With a little thought – and trust – we can accommodate both successfully.

Working smarter, not harder

We have come a long way in terms of working smarter in the last ten years. We now have around half the people we had before, a much higher workload and more demanding customers. More effective systems and more advanced technology have helped us to keep up. Ten years from now no doubt we'll have systems that make today's innovations look archaic. We just have to make sure that we continue to keep up the pace and take advantage of the latest technology.

The technology is only a means, not an end. It is helping our people to realise their full potential in ways that we could never have imagined. There is less drudgery in the tasks; the relationship between our front-line people and our customers is amazingly sophisticated. Today in our service centres people talk on line with a video link, so as to deal face to face. We even have customers inputting orders directly to our systems, without any interaction from BT people.

This trend moves our people from being part of 'just a good service organisation' to being the drivers behind 'BT the expert supplier'. People, not the technology, make the difference.

The style of an organisation has an overwhelming influence on how it treats its customers. These are the key issues from this chapter:

· · · · ·

Treat employees as adults and trust them to do a good job.

· · · · ·

Ensure that decisions are taken by people who understand the issues, not just by those who are in some way 'senior'.

· · · · ·

Invest in technology that enables the company to serve customers in the way it needs to.

· · · · ·

Ask employees what they think – and take their comments seriously.

· · · · ·

Don't expect change to end. Develop a style that gets the best out of changes.

· · · · ·

Keep the customer focus on any changes.

· · · · ·

5

Creating a new corporate identity

*M*ost large organisations have to consider a change of corporate identity at some time. At the end of the 1980s we had to look at the options for a complete change of identity. We were prompted by three factors in particular:

- Shifting our emphasis further towards customer service meant that we needed a new look to match.

- It was essential to let everyone know that we were making important changes that would affect all our customers in the future.

- With all the advances in technology and the changes in the industry, we needed an identity that would still fit however much the organisation changed in the future.

It was becoming clear that it would be unwise to continue using our blue British Telecom logo and our yellow vans for ever. We were looking towards expanding into a global market, and other companies abroad were already using the 'T' symbol that we were using ourselves, along with similar lettering. We also realised that the name 'British Telecom' sounded parochial if we wanted to operate in an international market. It was also a fact – not that we liked it – that the word 'British' (especially in Japan and the Far East) was not synonymous with advanced technology.

We could have adopted a new corporate identity for our overseas operations only, but we wanted to show our customers in the UK that we had changed – that we were now putting them first. If we were going to change we had to do it properly; a half-hearted attempt would be no good. So we had to change our corporate colours as well. Our yellow vans were very familiar, but the colour was becoming a little outdated, and we shared it with a number of other utility companies. All in all, it was time for a complete change.

What did we want from a new identity?

We had decided that we needed to move on from the old identity. But to what? There were several things to take into account:

- **We wanted something to show that we had changed.** This had to be something that we could carry on using if we kept changing. In a high technology industry you can't be sure where you are going to be in a few years' time.

- **We needed an international identity.** We had to be able to move into the worldwide market that was opening up.

- **We needed an identity that reinforced our commitment to the customer.** We needed an identity that focused on the customer and not ourselves.

Improving our service first

We employed a top consultancy, Wolff Olins, to help us. One of the first things they did was to tell us, politely but firmly, that we were absolutely right about needing a new identity, but not yet. One of the biggest mistakes many companies make is to revamp their identity without changing their basic service. Customers aren't daft: if the changes you imply in a new image haven't really happened, they won't be impressed. We had to be able to back up our claims to be a new customer-oriented company with more than just an improved payphone service. So we put the new identity on hold. We kept working on the idea, but we kept it to ourselves for the time being.

> **It is a big mistake to change your identity but not the rest of your image with your customers.**

It would have been nothing short of hypocritical to launch the new identity claiming we had changed while we were still structured for our own benefit. So the first thing we had to do was to reorganise the company so that it was structured for the customer's benefit – Project Sovereign. The launch of the new identity had to wait until Project Sovereign was complete.

See Chapter 2.

We were also still a classic example of the old adage of the cobbler's children (who never have any shoes). While we were trying to persuade customers to buy the latest technology, most of our own equipment was anything up to 30 years old. We needed to start practising what we preached. More than that, we needed to start setting the standard. For example, if good customer service includes answering the phone within three rings, then that's what we should do. We had to set ourselves up as the experts, and then live up to our claims.

We concentrated on Project Sovereign and our other customer-focused changes but, meanwhile, we started planning our new identity so that, once we were ready for it, we could put it into place.

'We had to be able to back up our claims to be a new customer-oriented company with more than just an improved payphone service.'

A new identity for an innovative company

Wolff Olins spent six months collecting opinions about BT:

- people in the company
- customers
- other telecommunications companies overseas.

They found that, although the general views weren't that good, everyone recognised that we were starting to change. But we still had a long way to go.

The best news came from our counterparts overseas, who were really quite jealous of our position:

- We were based in London, one of the three top cities in the world from which to launch an international company.
- We had several years' head start on them when it came to learning how to operate in a competitive environment.

Wolff Olins surprised us completely by telling us that we were operating in probably the most exciting industry in the world, and that we were in a prime position to be one of the most exciting companies in the world. Once we had climbed back onto our chairs, we realised

'...we were in a prime position to be the most exciting company in the world.'

that they were right. We could do something really innovative, and different from what other telecomms companies were doing. Now we had to choose a new identity that fitted the bill. Project Sovereign was launched in spring 1990 and completed a year later; we had that year in which to find this new and innovative identity.

Choosing the logo

One of the first decisions we had to make was whether to have one all-embracing identity, or whether to use a different identity for different parts of the company. At the time we had a host of variations on the basic logo, and various separately named subsidiaries.

We decided that we needed to present ourselves as a single company – since that was how our customers saw us – and we needed to build a strong unified identity at home and abroad. The simplicity of a single logo would also speed up the time it takes for people to recognise it. This meant finding an identity that would encompass everything that we did or were likely to do in the future.

A customer-focused logo

The breakthrough came when we concentrated on finding a logo that was customer oriented. We realised that we had to focus on the benefits of what our business was about,

Focus on the benefits of the company, not its features.

rather than the features. Just as British Airways realised that they weren't essentially in the business of flying planes but of looking after people and bringing them together, so our business wasn't really about networks and wires and connections, but about communication.

BT's job was to help communication, and we decided to focus our new identity on that. But we didn't want to use the whole area of communication; we wanted to pick out the most motivating part of it. We decided that good communication is about trusting relationships and a two-way exchange of confidences, and that was what we wanted to build our reputation around.

This is very similar to what Apple did to the computer market. We wanted to get away from the bits and the bytes and the technology symbolism, and into humanity. So we deliberately picked a human figure. Wolff Olins came up with a number of ideas; we chose the piper symbol because it didn't relate specifically to the telephone, and it had numerous connotations, such as music and mythology, in both Western and Eastern cultures. It also contained some of the mischievousness of Pan with his Pan pipes, which gave a bit of a non-establishment slant to it – something that would help us to break away from our outdated civil service image.

We looked at the corporate identities of all our major competitors – overseas telecomms companies, computing and electrical organisations and so on. Apart from Apple, they all used hard macho images. Our idea was fundamentally different, much more geared to the '90s and towards the customers rather than the industry itself.

We went through well over a hundred designs between making this decision and settling on the final logo. The first ones we looked at used the theme of the piper, but in a very abstract way, as shown in Figure 1.

We decided that we wanted to get closer to a human figure. We also felt that

Fig 1. The original logo design

83

Fig 2. Mr Twister

we needed to make the two-way function of communication more central. Two-way communication is what our business is all about: you don't use the phone in isolation, you use it to connect with someone else. After several more design stages we came up with a logo that we called 'Mr Twister' (Figure 2). This was the first time we had used two figures intertwined, to illustrate both 'announcing' and 'listening'.

Fig 3. Researched logo

We liked Mr Twister, but he was still too abstract, and we wanted a more human figure. After a few more variations we came up with something more human that still fulfilled all our criteria (Figure 3).

At this stage we did some market research, mostly in the UK, the States, Germany, France and Japan. The response was generally positive, except for the colours. At that stage we were using blue and orange. We found that orange just wasn't a good colour for a big corporate organisation. There were some interesting national differences of opinion: the French loved it, but the Japanese hated it, and didn't see that any company of BT's stature could be taken seriously with orange in its logo. So we switched to red, which had more weight and seriousness about it than the orange. We were careful to avoid a red that was too similar to that in the Union Jack, because we wanted to stay away from the UK image and keep ourselves as international as possible. The red, white and grey had a freshness and quality about it. Eventually, after several more variations, we settled on the final version (Figure 4).

Fig 4. The final version of the logo

Fig 5. The final version of the logo with lettering

All the time this was going on, we were trying to decide on a name for ourselves. We were looking for something that we could use internationally, and that symbolised good communications. We played around with words such as 'unison' but, in the end, we simply couldn't come up with anything better than BT, and we were running out of time. We had to be ready to launch the new identity at the same time as completing Project Sovereign and launching our new organisation. In a sense it was a compromise solution, but it wasn't *overtly* British, and people in the UK already knew us as BT. So BT it was, with the new logo (Figure 5).

Making the change

The first thing that we had to do was to deal with the practical side of changing our identity. For a start, we had to persuade our senior management to accept it. Not because they could prevent it, but because we wanted them on our side. The most difficult thing was to persuade the people who were running sections of the company that had their own identity, for example the subsidiaries with their own logos. Taking away a subsidiary's identity and making them join in with the bigger company can make them feel that they are losing status.

The resistance was probably 90 per cent ego and 10 per cent lack of conviction that we were doing the right thing. We found that if we talked through the reasoning behind the change with our managers, and explained how it would benefit the customer, we could carry them. One of the most important things was to use customer research to back up the arguments – including the research Wolff Olins had done. We put in a huge amount of work talking people round. In the end we found that, by that time, we had taken the culture of customer service far enough for people to be persuaded once they were convinced that the changes were in the customers' interests.

Introducing a dress code

Alongside Project Sovereign, and as part of our identity change, we wanted to introduce a corporate uniform of some kind for the people who dealt directly with customers. Things had got lax – engineers often visiting customers' premises wearing jeans and T-shirts; this wasn't dreadful, given the job they were doing, but it wasn't the right image. Dressing smartly would show more respect for the customer, as well as being a good advertisement for BT.

The trouble was that most of the engineers just refused to wear corporate clothing. We didn't want to start a fight with them over it, so we decided to take a different approach. We had the corporate clothing designed and a fair number of outfits made up. We then loaded it into a few big vans and drove them out to the engineers' workplaces. We told the engineers that they didn't have to wear the new clothing, but suggested that they come to try it on and see what they thought. We made only one rule. We said that *if* they accepted the clothing and took it away with them, they had to wear it for work.

Once the engineers began to try on the corporate clothing they started to see the benefits of not having to pay out for their own working clothes. Most of them actually felt reasonably proud to be wearing it. A few years before it might have been a bit of an embarrassment; now it felt quite good to be sporting the new BT logo.

Slowly the number of engineers taking away their outfit once they'd tried it on increased. We never made the uniform compulsory – to this day it is still voluntary – but it sets the standard we now require. When did you last see a BT engineer working in jeans and a T-shirt? Nowadays, they don't complain about wearing corporate clothing; instead they put in requests for us to provide belts or shoes or socks to go with it.

The practicalities

The other huge practical task was physically making the change. We had about fifteen task groups working on the logistics of changing the vehicles, the kiosks, the stationery, literature, pens, screwdrivers and everything else over to the new design. It would have cost a fortune to throw out or repaint all our old equipment and stationery. We decided to wait until vans needed repainting anyway, or literature needed reprinting, and then to bring in the new design. Most of the change-over was completed in eighteen months, although it was about three years before all the vans were repainted.

Even so it was hardly a low-cost exercise. A lot of the press gave us a hard time for spending £50m on the identity change, but it really cost less than that. The total sum may have been £50m, but most of that went on painting and printing and so on that we would have had to do even without a change. The actual cost of switching designs was probably nearer £10m. That is a lot of money, but these things don't come cheap. In fact this is an average sum for an organisation our size to spend on a new identity.

Letting the customers know

In an ideal world it would be great to launch a new identity alongside a major change or a big success, such as the improvement in payphones. It would have been great to revolutionise the company all at once and to create a new identity at the same time, but we knew that we couldn't change everything that fast. We also knew that, although introducing the new design too soon would leave us open to charges of self-delusion (as Wolff

See Chapter 2. Olins had warned us), the act of reinventing our image would help to drive the remaining changes forward. Timing the identity change when we did was a high-risk strategy because we had to get the thing just right.

'We used the advertising campaign to highlight important improvements for customers and to show that we really were changing.'

We were making steady progress towards better customer service, but without any huge, prominent changes. So at the same time as launching the new identity, we went public with the 'BT commitment': a clear statement of our basic service principles and aspiration. This plus the benefits for customers arising out of the Project Sovereign restructuring were publicised in a nationwide advertising campaign. In line with the thinking behind the new design, this series of ads was focused on human contact and communication with the customer.

We used the advertising campaign to highlight important improvements for customers and to show that we really were changing. The ads illustrated things such as the fact that we now made appointments to fix phones, that we could offer itemised billing, and that one operator could now answer most customer queries without having to keep transferring them round the company. The storyboard for one of these advertisements is shown on page 90.

Positive customer reaction

So what did everyone think? Inside BT we were ready for a change. We had been trying to adjust to our new competitive world ever since privatisation. Over recent years we had had successes, and the pace had been picking up for some time, but we had reached the point where everyone really needed a very big and very obvious boost. We wanted our customers to notice the hard work we'd been putting in. We still had a long way to go in their eyes – our new customer focus hadn't been road tested yet – but our people needed some credit for having completed the first few laps. We wanted the public to share our growing belief that we were on our way.

The new identity gave us a psychological punctuation mark. Although the changes were continuous, running into each other and alongside each other and overlapping, it helped to have a visible switchover point at which we could say, 'That was the old style British Telecom; this is the new style BT'. It was rather like climbing a mountain and reaching Camp Two. There's still a long way to go, but it gives somewhere to stop for a breather and see how far we'd come. You also feel reassured that you're not going to slip back down again.

OPERATOR: Hello. BT Shazia Zasar speaking. Can I help you?

MALE VO: Yes, hello. I've got to speak to somebody about my Company's bill and I'd rather you didn't pass me on to six different departments and then keep me hanging on for half an hour.

OPERATOR: I can help you with your bill, Sir.

MALE VO: I also need to speak to someone about getting another line.

OPERATOR: I can do that too.

MALE VO: What about ordering an answerphone?

OPERATOR: And that.

MALE VO: And this Call Diversion thingummy?

OPERATOR: And Call Diversion.

MALE VO: Really... Can you tell me why my phone always rings when I've just got in the bath?

OPERATOR: No, Sir. I can't do that.

Storyboard for 'and that'

The reaction from the general public wasn't unanimous, but in general people seemed to like the new image. More to the point, they noticed it, which was a large part of what we wanted from it. Inevitably there were a few snipes about having better things to spend our money on, but that's the nature of the British press. In fact we thought the money very well spent. For an organisation of our size such a major confidence booster for our people, and a big chance to show our customers what we could do, was never going to come cheap. The received wisdom is that if you want to make a change that is really radical, you ideally need a change of image to signal it to the outside world.

> **If you want to make a radical change, you need to signal it to the outside world.**

Overall the reaction was good. If you judged the public's behaviour, rather than their comments, you could see a new confidence in BT emerging. This confidence came as a result of the real changes we were making, not just because of a new logo, but the new identity helped to drive it faster than would have happened otherwise. Our television ads were a big help as well, because they gave the public a concrete set of benefits to go with the new look, so we could demonstrate that we weren't making hollow promises.

For a big organisation with the number of customers we have, it takes a while for the public perception to catch up with reality. Our customers were probably about three or four years behind us in 1991, when we launched the new identity. They were only just beginning to recognise that we were changing. The customers we dealt with frequently had noticed the change already, but those we rarely had contact with hadn't really begun to see it. An identity change helps to speed up this process of recognition, so long as you live up to your new image.

It takes a few years to change your customers' view of you.

Our change of identity brought with it another challenge that we would have to meet. We were inviting our customers to have far higher expectations of us than ever before. We were telling them that BT was a company that put the customer first, and that they could expect to be treated as our top priority from now on. We had burnt our bridges. We were going to have to live up to the standards we had set ourselves every time we dealt with any of our customers in future.

KEY LESSONS CHAPTER 5

The key lessons we discovered when creating our new corporate identity were:
. . . . .

Don't create a new identity that promises the customer more until you can live up to that promise.
. . . . .

Radical changes to a company ideally need a change of image to signal them.
. . . . .

The identity should focus on the customer, not on the organisation.
. . . . .

Get top management on your side to promote the new identity.
. . . . .

Launch a new identity alongside a success story if you can.
. . . . .

Keeping our customer service promises

*A*t *the beginning of the 1990s we faced two main customer service problems that compounded each other:*

- *We had been living with serious backlogs of work over a period of years. These backlogs meant that we were failing to meet the dates we promised to customers for the repair or installation of their equipment.*

- *We didn't have the resources to do the work any faster.*

Tackling these problems required us to identify the causes of the backlogs and to address those, instead of merely continuing to fight to reduce the backlogs themselves.

Managing the workload

By the end of the '80s we had put into place TQM programmes, restructuring programmes, and the beginning of a whole new culture and management style. Unfortunately we also had a legacy of backlogs that was exhausting, and that prompted a 'fire fighting' response – with everyone focused on short-term survival and given too little time to think.

We were getting better by the early 1990s, but there was still much to do. We needed a second wind.

Looking back, we were a very slow organisation. For example, it typically took us 100 days to install a private circuit. A few unlucky customers even had to wait as long as six months to have a single telephone line put in. See Chapter 7 This was clearly unacceptable, but at this time our managers were so busy dealing with complaints and problems that they could barely see a day ahead, let alone a few months. We were too busy doing yesterday's work to deal with today's – and we had no time at all to worry about tomorrow's.

> '*We were too busy doing yesterday's work to deal with today's – and we had no time at all to worry about tomorrow's.*'

The question we had to answer was simple: how could we clear enough space to catch up?

Clearing space to think

It was evident that everyone was working hard; we could not suddenly just do everything faster, so we were going to have to do it differently. In the short term the solution had been straightforward: we recruited extra people to help clear the worst of the build-ups. There were no short cuts to this; we *had* to create some headroom.

We then focused on finding ways to stop backlogs from developing again. We found that part of the problem was to do with our basic network technology. We were still working with out-dated equipment, and many customers had to wait for a line to be installed simply because of lack of capacity, either in the exchanges or in the lines from the exchanges to customers' premises. So we set many of the extra people we brought in to work on those tasks, such as upgrading exchanges, that would ensure that we had the physical capability to meet customer demand.

We also examined the processes we were using to manage the work. We found that, with a few good process managers and with support for changes coming from the senior management team, we could identify some real time savings. Gradually we gained enough thinking space to look at the root causes of our problems.

Getting it right first time

When we analysed what was really happening, we found that we were working pretty inefficiently. We spent a lot of our time dealing with complaints, or going back to redo jobs that we should have got right in the first place. The strike in '87 showed us that a lot of faults were caused accidentally by engineers unavoidably disturbing outmoded equipment in the process of fixing other faults. Much of this problem could be removed by the use of more sophisticated equipment and, where necessary, providing better training for the engineers. The rest of the solution related to the other changes already happening within BT.

> **Going back to fix a bad job costs money and upsets customers. You have to get a job right first time.**

See Chapter 1

The view from inside

It's worth reflecting on what it felt like to work in BT in the early '90s when so much change was hitting us. Although it wasn't always obvious at the time, things were on the up and there was a notable difference because of a variety of influences:

- **TQM.** TQM showed everyone that if we could get the job   See Chapter 2
  right first time we would save time and money, as well as
  keeping the customer satisfied. But the more we improved,
  the more we realised what else had to be done.

- **Listening to customers.** We had been in the habit of relying
  on internal measures to monitor our performance. Once we
  started to pay attention to what our *customers* thought, we   See Chapter 3
  learnt a lot about which things we were doing inefficiently.
  We found out which mistakes generated the most complaints
  and caused the most rework, and this increased the pressure
  for further change.

- **Project Sovereign.** Project Sovereign gave us important
  economies of scale. Instead of 27 separate geographic units
  we organised customers so that each job was
  owned by one division working throughout
  the country. This fundamentally changed
  working practices and put the focus on the
  customer, but it also shifted BT from a geographic to a functional organisation.

  *'...if you let your
  customers set the pace
  they don't usually set it
  as fast as you fear, but
  they do feel more satisfied.'*

- **Company style.** The changes we had made by devolving responsibility and decision making down the line saved a huge amount
  of time, and enabled us to work far more efficiently. Better two-
  way communication meant that front-line people and first-line
  managers were starting to suggest ways to improve the system.
  The fact that we recognised their contributions made them and
  their colleagues more likely to keep the good ideas coming.

- **Efficient use of time.** A whole range of changes were taking
  effect here – just look at the time we had saved on buying

See Chapter 4
batteries alone, now that we trusted our engineers to nip down to the shops rather than trek all the way out to the BT stores.

- **Letting customers set the pace.** We found that if you let your customers set the pace they don't usually set it as fast as you fear, but they do feel more satisfied. This is partly because they get what they want when they want it, but also because they feel involved – it's nice to be asked. The challenge of See Chapter 3 meeting the deadlines for delivering private circuits for the National Lottery was a good demonstration of this.

> Recently we have begun to ask our business customers to tell us how critical a fault is when they report it. Most people are very rational: they realise that if they claim that every fault is critical, even when it's not, we won't be able to fix the genuinely important ones fastest. We find that only about 15 per cent of faults are described as critical. Of course, this only works when customers trust you. Ten years ago our customers would have claimed that every fault was critical, in the belief that this was the only way to get us to fix it at all.

Getting somewhere at last

The sum effect of all of this went far deeper than simply clearing backlogs of work. We began to work far more effectively and to feel that we were getting somewhere.

> Around this time, one of our managers took a complaint from a dissatisfied customer who asked: 'Why on earth do you work for BT?' Our manager replied: 'Because one day, BT is going to get it right. And when that happens, I want to be there.'

We were still bad at some things, but a confidence was seeping through the organisation, and people were starting to believe that it was only a matter of time before BT was really on top of customer service.

It now became obvious that almost every time we made a change designed to improve life for the customer, it also brought us significant cost savings.

Driving up customer satisfaction drives down your costs.

We couldn't have clawed our way back through the mountains of work we had built up without putting our focus firmly on doing precisely that. But nor could we have done it without the structural and style changes that we had made.

The need for continuous improvement

Throughout the early '90s we continued to improve, but there was a plateauing effect – we reached a level that was not quite good enough. Though we were massively better than we had been, we still had more to do. We also faced increasing competition, especially in the business market.

Despite all our improvements, our customers were still experiencing problems with our services. For example, we now managed to deliver to the date we had promised our business customers in about 90% of cases. That may not sound too bad, until you think that we carry out around 80,000 'provisioning' jobs for businesses every week. We were therefore letting down 8,000 businesses a week. This meant that we were still getting too many complaints, and this was demoralising when we had taken so many positive steps to improve things.

'We were letting down 8,000 businesses a week.'

We had to take a fresh look at what we were doing. When we did we found that the problem was a side effect of the changes we had made with Project Sovereign. Before Project Sovereign, each job was undertaken entirely by one geographic district, assuming it didn't cross any boundaries. After Project Sovereign, as a company divided by function rather than location, most jobs required co-operation between more than one division, and so we put in place what we called 'Service Level Agreements' (SLAs) between different departments.

> If someone ordered a simple exchange line, one division would process the order, another provide the line, another provide the engineer to go to the customer's premises, and so on.
>
> We had anticipated this change in working arrangements when we were planning Project Sovereign, and we had a way of dealing with it. We distributed each bit of the process to a different division, and gave them each a target, or SLA. If there were six stages and the job had to be done in six days, we would say to the first division, 'This needs to be completed by the end of Monday', to the second 'You've got until the end of Tuesday for your bit' and so on. Each division was measured on their performance for their own part of the job.

Unfortunately this system was flawed. We just couldn't see it until it had been up and running for a while. If anything went wrong with one section of the job, five sections of BT had performance figures that showed a success, with just one showing a failure. As the one failure meant a failure from the customer's point of view, what was the good of five successes? We had analysed and understood intellectually what needed to be done, but we had lost the spirit of the end product – delivering service on the day.

All the departments or divisions involved in a job must have methods in place to make their different functions work effectively together.

Inspiring self-confidence – the hundred days' war

We were in danger of becoming focused on allocating blame internally; we needed to get everyone in the organisation to see the real goal and decided to re-inspire confidence by enabling our people to share a success – something that we could all feel good about. We launched a 'hundred days' war': a hundred-day campaign focused on the achievement of six key targets that would make a step change in our service to business customers.

The targets

All the targets were important, but the self-confidence we hoped they would generate was more important than any one of them. Having said that, our approach wouldn't have worked unless everyone could see that we were working on things that really needed doing. The overriding target that affected every part of the organisation was that we should keep our promises to our customers. This meant everything from delivering on the date we had promised to phoning customers back when we said we would.

Another target was to reduce complaints by a half. This sounds dramatic and it was – but we anticipated that keeping our promises would take care of much of the problem, because such a large proportion of our complaints were quite simply caused by us not keeping promises!

The timescale

A timescale of a hundred days was an emotive way of expressing urgency. Any shorter, a month for instance, and we wouldn't really have had time to do anything. Any longer, and there was the danger that we would run out of steam before we reached the finish line. On top of that, to create a big difference in results, the system had to change, and it's very unsettling for people if that process of change takes too long.

Once you have decided to change, it's best to do it as quickly as possible.

A lot of people were sceptical about whether we could meet the targets on time. Although we did not know beyond doubt that it could be done, we were pretty confident. In any case, as long as we were most of the way there in a hundred days, it didn't really matter if meeting all the targets fully took a little longer. Our experience with the payphone service, the 5 hour repair targets and the challenge of the National Lottery had taught us that it's very valuable to set big – even heroic – goals, and then to publicise them. It galvanises people. We were also driven by the fact that we had to do *something* to reduce failures and complaints.

See Chapter 2 for details of the payphone improvements

People are inspired if you set apparently unachievable goals and then announce them to the world.

And sure enough, it worked. In a hundred days we really did reduce complaints by a half (we've halved them again since then). The key to our success was working out how to use the SLAs in a way that meant that we could keep our promises.

Making Service Level Agreements work

Once we had identified the SLA problem and examined it properly, we started to see how to resolve it. It wasn't that nobody cared about the customer, but the current SLA gave them an *internal* measurement to focus on, rather than an *external* one. We decided to continue to measure each division's individual performance, but to add a second measure for each of them: whether or not we achieved the overall objective of meeting the end promised date. This latter overall objective was to be the more important measurement of the two.

'The hundred days' war really made a difference. We believed in ourselves again. We felt successful and it showed.'

By shifting each division's focus, the separate sections of the organisation began to work together more effectively, which meant that we could keep our promises to our customers. This in turn was a large part of what brought down the number of complaints – as we had predicted.

The hundred days' war really made a difference. We believed in ourselves again. We felt successful and it showed.

> To deliver really good customer service people must believe in themselves and in the company. They need to feel that both are successful.

A customer promise must not be broken

It is obvious that we should keep our promises. But in terms of the hundred days' war it was also important that the message was expressed in the simplest possible terms. This is something that we haven't always been good at: it is relatively easy for management to go through the whole thought process of setting a policy or a target, and to reach the point where they understand it clearly themselves. It is much harder to keep that message clear as it goes down through all the layers of management to reach people who weren't involved in the decision and haven't a clue what the thinking behind it was.

People won't get onto your wavelength if you give long, boring presentations about what needs to be done. But if you can find a simple tag line everyone can get behind it: they will all know that they've understood it properly because there isn't any room for misunderstanding.

What we were saying to our front-line people and our first-line managers was really an extension of what the total quality programme was all about: focus on the customer. We were telling them that their job was to give the customer what we promised them. People grasped that if they used their initiative to give the customer what they had been promised, they would be praised and not blamed for it.

Our people are still growing more confident all the time about making their own decisions when it benefits the customer.

One of our engineers was sent out to install a line. When he got there, he found he couldn't do the job because there was a problem with taking the line across a local farmer's land. Before we revised the SLA system, the engineer would doubtless have breathed a sigh of relief and thought 'It's not my problem. I can leave that to the wayleave people.' Under the new system, the engineer understood that the object of the exercise was to keep the promise to the customer that the line would be installed that day. So he got on the phone, called up the wayleave people, and got them to arrange a wayleave (permission to run a line across private property) with the farmer then and there, and to agree a price. He then took the line across the farmer's land and the customer had the service installed by the end of the day as promised.

All this happened because the engineer understood that his task was to get the line installed, and that he had to take responsibility for anything that was necessary to get the job done.

To keep your promises, you need to be flexible.

One of the biggest problems in large organisations is when people blindly follow pre-set rules for how to do things. There's a procedure laid down, and they can't vary from it. That may work well in about ninety-five per cent of cases, but as far as the other five per cent are concerned, there has to be some built-in flexibility in order to keep promises to customers. It's much easier to build the flexibility into the people than to build it into the processes.

We were looking to recruit project managers a year or two ago, and we had an application from one of our accountants who wanted a career change. Her knowledge of the subject wasn't great, but we could train her in that. More importantly, she was one of those people who could be guaranteed to stick with a task until it was done, and that was a quality we wanted. So she got the job.

Soon after her appointment, she was dealing with a customer who had one of our switchboards and a piece of peripheral equipment. The two were linked by some software that was written by a fairly small American company. There were problems getting the thing to work. The suppliers of the switchboard and of the peripheral both insisted that the fault wasn't with their equipment, and it was beginning to look as if it must be a software problem.

The new project manager started to get fed up with the fact that, while the two suppliers were debating the problem, the customer still had a fault on their service. So she decided to do something about it. She found out who owned the American software company, got his home phone number, because he'd left work for the week, and phoned him at home over the weekend.

She explained the situation to the American and found that he was horrified to think that two large organisations 5,000 miles away were having problems, blaming him, and he didn't even know about it. So he put someone on a plane on Monday morning and by Wednesday the problem was fixed. The American owner was so grateful that he flew over the next weekend to thank the project manager in person.

No one told the project manager to act as she did. There was no process in place that allowed for that particular situation. But no one had told her that she couldn't take such action, and she couldn't see any other way to keep the promise to the customer to get the fault fixed.

It isn't possible to tell your people what to do in every situation that isn't covered by normal procedures, but it is possible to give them a rule against which to measure every option. If it means breaking a promise, it's the wrong solution; if it means keeping our promise to the customer, it's the right solution. Everyone understands that.

Adopting this approach takes a degree of trust in people, but they won't deliver at any cost if there's a cheaper solution that also meets the promise. As long as you keep the message clear and simple, people will understand it, and if they understand it, they can do it.

Keeping more difficult promises and learning to manage complexity

All promises to customers are important, but some are more difficult to keep than others. We found the more difficult to keep

'If it means breaking a promise, it's the wrong solution; if it means keeping our promise to the customer, it's the right solution. '

promises required us to use project management techniques – common in other industries but not to us in BT a few years ago. Project management allows us to deliver excellent service to customers in the more complex situations. This complexity is increasing for us as customers rely on us to deliver business solutions, rather than just products or services. It is now common for a single installation to involve many locations across the country, several different products, third-party suppliers and so on; all of these need to be co-ordinated.

Ten years ago a large project would have meant, say, installing switchboards in several geographic locations with some private circuits linking them. Now we can be installing a product

FeatureNet is a virtual private network. See Chapter 7

such as FeatureNet at hundreds of locations all round the country, or putting National Lottery terminals at literally thousands of locations.

We also work faster than we used to – we have to, because that is what our customers want. We might get six weeks now to install something that, ten years ago, we'd have had six months to put in.

Ten years ago the vast majority of our customers could tell us months in advance what they wanted organisationally. Now, because businesses move so much faster, the customer might be changing their organisational departments (and therefore their telecommunications requirements) even within our six weeks' installation time.

Our project management teams have two roles. One is to take worry off the customer's hands, and see the project through smoothly. The other is to highlight within BT where our underlying processes need to change and to build failsafes into the system so that problems can't recur. We've had to get smart at smoothing out processes and then ensuring that they are put right and, most importantly, to develop solutions that can deliver automatically in situations that previously required project managing. If we still project managed today some of the things we project managed ten years ago, we would need far more people than we could ever afford. We've learnt to work smarter.

Adding value – managing change for customers

Project management is a significant way in which we can add value to a major project for a customer. We've built up a good reputation, and often customers will choose us over our competitors because they have confidence in our project management – it gives them peace of mind. We have enough experience that we can often also advise on things that aren't strictly in our remit. That is one of the key ways we can really delight our customers – by giving them that bit extra.

Project management adds value to a product.

Often our customers may be instigating some kind of business re-engineering by, perhaps, cutting down on people and using new technology instead. At the same time they may be reducing the number of sites they have and changing their working practices. We now have a lot of experience in this sort of thing, and we can often look at a customer's own project plan and suggest that certain changes will give them a better result. Then we can help the customer to plan their communications in the new environment as well.

There are no hard or fast rules between project managing and 'business as usual', but in a fast changing industry where bespoke projects are becoming more commonplace, we often find that the reassurance of a personal touch makes all the difference. This is particularly true for new recently launched technology. We now find that our most experienced project managers work on new launches, and they create the processes to move these into a 'business as usual' way of working as they nurse through the early installations.

Customer service now

We have achieved huge improvements to our customer service by:

- getting our processes sharpened up
- clever understanding of the end goal – the customer – and
- overlaying our day-to-day business with project management to handle complexity that our processes and systems cannot handle.

It is not possible to create perfect systems overnight. The approach we have followed is to use *people* to handle the complexity while the *systems* are being developed. Once these systems can do the job we move the people to tackle other more difficult developing areas. This might be seen as a 'hand-to-mouth' existence, but with the rate of change we are experiencing we have found it to be the only realistic option.

We have come a long way since we had lead times of a hundred days, and the key to making the change was surprisingly simple: focus on keeping your promises to the customer.

**KEY
LESSONS
CHAPTER
6**

These are the key lessons:

.....

Do the job right first time.

.....

It is *everybody's* job to see that promises to customers
are kept.

.....

It is far easier to create flexible people than to create
flexible processes.

.....

Concentrate on acquiring good project management skills.

.....

There are two key guidelines for motivating people to
achieve quick successes:

.....

If morale and self-confidence are low, give people a success.

.....

Keep messages to the company clear and simple.

.....

7

Learning to embrace new technology products

*B*y the early '90s, things were so much better and self-confidence around the organisation increased but we got caught out as we moved from our traditional products to newer technologies. FeatureNet was a very popular and successful product. Its very success caused us a lot of problems. The process of resolving these taught us a lot of often painful lessons, which we have been able to apply to subsequent launches of high-technology products:

- *It is difficult to time a launch. Do it too soon and there may be too many teething problems. Leave it too late and the product may be overtaken by others, or competitors may steal the market.*

- *It is easy to underestimate the demand for a good product and be unprepared for the problems this causes.*

- *It is important not to become complacent about being able to fix things on the hoof – sooner or later things will go badly wrong.*

At some stage every company has to face the challenge of introducing new products or services. This can be difficult enough when the product uses well established methods or familiar technology. When it involves brand new technology and radically different ways of doing things the problems are usually multiplied. BT went through these difficulties with FeatureNet, which we introduced in the UK in the early 1990s. This chapter tells the story – warts and all – in terms of what can go wrong. More importantly, it explains how we now try to avoid the same thing happening again. There are lessons here for everyone who has ever tried to launch a new product to customers – especially one that was in heavy demand from day one.

FeatureNet was introduced at a time when our service in BT was very much on the up. In a way we were caught out by our own self-confidence. We had always had difficulties with product launches, but had been able to pull the irons out of the fire to avoid the worst consequences. People working in the service world are really quite proud of their ability to fight the product launch fires and, looking back, we probably expected to do this again with FeatureNet. That's where we went wrong. We soon learned that a high profile new technology product like FeatureNet doesn't lend itself to the 'skin of the teeth' approach. If we didn't launch such products properly we weren't going to do it at all. The FeatureNet experience brought this home to us, and taught us to change our ideas. It also taught us that we weren't as good as we thought we were.

'...a high profile new technology product like FeatureNet doesn't lend itself to the 'skin of the teeth' approach.'

Setting the scene
....

We had been launching products successfully – in our terms at least – for many years. The problem was that these products were in the main based on technology with which everyone in the organisation was very familiar – switchboards, telephone equipment, private circuits and the like. And most important was the fact that our customers had over the years become conditioned to accepting that 'things can go wrong'. The waiting lists of the 1980s were still remembered. So why is FeatureNet different? In simple terms, it does pretty well what a sophisticated switchboard does – clever things with telephone calls, diversions, messaging, etc. If you connect several switchboards to a traditional private network, these facilities are available throughout an organisation at locations all over the country. FeatureNet goes one better. It is what we call a 'virtual' private network.

The problem with the traditional switchboard system from the customer's point of view is that, even if they buy the most up-to-date equipment, in time it is likely to need upgrading. Customers want to add new features that didn't exist when they bought it, and so on. This is not so with FeatureNet, because the customer never owns the network, BT does. We ensure it has the very latest features available.

FeatureNet means that the customer doesn't have the capital expenditure, or the risk, involved in investing in their own private network. There are also cost benefits, since calls on private networks are cheaper. It was a technology whose time had come – a solution to a very real set of business problems relating to the issue of communications and technology management. Companies whose core business was nothing to do with telecommunications – such as retail banks – had over the years found themselves building up an increasingly complex set of telecomms assets and a growing number of people supporting them. The rate of change in this area was accelerating, so that the demand for upgrading and reskilling was growing too. FeatureNet gave these organisations the opportunity to re-think their strategy relating to telecomms equipment purchasing, and the ability to bring tight central control on costs and standards, which, in many cases, had been surrendered to the outer reaches of the organisation many years before.

It is not hard, therefore, to see why FeatureNet was immediately popular with large companies. What was not so obvious was that it would be equally popular with many smaller ones. A further complication was that many of the larger companies wanted to introduce FeatureNet as rapidly as possible across a large number of small sites that were spread right across the country. This was good business for us, but very difficult to manage at the rate we were being asked to achieve.

Lastly, FeatureNet had enormous visibility in companies. It is a very big decision to give up your long established telecomms assets in favour of a completely different approach. This sort of decision is usually taken at the very top of the organisation, so when things went wrong it became very obvious.

Planned launches are better than product escapes

FeatureNet started life with BT when one of the major high street banks approached us and told us that they wanted this technology in the UK – it already existed in a very similar form in the United States. We could see that it was only a matter of time before one of our competitors would offer the product if we didn't.

Perhaps we were too hung up on breaking away from our old image – this was the 1990s and we were really getting into the new, improved BT way of doing things. FeatureNet was launched and we found that it was a big hit. But as we started installing it the problems began.

Everybody wanted FeatureNet, but unfortunately the basics weren't as right as we hoped. The problems weren't huge, but it was noticeable to users that we weren't on top of them, so pressures built up. Anyone who worked on FeatureNet then would say that the product wasn't launched, it escaped. By mid 1994 things came to a head. We had three main problems:

- **Not all the features were available from day one.** Our promotion of the product had raised expectations and customers wanted, quite reasonably, all the bells and whistles straight away. There was a direct comparison being made between the functionality of previous switchboards and FeatureNet.

- **We lacked the courage of our convictions.** We built an entirely new network to meet expected demand, but this was not enough. We experienced problems in meeting the growing order book. The popularity of the new system with our own sales people was immense, because it offered a solution to customers' real business needs. Tensions built up around the prioritisation of loading of new customers.

- **Many of the first people working on FeatureNet were inexperienced with the product.** This was probably the most important issue of all. Often relatively simple problems bogged us down. These people took a while to be trained; meanwhile everyone working on FeatureNet knew that workloads were building up. Confidence that we could get ahead of these problems was a real issue.

Customers became extremely irritated with us. We were in danger of souring the relationships we had spent so much time establishing. Within BT the frustrations mounted between the marketing, sales and service operations. The problems had to be brought under control – fast.

Regaining control

We pulled the top people from each of the key departments together with a clear remit of fixing things. The overall responsibility was with the Service Director to pull back the problems and rebuild the confidence of the sales and marketing people.

We needed to list the problems, to share with everyone involved just what needed to be done and who was (and was not) doing what, and to plan activity to get things right within realistic timescales.

Top of the priority list were two goals. First, to clear backlogs of work that were bogging people down – often relatively straightforward faults that our engineers simply lacked the expertise and skills to get on top of. Secondly, to control selling activity so that we could get ahead of the game.

We spent a lot of time getting views from our front-line people. We found that the lack of skills was a serious issue. We had 70 or 80 engineers, very experienced in many fields, but not properly trained on FeatureNet. Within weeks we built a dedicated FeatureNet training centre so that all our people could be properly trained in at least the basic skills they needed for the product.

Just as important was the management team who ran FeatureNet operations. They were almost entirely new to the job, and many of them were relatively young and inexperienced. Interestingly, these managers were doing very much what all of us had done in the mid '80s. They were fully occupied solving problems. They were under such pressure from customers to fix problems that they didn't have time to address the underlying issues. Instead of listening to their teams and understanding the root causes of the problems, they focused on fire-fighting.

We had been through all this several years before, and we had learnt the answer back then. We were absolutely firm that the managers' job was to deal with new work, not day-to-day problems, and we got the managers to delegate the job of dealing with customers to their teams – who were becoming more expert as the training advanced. This left the managers free to focus on how to prevent the faults in the future.

Gradually the people talking to customers felt that they were at last really able to deal with customers' queries, and the customers realised that they were dealing with people who understood the system. Meanwhile the managers gained the headroom to concentrate on the problems their teams were expressing.

Of course there were a myriad of other problems we had to sort out, often involving additional investment, but it was amazing how 'getting the basics' right was the key to changing the mood all the way through the organisation.

Communication of what we were doing was vital. Handling sales reaction to a slow down in selling was pretty high on the list. We had to make sure that everyone understood the issues and to gain the commitment of everyone at the top of all the departments involved to get things put right.

In short, the senior managers took a grip and set priorities. Steadily through 1994 and 1995 things got better. The improvement was slow at first, but momentum built up as confidence grew that we had a plan.

Most important – and surprisingly perhaps – our customers' confidence may even have grown faster than ours, because they stayed with us despite all the problems, and in many cases they ordered more. They experienced serious frustrations, but we kept explaining what we were doing as honestly as we could. Our relations had been strained, but at least BT retained a level of trust.

By the end of '95 things could be said to be 'run well'. Our external customer satisfaction ratings (we measure the FeatureNet service separately) steadily improved. Then something happened that not only shocked us but that had a completely unexpected effect. A huge IRA bomb went off in London's Docklands in early 1996, and one of our main buildings was hit.

The Docklands bomb

About a third of the FeatureNet people are based in the building that was hit. The bomb had been left in a van that was parked right outside; some of our staff had walked past it not five minutes before it went off. Windows were blown out, desks were blown up, and some people were thrown across the room by the force of the blast.

Our people coped incredibly well. They had the whole operation moved to another location. The bomb went off on a Friday; by the next Monday they were up and running again and customers didn't notice any difference to their service. But news of what we had done spread

'Windows were blown out, desks were blown up, and some people were thrown across the room by the force of the blast.'

by word of mouth, and they began ringing to congratulate us.

In the same way in which the 1987 hurricane proved to be a turning point, the Docklands bomb was the point where things started to go right. BT people all pulled together to cope. A spirit of teamwork went right through everything – not just the practicalities of providing a service after the destruction of the building, nor just emotional support for the people who had been in the building when the bomb hit, but through every aspect of the job.

Suddenly FeatureNet has really come right. People were all pulling in the same direction, and it showed. It was going to happen anyway, but it happened sooner than it would have done otherwise. It took three or four months for things to get back to normal, and by then FeatureNet was no longer a product in trouble. It was a successful product with a few creases to iron out.

When we started on our get well plan our customer satisfaction figures showed that virtually none of our customers described themselves as satisfied. A year after we'd started to tackle the problems with FeatureNet, over 60 per cent of customers said that they were satisfied. The percentage has been increasing ever since. There are always going to be faults that need fixing, but we're now dealing with the fine tuning that we'd have liked to be dealing with when we first 'launched' the product.

KEY LESSONS CHAPTER 7

Even with hindsight, it's hard to see how we could have spent much more time developing FeatureNet before we brought it on line. But there are lessons to be drawn from the experience:

.....

The most important thing is to anticipate demand in plenty of time.

.....

Do as much research as is feasible; a vague guess won't do.

.....

Make sure that the resources are there, the people are properly trained and so on, so that when the demand hits, you can react quickly to cope with it.

.....

Stick to product launch disciplines. No matter how good you are, you can't 'wing it' every time.

.....

Be prepared for the unexpected; you cannot predict all the challenges that new technology brings.

.....

Carefully consider your marketing strategy, and do not oversell.

.....

Communications with customers and with your own people are key.

.....

Positive action on complaints

Complaints are an important gauge of a business as whole.

- *We started by compensating customers with serious complaints.*

- *Next, we addressed how to prevent the complaints from happening.*

- *Then we learnt how to handle the remaining complaints in order to satisfy the customer.*

- *We performed rigorous analysis to find out whether we were fixing the symptom or the root cause.*

To understand how far BT has had to travel, you have to go back to the days before privatisation, when our original attitude to complaints was formed. Back then customers got their phone fixed within the timescales we set if they were lucky and not if they weren't. There was nothing else for them – no rebates or compensation. Customers' contracts made it clear that they had no right to anything; if they weren't happy there was little they could do. We were a part of the Post Office, and we had Crown immunity from prosecution, so there was no way in which anyone could take legal action against us. There was no OFTEL to appeal to, so the customer was always wrong!

In the run up to privatisation, the government placed certain conditions on us. One of the big changes was that customers were allowed, for the first time, to take legal action against us if we were at fault. As our contract terms and conditions with customers began to change, we realised that we had to be more pro-active in dealing with complaints. We would have to be sympathetic, at the very least, to the idea of offering rental rebates. It was a huge leap forward for us.

By the mid to late '80s we were learning to take complaints seriously, but while we were genuinely doing our best, this often fell far short of our customers' expectations. We also went through some very rough periods in the '80s when our complaints departments were just overwhelmed. 1987 was a good example, when the after-effects of the strike caused huge backlogs of repairs and installations. The following year we had to See Chapter 1 modernise our King's Cross exchange and thousands of customers lost all service for months.

A GP lost his emergency line for three months, and went on television to talk about it. The complaints department for that district was so flooded with calls from everyone affected by the disruption that the complaints manager had to use schoolchildren from the East End on work experience to answer calls.

The customer service guarantee scheme

In 1989 we introduced a completely new idea: the customer service guarantee scheme. This approach is now fairly well recognised as part of the Citizen's Charter initiative but at the time it was seen as pioneering.

The customer service guarantee scheme promised customers that if we failed to repair a fault or to supply a service within a fixed time limit, we would pay them compensation. In those days we offered £5 a day, but people could also claim up to £5,000 for actual financial loss – these limits have increased considerably since then. When we introduced the scheme it not only offered a commitment to customers, it showed to everyone in the company that we were really serious about our drive to improve service.

'...no customer ever really wants to claim, they want everything to go right in the first place.'

There was a risk to this scheme: we didn't want our people to relax and think it didn't really matter if we got it wrong because the customer would be compensated. This would absolutely have missed the point: no customer every really wants to claim, they want everything to go right in the first place. We tried to move away from broad indicators of complaints by publishing internally just how much we paid out, rather than simply telling our people how many customers we had compensated.

Customers would rather have good service than compensation.

> If in a particular part of the company there are 250 installa-
> tions in a month and only seven of them are late by three days,
> it's not unreasonable for the people involved to think that
> they're doing pretty well. But if you tell them that as a result of
> those late installations BT had to pay out £47,000, they realise
> the cost impact.

These paybacks run alongside complaint measurements as indicators of our performance. Only a few years ago we were paying
out around a million pounds a month across the whole organisation for loss of service. That has dropped by over 90 per cent
and is still falling. Our complaint numbers have gone down cor-
respondingly – each set of figures supports the other.

Satisfying the customer who complains

After the customer guarantee scheme, we looked hard at how
we could improve our complaint handling, and at how we
could use the complaints we were getting to teach us how to
prevent future mistakes.

It is a terrible admission, but at one time we had so many
complaints that we got pretty good at dealing with them. Our
legacy from the bad old days is that now we have a system that
we think works well. There is always scope for improvement,
but now we know we have the right basis to build on. We have
been to other large organisations to ask them how they do
things, and they almost invariably end up asking us for advice.
It's encouraging to know that we have as much to teach as we
have to learn.

What exactly do we do with complaints? First, let's define what
a complaint is: we classify any expression of dissatisfaction from a
customer as a complaint. If they ring up and say, 'My phone is out

'...at one time we had so many complaints that we got pretty good at dealing with them.'

of order. Would you come and repair it?', we don't count that as a complaint. If they say, 'My phone has been out of order for two days and you still haven't fixed it.', we would call that a complaint. Sometimes the tone of voice, rather than the words, can make the difference between what constitutes the report of a fault and what constitutes a complaint.

We discovered very early on that if we give the wrong response we can turn a fault report into a complaint very quickly. Most of our customers recognise that things will go wrong from time to time, and they don't automatically complain about it. Once we've decided that what we are dealing with is a complaint, we have to make sure that it is dealt with efficiently. First of all the call is logged on a computerised Customer Complaint Handling (CCH) system where all the information about the complaint is recorded. We categorise the complaint by type, so we record whether it is a payphone problem, a network problem, a chargecard problem or whatever. We also categorise the complaint geographically.

The wrong response can turn a fault report into a complaint.

The customer hasn't had to ring the complaints department to make the complaint; they ring the fault reception team or whoever is appropriate and our CCH system logs the complaint regardless of where it arises in the organisation.

If as the problem is being dealt with the customer isn't happy they will then be put through to a specialist complaint department.

Customer satisfaction is improved if you contact the customer after resolving the complaint.

And finally, once every complaint has been resolved we contact the customer again to check that they are satisfied and we 'close' the complaint. And at this stage we look again at how we classified the problem. This is because the original classification – what the customer told us the problem was – may not have been accurate. For example, the customer may have told us that their switchboard wasn't working when, in fact, it was the network serving the switchboard that had a fault. This 'closing' stage of the process is hugely important in terms of how customers rate our handling of their complaint.

High level complaints

We still handle separately what we call 'high level' complaints. These aren't just defined by the nature of the complaint or by the complainer, but by a mixture of the two. The customer may be someone running a one-person business whose phone is out of order for only a short time, but if they write to the Chairman of BT to complain about it, that makes it a high level complaint. 'High level' might sound a bit of an old fashioned term, but in a large organisation it is not unusual for some customers to complain straight to the very top, even though the normal channels are usually a more effective way of sorting out most problems. Having said that, the majority of high level complaints are either very serious or very complicated, and they certainly require a great deal of expertise to ensure that they are handled properly.

Measuring complaints

We measure the quality of our complaint handling as we measure most things, using customer satisfaction measures. This has its problems, because it is much harder to get a customer who has complained to say that they were very satisfied: we may only be asking them to judge us on how we handled the

complaint, but their view is bound to be coloured by the fact
that they had cause to complain in the first place. We do find
that a well handled complaint can do much to redeem things,
and indeed we get a lot of 9 and 10 out of 10 scores. This
is where the skill and expertise of the people handling
complaints make all the difference.

It is important to analyse what went wrong.

We use the satisfaction surveys to follow up any
particularly poor scores and pass all these back to
the line people who handled the complaint so they
can see what went wrong.

We keep close track of what things people complain about. This
means that we can pick up whether complaints are high on payphones, repairs or whatever. Sometimes there is a specific reason –
repair complaints tend to be high following severe storms, for
example. We check on how fast we fix complaints, how much we
pay out under the customer service guarantee scheme, what our
overall customer satisfaction scores are, and so on.

The table shown on page 133 is just one example of the kind
of information we extract every week from the system. It shows
a breakdown of the number of complaints for the week by
region and by type of complaint. As you can see, it also high-
lights (along the bottom) any areas where there is a significant
increase in complaints, so that we can investigate further.

The psychological angle

The way we handle complaints can make all the difference between
a customer with a minor gripe and a customer who is livid. In fact,
it's arguably more important than how we fix the actual problem,
assuming we fix it reasonably efficiently. This isn't just a gut feeling,

Business communications complaints received profile: by zone (week ending 14 June 1996)

	LONDON	H.COUNTIES	MIDLANDS W&W	NORTH	SCOTLAND	GRAND TOTAL	%
31 Inbound sales	32	37	26	22	16	133	9%
02 Provision	58	56	63	52	11	240	17%
3/6/35/36 Billing	86	58	38	35	14	231	16%
07 Repair	61	41	56	57	8	223	15%
8 Payphones	48	23	57	26	4	158	11%
9/30 Outbound sales	12	14	5	4	2	37	3%
10 Local network	7	16	12	24	11	70	5%
11 Operator svcs	6	1	1	1	0	9	1%
12 Phonebooks	16	25	25	18	8	92	6%
13 Chargecards	13	10	18	16	2	59	4%
14/1 Private svcs	3	0	2	0	0	5	1%
16 Exchanges	3	1	3	3	1	11	1%
18 Calls in error	5	0	1	2	3	11	1%
19 Misc: BT policy	12	17	7	6	2	44	3%
20+ Others	7	5	8	9	3	33	2%
27 Telecom red	4	2	4	1	1	12	1%
32 Service channel	3	8	19	5	5	40	3%
34 Telemarketing	8	6	12	3	2	31	2%
Grand total	384	321	357	284	93	1,439	100%

> *'The way we handle complaints can make the difference between a customer with a minor gripe and a customer who is livid.'*

this is what our customer satisfaction measures tell us. Fix a fault an hour faster and the score may go up by a few percentage points. Call the customer afterwards to check that they're satisfied and it can go up by 10 or 15 per cent.

One of the most important things is to look at the problem from the customer's point of view. This means taking the customer very seriously – letting them know that their problem is important to us. People are often nervous when they ring in. They think that we won't understand how important it is to them to get the problem fixed. It makes a huge difference simply to let them know that we aren't going to shrug them off, but that we're going to do everything we can to put things right.

In most of our operational units we aim to answer the phone quickly and, quite rightly we monitor this. But this can create tensions for the people dealing with a customer – spending a little longer on the call can make all the difference. So whilst speed of answering is important we have shifted the emphasis towards how well customers tell us they have been dealt with when we measure their satisfaction with our call reception.

Treat each customer as if they were the only one you have.

We also go out and visit customers, and it's amazing the difference it makes to them. They feel important enough for us to spend time on. We can't afford to do this every time someone complains, but there are occasions when it really helps.

One of our customers had a switchboard installed, and we got it wrong. The customer had used a consultant to supply the switchboard, and us to install it. Somewhere along the line we'd all managed to make mistakes.

satisfaction in general and complaints in particular. These gatherings draw people from all the parts of the organisation that can have an effect on the customer's experience: field engineering, sales, exchange operations, billing. They look at a common set of data, come to a common understanding of the problem and have the authority to do whatever is necessary to fix it.

The main point about Quality Councils is that they enable people to confront other parts of the organisation face-to-face, to understand the issues involved and to work collaboratively to solve problems.

> One manager was heard to remark at a Quality Council meeting, 'That was a good presentation. I can now see what they are talking about ... Why didn't they tell us that in the first place?'
>
> The fact is that they probably had, but in slightly different terms, using slightly different statistics. The Quality Council had brought these different views together and enabled a common understanding to be reached. At the root of all this was the fundamental acknowledgement that we had to get it right for the customer.

Turning complaints into opportunities

Complaints can be opportunities to build a better customer relationship. Think about it from your own point of view. All organisations make mistakes from time to time and a well handled complaint will make a customer more loyal than no mistake at all. Every complaint is an opportunity to create a more loyal customer.

Every complaint has the potential to create a more loyal customer.

A complaint is also free market research. It would be better to have no complaints and to pay for the research, but if you've got the complaints, why not get all the

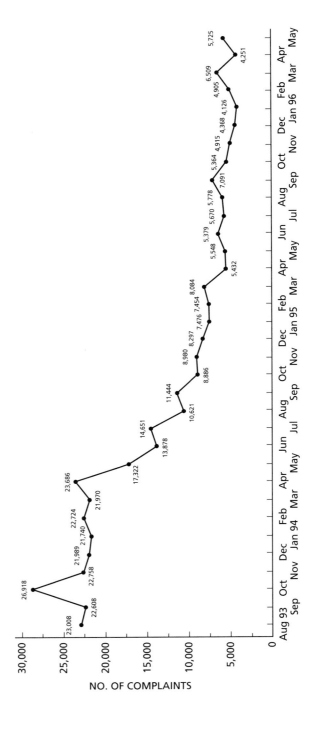

Total business complaints received: (1993–1996)

benefit you can from them? It's all for the customer's benefit, because the aim is to prevent a recurrence of the problem.

A complaint is free market research.

It is also surprising how often a complaint can be turned into a sale. Our complaint handlers aren't specifically trained to sell, but they are trained to spot opportunities.

> Suppose a customer calls at ten o'clock at night and complains that their phone doesn't work. Their contract states that they are only paying for repairs during working hours. If we can we will turn out anyway at ten o'clock, but explain that we can't guarantee to do this again, unless they would like a better maintenance contract. Or they might like a second line, per- haps. When you handle it the right way, people don't resent you selling to them, because they see it as BT trying to help them to prevent a recurrence of the problem.

As far as our complaint handlers are concerned, that is precisely the point. Their priority is not selling, it is on reducing complaints. If the best way to do that is by selling something to the customer then everyone gains.

Complaints can often be converted into sales.

Raising expectations

The complaints we get now are not essentially that different from the complaints we used to get 10 or 15 years ago, except that customers expect more than back then. Ten years ago a cus- tomer might have complained because it took longer than two weeks to provide something. Now they will complain because it takes us more than two days.

Expectations are rising because our industry is all about speed, doing things better and cheaper. People generally today expect

. . . .

'Ten years ago a customer might have complained because it took longer than two weeks to provide something. Now they will complain because it takes us more than two days.'

. . . .

Chapter 6 describes the customer service guarantee scheme

more than they used to; customers are beginning to recognise their own power to push standards up. And at BT we have quite deliberately pushed up our customers' expectations with things such as the customer service guarantee scheme and by promoting our BT Commitment.

The end result of all this is that we expect people to complain about shorter delays and more minor hitches. That is because we want them to be totally satisfied, not just prepared to settle for what they're given. So we keep the pressure on for better ways to prevent complaints and better ways to handle them when they do arise. But we now know that we have a system that can incorporate all the improvements we want to make, and that can keep meeting our customers' expectations even when we raise them.

KEY LESSONS CHAPTER 8

The key lessons we have discovered are:

.....

Whenever possible, complaints should be handled by whoever the customer speaks to first, not by a specialised complaints department.

.....

You need to give your people the authority and flexibility to solve problems themselves whenever possible.

.....

The response the customer receives is crucial; badly handled, a notification of a fault can quickly turn into a complaint.

.....

You must keep customers informed of what is happening with their complaint.

.....

It makes a big difference if you contact customers once the problem is resolved to make sure that they are satisfied.

.....

You need to measure complaint handling according to the customer satisfaction it generates.

.....

A well handled complaint can make a customer more loyal than no complaint at all.

.....

Downsizing
without disaster

Streamlining the organisation and efficiency savings from new technology came at the same time for BT, with the result that our workforce was far bigger than we needed it to be. This led to some difficult conclusions:

- *Although we didn't need to keep all our staff, we had to keep a focus on customers during what would, inevitability, be a very difficult period.*

- *We decided that we needed to downsize the organisation without any compulsory redundancies at all. This was not an easy task, but we found that it was possible and desirable.*

- *Our employees had worked hard for the company for many years. How they were treated during this period would set a tone for the future.*

In 1989 BT employed 240,000 people. Now the number varies depending on need; at the time of writing is about half that. One of the biggest challenges of the last few years has been this dramatic downsizing. The word may have been redefined as right sizing but at the time there were no euphemisms. It was downsizing. What made it particularly challenging was our determination to do it without any compulsory redundancies.

The pressures for downsizing

As we started to pull the organisation into its new shape in the mid to late '80s, it became clear that the impact of new technology meant that we simply couldn't justify having so many people. In addition, Project Sovereign was about to restructure the company in a way that would give economies of scale. Our failure costs would also be reducing as our quality improved.

See Chapter 2 for information about Project Sovereign

The technology impact was huge. Jobs that had once needed an engineer to wire up a complex installation now only needed someone to flick a switch, or to swap over a computerised card in an exchange. Repairs that once called for a visit could now be fixed remotely by computer. It just did not take as many people to do the job as it used to. We were also bringing in improved and more effective working practices.

Maintaining loyalty to our people

We needed to reduce numbers, but our old civil service mentality and public-service ethics had their benefits, as well as the drawbacks we've already seen. There was an enormous loyalty to our people. Most of them had joined the organisation when it was still part of the civil service, and they expected a job for life. It was clear that the way in which we handled the need to downsize would play a major part in defining the kind of company BT was to its people. We made sure that we never forgot that we were dealing with individuals – not just figures on a page – and most of these people had made a considerable contribution to the organisation.

'We made sure that we never forgot that we were dealing with real individuals – not just figures on a page.'

The way in which we dealt with downsizing would be important:

- **Those who remained needed to know that they were working for a caring company that treated its employees well.** The morale of staff who stay after redundancies can suffer badly. We did not wish to have an unhappy and apprehensive workforce.

Your whole approach to business can be defined by the way in which you treat your employees.

- **Our actions would define the approach of the company as a quality long-term organisation.** We care about our customers; you cannot be successful without caring about the employees.

We ran a series of voluntary 'early-release schemes', over several years. Initially, these only applied to managers. With Project Sovereign on the horizon we were clearly not going to have room for them all. We were making the organisation much flatter – cutting out half a dozen layers of management – and we didn't have anywhere to transfer many of these people to.

Helping people to make the break

It was useful that the need to reduce our numbers was closely tied in with the changes we were going through to become more customer-focused. We were in a position to begin to describe the sort of company and skills that would be required. Because our release arrangements were voluntary there was no shortage of volunteers. Many of these people were those who had been used to the routine of the past and who could see the extent of the changes that were to come.

One of the most important decisions was to communicate early and regularly – and to be as open and honest as possible about the reasons for the changes and the effects they were likely to have on everyone. In this situation the rumour machine

'In this situation the rumour machine defaults to the worst case scenario.'

defaults to the worst case scenario. We had to ensure that all our people had access to accurate up-to-date information so that they could make informed choices.

A great deal of thought went into designing our early release schemes. We looked hard at industry best practice and calculated carefully how these schemes could be funded to ensure fairness as far as possible to all sides: those leaving, those staying, our shareholders and our customers.

Once the unions recognised the inevitability of redundancies they worked with us at the design stage to ensure that the interests of their members were represented. This co-operation was a vital and invaluable contribution to the overall success of the project.

We launched the first release scheme for people who were not managers at a time when a number of engineers weren't comfortable with the way their roles were changing. The job was no longer as technical as it had been. It didn't involve the traditional engineering skills. The result was that we got a huge voluntary take-up of the scheme. There were other reasons for this as well – not least that we were offering a very good severance

Some people don't want to stay in a fast changing organisation.

A good severance package shows people that you appreciate the work they have done.

package. This was not only relevant to the people who were leaving, but was an equally important message for those who stayed. It showed that we appreciated the work of everyone in the organisation.

Some people were due to retire in a few years; for them a lump sum at the right time provided the opportunity to leave a little earlier than they might have planned.

Another factor was that we were in a growing industry, with tremendous opportunities. There were jobs available, and BT's training was regarded as just about the best anywhere. Some of the people who left us but who wanted to stay in the industry ended up employed by our growing band of competitors.

It is easy to find the first volunteers for redundancy, but it becomes harder as time goes on.

As time went on there were fewer applications for voluntary redundancy with each release scheme. Whilst there were always some people who were getting close enough to retirement that they liked the idea of a lump sum, and others who decided that BT wasn't for them and that this was a good time to go, it became harder to reduce numbers.

The detailed mechanics of handling release were very important. At the outset we made line managers responsible for managing the arrangements in their own units. We trained them for this, and it made a huge difference to the way the scheme operated. The managers knew how many people they had to lose, and they talked to the individuals and agreed voluntary redundancies. It wasn't an easy job. It's one thing for senior management to say, 'we need to lose a considerable number of people', but by the time it gets down to line-manager level, it gets very personal.

It is true that there were no compulsory redundancies, but there were people who needed to be persuaded that it was in their own and BT's interests for them to go. If these people had refused to do so they would have been allowed to stay. The reason we encouraged them to go was because we did not feel that they were suited to the way BT was heading. We really didn't think it was any more in their interests than ours for them to stay. Once we had explained this they usually chose to go.

'It's one thing for senior management to say, "we need to lose a considerable number of people", but by the time it gets down to line-manager level, it gets very personal.'

Generally speaking, release worked out in everybody's interests.

Downsizing and morale

Some people imagine that downsizing can be achieved without too serious an impact on morale so long as it is voluntary. This wasn't the case for us. Although it could have been far worse, it was still an extremely unsettling period for everyone. The people who have stayed are those who are most enthusiastic about change, but that doesn't mean that they find it easy to cope with while it's happening.

The biggest problem, as far as morale was concerned, was the constant fear in people's minds that not enough of their colleagues would go voluntarily and that compulsion would be necessary. This is hardly a basis for individual confidence. There were also concerns that, despite improvements in working practices, those who stayed would be required to work longer and harder.

Another problem was that new recruits were minimal. We did recruit a few people, but very few. On top of that, promotion prospects appeared to disappear with the reduction in both jobs and organisational levels.

The counter to all these negative aspects was the extent to which individual jobs were becoming more challenging. As a result of the things that have gone on along with the downsizing – the changes, the way we work, and so on – we have given our people far more responsibility than we ever used to. We have learnt the importance of training people who want a greater challenge, so that they can move into the jobs where we are growing our numbers. For example, we have reduced the numbers of traditional engineering jobs but continue to require salespeople, project managers and systems engineers. The trick is to help people to face up to the need to change their skills and to offer them practical help to do so. We put a lot of effort into this.

Another morale-related development that occurred during the release programmes was that many people started planning to leave well before their normal retirement. They thought that downsizing would go on forever, and they started to think, 'Maybe in a couple of years' time, when the mortgage is paid off...' When a lot of people are all thinking about going they tend to lose their focus on and enthusiasm for what they're doing. After a while this attitude can permeate to the people who don't have any intention of going, and morale can be undermined more widely.

For this and other reasons, it would not have been wise to run a continuous series of release schemes indefinitely.

> Career prospects diminish with downsizing. It is important to make the remaining jobs more challenging.

> Chapter 10 gives an insight into how we have shifted the focus from 'downsizing' to 'reskilling'

> It is not a good idea to run a release scheme indefinitely.

Life after downsizing

The downsizing programme went on for five years. That is a long time for people to feel uncertain about their jobs, especially when they grew up in a job-for-life culture. There are still jobs in BT that will become obsolete, but there are other new jobs opening up, and we want to focus on developing and reskilling people so that they can move inside the organisation rather than leave.

It became important to bring in some new blood. Every organisation needs fresh new people, and one of the disadvantages of redundancy schemes is that the company could not recruit to replace leavers during this period. That is not to say that we haven't recruited anyone since 1989, but recruitment has been on a fairly modest scale. We have managed to keep the support of the unions throughout the downsizing, largely because it was voluntary. We would certainly have put that support in jeopardy if we had recruited new people as fast as we were losing our long-term people.

'Our people have to be able to learn new skills constantly, just to perform the same job.'

Along with the downsizing, we also needed to tackle other significant changes – not least the big shift in skills, in a fast moving technical industry such as telecommunications. Our people have to be able to learn new skills constantly, just to perform the same job. If they want to move around, or if we want them to, that can involve another whole set of skills too. In a way, downsizing has proved valuable experience for this, because over the next ten years or so everyone (not only in an industry such as BT's) is going to have to be able to adapt to new technology faster than ever before. Flexibility and willingness to change are going to be key skills, and the people who have stayed with BT have had to learn them.

Looking back at the years of downsizing makes us realise just what a tough time they have been. The amount of turbulence caused was huge. Our people showed great flexibility in handling some very difficult situations. It wasn't unusual for some people to have three or more bosses in a year – the organisation and people shifted so fast. The fact that it was tough doesn't mean that the overall changes weren't right. But, at the same time, we had to learn to manage them so that people had some stability. People who enjoy change will be challenged and stimulated by having to learn new skills, but interpersonal relationships aren't so easy to change. It takes time for a team to learn to work really well together; you can't keep disrupting it and expect the same performance.

Significant downsizing is bound to entail significant change to the organisation.

People have responded tremendously well to change, perhaps even to the extent that we need to be conscious of the possibility of going too far the other way. Everyone is so used to change now, and they cope with it so well, that there is a real risk that they will become restless when things don't alter for a while. That could have a detrimental effect on routine work: people need to feel challenged if they are to retain their focus and commitment.

Change needs careful management. You can have too much of the wrong kind of change.

The secret is to harness people's enthusiasm for change and not to suppress it. In our industry they are bound to get all the change they want sooner or later. Nevertheless, it is important to be aware of people's raised expectations of the excitement of the job. It is also an interesting reflection of how far we have come in a relatively short time from the days when change was virtually unheard of in our organisation.

What does it all mean for the customer?

There has been a real correlation between reducing costs and improving service in BT. We had to focus much harder on working effectively, and downsizing was only one of many factors making us do that. The result has always seemed to be better quality for the customer, even when this wasn't the original driving force. As our costs have come down we have been able to pass on the savings to our customers. We couldn't offer the service we do now at the cost we do if we still employed a quarter of a million people.

'We couldn't offer the service we do now at the cost we do if we still employed a quarter of a million people.'

Our next big challenge is to find ways of retraining our employees so that their jobs are secure and we have a skilled workforce that can cope with new technology and ever rising customer expectations.

It is possible to downsize, improve service and maintain morale all at the same time. However, it is not easy. Some key considerations are:

.....

Communicate early and often – be open and honest and don't avoid difficult issues.

.....

Explain the 'why' just as much as the 'how'.

.....

Be as generous as you can be with severance packages – but remember that there are many interest groups to consider.

.....

Devolve responsibility as far as possible *and* train and support the managers involved.

.....

Don't run release schemes indefinitely. Set a target and manage to achieve it.

.....

Ensure that leavers go with dignity, and that those staying still feel valued.

.....

Getting in shape and staying fit:
building a flexible workforce

A flexible workforce is the most valuable asset a company can have. We have taken the first steps towards this, and have learned some important lessons:

- *Many people are suspicious about the reasons for re-training.*

- *People need to understand that re-training will often mean a career change – not just coping with new technology.*

- *Regular change must be viewed as an opportunity; sometimes that goes against the 'conventional grain'.*

- *Motivation and morale will be key factors in any retraining. Don't underestimate the in-built worries people will have.*

- *Be prepared to invest in your people. Show them that you're in it for the long term.*

- *Don't underestimate how much support large-scale change will need.*

BT's company-wide release schemes came to an end in 1995. Making people redundant, even on a voluntary basis, was uncomfortable, but it was one of those things that was unavoidable if we were going to remain competitive and ensure jobs for those that stayed. We always preferred to find a way of keeping as many people as we could.

'It is ingrained in our culture to give everyone a job for as long as we can, even if it isn't always for life these days.'

The type of skills we need in BT have been changing for many years. As people's jobs become obsolete we would much rather retrain them for the new jobs we are creating than lose them and bring in new people who already have the skills we want. It is ingrained in our culture to give everyone a job for as long as we can, even if it isn't always for life these days. It also makes financial sense. It is better to retain the people we already have, with new skills, than to give them money to go and then recruit people who already have those skills.

> It is better to retrain existing employees than to lose them and have to bring in new people.

Each part of the organisation has the responsibility for dealing with this problem according to their particular situation. Different parts of the organisation need different schemes, appropriate to their people's qualities, background and skills.

This chapter describes how we went about retraining and redeploying people in the part of BT responsible for business customers and how we have moved this on to a completely new approach to learning and reskilling.

Finding permanent placements for displaced employees

As the numbers of people we needed began to reduce we couldn't offer a release package to the displaced people but we did have to take the surpluses out of the day-to-day operations or productivity would have simply collapsed. So we moved these people into what we called the Resource Management Group (RMG). The name tried to illustrate the fact that the people who were in the unit would work on specific projects away from the normal day-to-day jobs they had been doing. During their time in the RMG new 'permanent' jobs would be sought for them.

That was the theory. In practice the RMG was seen by many quite simply as the place for surpluses to go. As a result it soon had very negative associations. It was seen almost as a staging post on the way out of the company. One of the first redeployment tasks attempted by those running the RMG was to place engineers in clerical jobs. Because of the way our technology was changing, the engineers in the field took the brunt of the non-management redundancies. It was these jobs that most often became obsolete.

We found that it was difficult to retrain engineers simply to move to office-based work. It's not that engineers aren't flexible people, it's just that there are limits to how far anyone can change. Our engineers had always worked out and about, meeting customers face-to-face and using a very practical set of technical skills. We were asking them to sit in an office all day, operate a computer and talk to customers on the phone instead of face-to-face.

You can't force managers to take on redeployees. You have to persuade them.

The managers who had agreed to take on engineers in clerical roles were cautious – and their early experiences weren't always too good. We didn't order managers to take on people from other parts of the company. We had to sell the idea.

And a particularly important role was that of the managers of the people in the RMG. They had to go round the company selling the idea of taking on these technical people. It wasn't an easy task and meant visiting managers right down the line, convincing them of the skills and potential these technical people offered. By the end of a year they had begun to make significant progress, but only by sheer hard work on an individual basis. And choosing the managers to work in the RMG wasn't easy – we recognised early on that we had to handpick the right people and give them all the right career assurances!

Could the RMG add value?

Simply training engineers to turn them into clerical people was proving tough – and it was far too limited a view. The scale of downsizing meant that permanent resource levels were being set against a 'standard' amount of work. When demand for the new services went up and the weather made it difficult to cope with an increased number of faults then the new operational units on their own didn't always have sufficient people to cope. As a result they were often turning to outside contractors to fill the gaps. Clearly this made no sense and the RMG took on the function of a kind of internal employment agency to call on skilled engineers as a safety net to cover peaks of work.

'Simply training engineers to turn them into clerical people was proving tough – and we sensed that it was far too limited a view.'

Gradually we had persuaded the bulk of BT managers that the idea of an RMG was a good thing. We took things on a stage further to include people with a much wider range of skills. We had to learn to cope with variable demands for extra people. A manager might call up one day with 30 people for the RMG – surpluses in a particular skillset. The next day there might be a call for 30 people working in another part of the country with a very different job content. The RMG managers had to really understand the skills, numbers and locations of the people to be placed, and make sure resource priorities were clearly agreed before sending people to particular tasks. They discovered very fast that if we didn't do those things we ended up with a shambles. Managing surpluses became an important new discipline.

'Very good people had skills that simply weren't needed in the new organisation.'

The RMG had been a bold and innovative initiative, but there were limits to how far that approach could go on its own. It became increasingly clear that the problem wasn't just one of numbers – it was really one of skills. Good people had skills that simply weren't needed in the new organisation. It was very often the case of 'right person – wrong skills'. We needed to face up to this issue, and the way in which we tackled this would have a fundamental impact on the type of organisation we would become. Was our commitment to our people big enough? Were we prepared to see an investment in their future as an investment in the company's future?

Skillbank: focusing on skills for the information age

Skillbank was a new identity for the old RMG. Once we knew that we were going to call a halt to the release schemes, we could see that we were going to have to find a way to retrain people for new jobs in BT once again. These were people with valuable skills whom we didn't want to lose, but whose role had to change. Although the RMG had been reasonably successful, its reputation had never quite caught up with its achievements. We decided on a new identity and a role that was broader in scope. The RMG had been seen as a last resort before voluntary redundancy. This time we had to be able to retrain valuable people we really didn't want to lose, so that we had the right skills for the future.

We wanted to shift the emphasis towards individuals predicting, and even initiating, the development required to enhance their skills. We said to people that if they were prepared to be flexible in terms of accepting a job, we would do what we could to find them one and to train them. We weren't talking about flexibility in terms of being prepared to work completely different hours, or move to the other end of the country. We meant being prepared to move to a very different type of role – almost always in IT and office-based skills – and maybe at a different grade from before, and we weren't asking people to take a drop in pay.

It is often the case that people simply aren't aware of exactly what skills they have. We now actively encourage staff to volunteer to join Skillbank; this enables their skills to be assessed and their career preferences to be discussed. A development plan is then agreed that is matched to the type of vacancies that exist or that will arise in the company.

We want people to realise that they are not surplus to requirements in themselves – it's just that their old job can become surplus. This has led to a whole new way of thinking about the nature of employment and careers. And it is paying off. A manager with extra people may suggest that a particular individual is a good candidate for Skillbank which may offer new career opportunities. People are also volunteering to join – some specifically because they want to switch from field-based to clerical jobs.

We have divided Skillbank into three units, each with a name based on the skills theme.

Skillfast

Skillfast is a group of engineers who operate as a kind of flying squad. They are trained to be highly skilled and flexible, prepared to travel anywhere in the country where there is a demand for them. We avoid the problem we had at times with the RMG of these 'temps' being branded as redeployees, because they are highly skilled. They are, in a sense, already in a permanent job.

Skillplus

Skillplus is the main retraining unit. Here we look at people's development potential and retrain them to fit the type of vacancies that are likely to arise that they could become suitable for. Skillplus is purely voluntary, and people have to apply to be part of it. If we don't feel that they are ready to move on to a new job yet, we delay accepting them into Skillplus.

Once someone has joined Skillplus they are counselled on job options and on their own training needs. We even start to train them while they are still in their old job. Once they move into a new post – often on a trial basis – we can go on training them. We reckon that no one should spend more than six months in Skillplus before they find a job, although if they seem to be on the verge of a job we'll keep them in the scheme for a little longer.

> It shouldn't take more than six months to find someone a job once they have retrained.

Skillpro

Skillpro includes the people who are not yet ready to move into Skillplus, or who have spent six months in Skillplus and have not managed to find a job. Either way, we examine why they aren't ready to be employed elsewhere in BT and then we agree to work with them on improving their performance or whatever it is that's holding them back.

Managing Skillbank

Skillbank is run day-to-day by a team of managers, each of whom is responsible for about 30 people. These managers are trained in career counselling, and their job is to assess each of the people they are responsible for: their employability, their aspirations, the job market, and so on. They work with each of their people individually, talking them through how realistic their hopes are and where they need extra training. Sometimes people have been overgraded and we have to help them to accept that they are unlikely to find another job at the same level.

Once someone has been accepted into Skillplus, the Skillplus manager helps them to find a suitable vacancy, supports their application and provides any training they need if they are offered a trial period in the job.

The Skillplus managers have another important role: they have to find the vacancies in the first place. Some are advertised internally, but often we have to sell the benefits of Skillbank around BT to make sure that managers come to us – just as we did with the old RMG but this time there is a really positive story. Our Skillplus managers visit units where vacancies are likely to come up and talk to them about Skillbank. If a unit has no vacancies now but is likely to in six months' time, we can start working with them early on to prepare our people for the jobs when they do come up. This is the world of an 'assignment culture'.

The assignment culture: the key to a flexible workforce in the information age

The traditional 'job for life' culture is of course changing but there is actually nothing wrong with the idea of working for the same organisation for all of your career! The trouble is that in the BT culture that has usually meant staying within a fairly narrow discipline for most, if not, all of that career. In the case of our traditional engineering functions it has almost always been a case of 'once an engineer – always an engineer'. Even promotion was usually within this discipline.

> *'We need to face up to changing the traditional open-ended nature of jobs.'*

This was acceptable in a largely static organisation, but in a company aiming to become a driving force in the information age this sort of rigidity just can't work. People doing a particular job used to expect it to last forever. There really was no need to think about developing for a future move unless you were the ambitious type. The emphasis for many BT people was on doing an adequate job within the same function unless or until the mood for a change seized you.

Our experience of downsizing, and of setting up first the RMG and then Skillbank, has led us to question this pattern of employment. It is a pattern having the characteristics of a 'parent–child' relationship: the company as the parent will look after the employee as the child so long as that child is well behaved. The responsibility for decisions about the relationship rests with the parent.

This model is becoming obsolete for three reasons:

- First, people within the company – like those in the market as a whole – are going to have to change their roles and update their skills several, perhaps many, times in their career. This will reflect the rapidly changing technologies, customer demand and global economic conditions facing all companies who wish to compete successfully.

- Secondly, to make this transition people are going to have to re-skill and develop themselves – not alone and unaided but in partnership with their employer, their professional organisation, their government or some other body. It is not possible to make people learn: those who want to be flexible will have to take responsibility for the changes they need to make.

- Lastly, we have to have a framework that will promote – drive even – this pattern of career change and self-motivated development. This framework is an 'assignment culture'. It is already successfully adopted by many leading companies around the world. It is very different from the model of employment that we and most other telecommunications companies have inherited from the public sector.

What is the assignment culture?

Essentially the assignment culture is about allocating people to defined tasks (assignments) for a fixed period of time depending on the nature of the work. During an assignment a person is obviously expected to achieve the goals set for that task but also actively to prepare themselves for a move to their next assignment. How they do this is agreed with their line manager (who is also on assignment) as part of their 'assignment plan' (a combination of a job description and personal development plan). At the end of the assignment the person moves to another role, either directly because he or she has spotted an opportunity and has the right skills, or via an intermediate body which works with the person to identify further opportunities and to help them to acquire the necessary skills.

'The company–employee relationship therefore becomes a partnership and more of an adult-to-adult relationship.'

Over time new assignments are created in those areas where they are needed by the company. As assignments end in declining areas fewer (and eventually none) are created. Career change and self-development therefore became the natural order of things which everyone in the company has to go through. The company–employee relationship therefore becomes a partnership and more of an adult-to-adult relationship. In this pattern of employment the idea of 'redeployees' in the sense in which we have them now no longer has any meaning. The organisation we now call Skillbank becomes a retraining and reskilling unit open to everyone. It functions as a 'gearbox' via which our people are able to switch to the roles that suit their talents and the company's needs.

Not only does the assignment culture allow resources to move much more smoothly around the company by enabling change to be natural, it will also – if we so wish – allow us to reward people differently depending on the nature of the assignment they undertake. This would inevitably have the effect of attracting more skilled people into certain areas, so that the best people do the most valuable work.

'...the old idea of a "job for life" – essentially staying within narrow functional boundaries for most of your employment with the company – has gone forever.'

At the moment we are a long way from realising this vision. Change is still seen as difficult and sometimes painful. But we have recognised the need to reshape our employment patterns if we are to compete effectively in the information age. Certainly in the future many people can expect a 'career for life' with BT, but the old idea of a 'job for life' – essentially staying within narrow functional boundaries for most of your employment with the company – has gone forever. What will replace it will be far more dynamic, challenging and, ultimately, far more rewarding for the individual and for BT. It is a challenge that our experience with Skillbank is enabling us to face with confidence.

Raising our game

....

Skills development for managers

One thing that we have learnt to do is to take personal development very seriously. Everyone in BT is encouraged to look at their skills, to consider the type of people the company will need in the future and to work towards acquiring or improving their skillset. In order to do this personal development plans are discussed at one-to-one meetings, and we've taken some bold initiatives to help people to assess themselves and put development plans into actions.

Different parts of the company have adopted different approaches to suit their particular situations. All of them have this end in mind.

> All the managers in customer service have been on a two-day Skills Development workshop – all about facing up to a very different future and considering their own skill requirements. They were set a number of tasks and assessed by trained observers. The resulting feedback was used to help them to understand their strengths as well as to identify areas for development. This then became an integral part of their development plan.
>
> At first these workshops were viewed with apprehension by the managers, but they soon came to realise that they were genuinely there to help – not an exercise designed to catch people out. The feedback from every event was overwhelmingly positive. A senior manager attended every session, and there were two every week for over two years. This was an invaluable opportunity for participants to ask difficult questions and for senior managers to stay in touch with the people. The programme was even used as a benchmark by some of our customers for use in their own organisations.

Going on the road: taking training to the people

The Skills Development workshops were good, but they were only aimed at managers. One of the early requests from participants in them was for all our people to be included – but only if events could be run locally to avoid travelling time and time away from the workplace. We considered several ways of doing this. We finally decided to 'take the show on the road' and build a whole multimedia learning environment inside two 40ft articulated lorries. This is designed to deliver training to many thousands of people all over the UK. The vast majority of staff do not have to travel more than a short walk from their workplace. We call this programme the 'Development Fair'. Quite apart from the training it delivers, it is a very visible demonstration of how seriously we take the development of our people.

The Development Fair delivers training (presentation skills, stress management, and so forth) as well as giving an opportunity to see what the future will look like and to try some of the new

'We've discovered that people do want to learn, and that our responsibility is to make it easy for them to do so.'

technologies. The precise programme differs from person to person, because it is tailored to suit the individual's needs as part of their personal development plan. This style of 'taking training to the people' in a very high-tech and high profile way has sparked a huge interest amongst other organisations, as well as being a real confidence booster for our own people.

People really do want to learn and our responsibility is to make it easy for them to do so. Given the emphasis we place on customer service it's not possible to have large numbers of people away from the workplace for extended periods. The mobility of the Development Fair helps people to have high

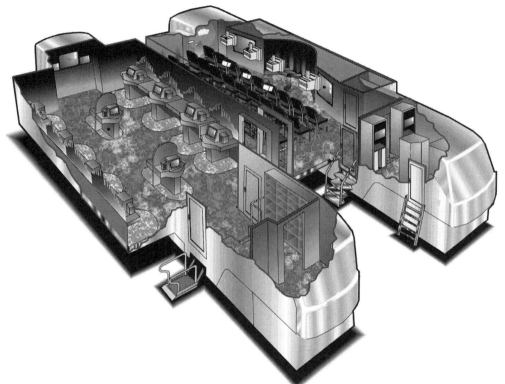

The Development Fair

quality training in short bursts with the minimum time away from the 'coal face'. Someone asked if this approach wasn't rather expensive. The reply from one of our senior managers was, 'if you think that's expensive, try ignorance'.

Measuring ourselves against national standards: are we as good as we think?

Another major part of our drive to re-skill and develop our people are NVQs (National Vocational Qualifications). These are a range of recognised national qualifications in virtually all vocational subjects. We strongly encourage our people to work towards NVQs because they're a valuable qualification anywhere, not only inside BT. We have significant numbers of people working towards NVQs in customer service – in fact one of the biggest NVQ programmes in the UK.

NVQs aren't about acquiring academic knowledge and taking exams. There aren't any courses for NVQs, the employee works on them in the workplace. Achieving an NVQ involves demonstrating certain skills that are important in customer service, or whatever the subject is. We also encourage our managers to qualify as NVQ assessors. If this is done well it fits in easily with the way in which their role is changing towards that of being a coach and a guide. The NVQ process links the individual taking responsibility for their own development with the need for managers to be close to their people.

We're using the customer service NVQ as a benchmark that we expect all our customer service people to achieve. When someone does obtain the qualification it is a recognition of their professionalism.

One of the reasons we have had such a good take-up on the programme is because people really do value this recognition.

Customer service can be a 'twilight world' compared with other professions such as marketing, accountancy and engineering (all of which have their formal qualifications, governing bodies and the like). Customer service people, who do such important jobs, weren't able to get that kind of status. Now that is all changing. Clear evidence of that change is the ability to have hard won skills formally recognised by a national qualification; not one that just relates to BT, but one that has national – and increasingly international – validity. Such a qualification not only provides a benchmark for service standards, but also gives our people greater mobility both inside and outside the company. With the emphasis now on flexibility the customer service NVQ – and indeed any other NVQ – gives people the confidence to contemplate change and tells others exactly what they are capable of doing. Both of these will be the bedrock of any successful career as we move into the 21st century.

We have discovered that there are certain guidelines to follow when introducing the concept of career change to any organisation:

• • • • •

Help people to recognise their own skills and give them the confidence to contemplate change.

• • • • •

Make it as easy as you can for people to acquire new skills and to see new opportunities.

• • • • •

Use recognised standards and qualifications to measure your performance.

• • • • •

Review the pattern and style of employment within the organisation. Does it encourage career change and reward people who move into areas that are important for the company?

• • • • •

Try new things and show people that you mean business by taking development activity seriously.

• • • • •

Make development and training high profile and exciting.

• • • • •

The most exciting job in the world:
meeting customers and making money!

In the past customer service people met or talked to customers, did the job they were there to do and went away. If, by chance, staff could see some way to help both the customer and BT (for example, by an additional BT sale) they were extremely unlikely to see how they could benefit from it themselves. Why should they? That sort of thing was only for sales people.

We realised that:

- *customer service people have a great opportunity to bring the needs of the customer and the resources of BT together for mutual benefit*

- *BT customer service staff need to be given the confidence to think in this way*

- *people need to experience the finding of these opportunities as exciting and worth their while.*

Customer service should be an exciting place to work, but during the 'different years' people hadn't seen it like that. We became convinced that if we put a 'buzz' into the service we would see real benefits – and we were right. In addition to incentives programmes we also run:

- *the 'Local Partnership' programme, to reach out to customers, the community and BT's own people*

- *schemes to give to the communities and charities with which BT employees are involved.*

Increasingly over recent years we have given our people more responsibility and more recognition, rather than stifling initiative. We have thousands of customer service people in daily contact with our customers which meant literally millions of customer contacts each year that could be used as selling opportunities – but we weren't seizing the opportunity.

'...we had millions of customer contacts each year that could be used as selling opportunities – but we weren't seizing the opportunity.'

Customers often ask engineers, or service people taking fault reports, for information on products and services that can prevent their problem from recurring, give them a back up, or make their lives easier in some way. In the past our people were not really able to help: we didn't equip or train them to talk about products, or give them any incentive to do so.

This is a BT-wide issue, which has to be dealt with according to the types of people and their roles in different parts of the company. Our service people who deal with business customers almost always have a great rapport with customers, and they ask for their advice and guidance and expect them to be able to help. Often this is the sort of 'consultancy selling' (albeit at fairly low level) that many sales people aim for.

Bringing in business: *everybody's* responsibility

The challenge was to broaden our service people actively to seek new opportunities. So a few years back we launched a scheme called 'Lucky Numbers' and asked anyone seeing an opportunity for a sale to call a telephone number designated the 'sales lead line.' The lead was then passed to sales staff to follow up.

Everyone who gave a sales lead was entered into a prize draw with the chance to win store vouchers. People were entered into the draw once for every lead put in.

This scheme sounded good on paper, but it didn't work properly. We soon identified two drawbacks. They seem obvious now, but they weren't at the time:

- **The system didn't allow us to trace the revenue being generated,** so we had no way of measuring effectiveness.

- **We gave incentives on the generation of a lead, not on its conversion to a sale.** Someone who put in 20 leads a day that didn't result in a sale would get a greater chance of reward than the someone who put in one lead that led to a really valuable sale. The lead line began to generate many poor leads, and to get a bad name amongst sales people.

Make sure that you recognise the potential for sales and find ways to make the most of them.

We tried again to find a better system and to rebuild the confidence of the sales force. The challenge was to shift the traditional sales and service boundaries closer together.

Getting warmer: some early successes

We improved the system so that we could track the leads. We then only gave an incentive to those leads that were converted to sales. We allocated points according to the amount of revenue from each lead, and collated each individual's points. We rewarded the most successful leads each month, so people competed to be amongst the top few to be awarded store vouchers.

It is best to give incentives only to those leads that result in sales.

Each quarter the most successful people, with their partners, were invited to an event hosted by a senior manager. The events were always different. One was to the Eurovision

Song Contest in Dublin, one to a haunted house weekend, another was a trip to Portugal. We tried variations on scheme names and themes over time to keep interest going.

Clearly people could generate good leads more easily if they had the relevant product and service information. We gave engineers and office-based support people information packs containing all the details they needed. Everyone had a common set of information to help them to sell each product:

- **What do I need to know?** This section gave the basics on the product or service.

- **What do I need to say?** This gave prompts on what to ask the customer.

- **What do I need to do?** This section told staff whether to give a telephone number for the customer to ring, or to pass on a lead.

Non-sales people need product information if they are to maximise sales opportunities.

We had learnt that it is not enough just to ask people to spot opportunities; they have to be given the support they need to follow this through.

The scheme ran quite successfully, with just the top performers being rewarded, for 18 months. But it was not perfect. It became clear that many people had stopped trying because they believed they would never be in the top few. Typically these people had limited opportunity to spot sales because, for example, they worked in an administration office or only dealt with a limited number of customers. The participation level was low, and although we were certainly generating more revenue, most of it came from a few very big sales.

Getting people to join in

We revised the scheme again and relaunched it as 'Winning Deal'. We had carried out a lot of research with our people and realised that it was important to change the 'look and feel' of the scheme periodically to keep it fresh and exciting. Boredom (and the threat of boredom) was one of our greatest enemies. The new scheme had two objectives: to generate revenue and to increase participation. We decided to quadruple the budget: experience showed that for every £1 spent £100 extra revenue could be generated.

> **You have to be prepared to invest in an incentive scheme.**

We gave everyone a revenue threshold. This meant that if they reached a certain number of revenue points they could start changing these for store vouchers. Thresholds were set for different teams depending upon their roles and selling opportunities. For example, people in a fault reception centre had a threshold of 2,000 points, whereas senior systems engineers had a threshold of 5,000.

> **Team awards can help to include people who never talk to customers.**

We also extended the scheme to include team awards, so a back office person could be included to recognise his or her contribution.

We found that participation rates shot up. In certain office-based groups 80% or 90% of people became involved. Not all achieved their threshold, but they did at least put in some successful leads and orders. In the previous year 200 people had been given rewards, this time 4,500 people qualified.

> *'With this rate of success we had to think on our feet if we weren't to turn people off, run out of money, or both.'*

With this rate of success we had to think on our feet if we weren't to turn people off, run out of money, or both. We had set a maximum award, and this ceiling was being quickly reached, so half way through the year we introduced a 'super league'. Once individuals reached this they had earned the most they could, but they were entered into a super league prize draw at the end of the year. Some people continued to participate, but others lost interest as there were no further points to be gained.

We had abandoned the monthly and quarterly targets and events, and were simply holding an end-of-year event for those in the super league. But we discovered that people really wanted the more regular events. In fact, because partners had been invited, much of the motivation for participating had come from them. Overall the scheme was shaping up well but, as ever, there was room for improvement.

Winning people really appreciate regular winners' events.

More developments – more excitement!

The next version of the scheme was called 'Superstars'. The super league was changed so that people could not reach the very top unless they kept doing more. One huge lead would not work – they had to generate more leads month on month.

We reintroduced the quarterly event for top performers, with about 30 individuals and their partners attending each of them. The year-end event also included team winners, so it involved about two hundred people plus their partners.

Participation rates are the key to success.

We conducted a lot of research and obtained feedback from our people. It became clear that peer pressure is vitally important: once the majority of the team were involved the others soon joined in. The bottom line was, and is, participation rates. They are the key to any successful incentive scheme.

Our plans are now to focus the selling effort on profitable or strategic products and services. In the early days any revenue was good revenue – and that's still true to some extent – but we will be missing a trick if we don't concentrate on those things that are especially important to us and to our customers.

Reward people for selling specific products or services that you want to focus on.

It takes time to establish a good incentive scheme.

It is about five years since we launched the first scheme. We've discovered a huge amount along the way, and the participants have learnt with us – becoming more confident and clear about the aims of the scheme. Over time we have shifted up a gear, increased funding and extended the rewards. It takes time to go through that process.

Now that we have a robust programme we just need to change the packaging to keep things fresh and stimulating for participants. We vary the presentation, themes, product emphasis, winners' events, and so on. The core scheme is highly effective, partly because its objectives are clear and are clearly communicated, and also because we listened to feedback from service people, gave them the support they said they needed and made participating exciting and rewarding. Above all we made it easy to participate. It is almost easier to take part than it is not to. When most people are having fun it is hard for others to opt out – and that is just what we want.

Keeping the momentum going

We publish quarterly newsletters to keep people updated and tell them of any extra product-related schemes. The newsletters include stories about the big sales, and also about the little things where people have helped customers by giving advice.

Give all the participants regular statements to show how they are doing.

Individuals are kept up to date with how they are doing, and line managers receive a monthly statement showing individual and team attainment within the scheme. We've found the incentive schemes to have a real effect on people's performance and morale. Many staff have are now more keen to interact with customers; they show an interest in customers' queries and problems, in case there's a sales opportunity in them.

*Winning Deal and
Superstars launch
brochures*

Awards for excellence: recognising the very best

We now run another motivation scheme that is broader than the Superstars programme. It is called 'Awards for Excellence' and was launched in 1994 to give awards for quality performances – not just for new sales. Originally for managers only, the scheme has been widened to include anyone who shows an exceptional standard of work. One of our customer service managers, for example, increased revenues and customer satisfaction on a team where both staff morale and customer perceptions of BT were low. Another won an award simply because his customers love him – he is always receiving letters of thanks for his care and attention. He won his award for exceptional customer service rather than for a one-off achievement.

Motivation schemes are as important as incentive schemes.

Each quarter nominations are compiled and ten people receive an award. Colleagues from other divisions are also nominated where they have been instrumental in the success of a cross-divisional project. The main motivation for Awards for Excellence has become recognition rather than money. We tell all nominees why they were put forward and pass copies of the letters down the management chain so that everyone can see who was given an award and why.

People are often motivated by recognition, not money.

A small but important element of the scheme provides money for the whole team to celebrate when a manager is an award winner. There are also prize vouchers and all individual winners are invited to an event such as a senior management dinner or conference.

A bit of 'showing off'

Awards for Excellence is a very effective scheme for making individuals and teams feel special. The well-deserved glow seems to

sentation and then give people the equipment to go and deliver the talk in schools. Once again we benefit, of course, but so do the schools and the people involved.

What does it all mean?

We all know that partnership – with customers, suppliers and employees – is the way forward for successful companies. What we have now come to realise is that there is another vital element needed to complete the partnership model: partnership with the community. This type of partnership creates and reinforces the 'feel good' factor for employees about the community, for the community about the company, and for the company about itself. Through initiatives such as 'Helping Hands', and many other corporate, local and individual activities besides, we are trying to show that our commitment is to more than just large-scale charitable donations; it is about encouraging individuals and offering the support of BT beyond just the day job.

It can take a few years to develop a really effective incentive scheme, and there are certain guidelines to be followed:

• • • • •

You must be prepared to invest in the programme.

• • • • •

Be absolutely clear about your objectives.

• • • • •

Ensure that people participate.

• • • • •

Equip service people with product information to help them to maximise sales opportunities.

• • • • •

Team awards are a good way to include people who don't deal with customers themselves.

• • • • •

Winners' events are really appreciated: involve partners in them because they provide behind-the-scenes motivation.

• • • • •

Focus on profitable or strategic products by giving incentives for those in particular.

• • • • •

Keep the communications and the interest going for maximum effectiveness.

• • • • •

12

Putting the jigsaw together:
realising we all have customers

*T*eamwork is not just about individuals coming together to achieve a goal; in a large organisation a network of teams has to work together. We have identified five key points that help us to achieve this:

- *recognise the strength of small team identity*

- *make sure team goals interlock and complement one another*

- *ensure that each team sees each other team as either a 'customer' or a 'supplier'*

- *recognise that every team has customers; some of these are internal (within the company), and some are external (outside the company)*

- *make the ultimate test for every individual and every team: 'Is what I am doing benefiting the end customer?' If it is not, something is wrong and no team goal can justify it.*

In BT we have worked hard to bring individuals together, giving them a sense of identity and purpose so that 'the whole is greater than the sum of the parts'. However, as in any large organisation, this is not the whole story because BT has within it literally hundreds of teams. It is the identity and goals of a group of individuals that makes them into a team in the first place. This can and does drive them to achieve great things, but it begs the question of how a multitude of teams can be brought together so that conflicts are avoided and the power of the larger 'team' is released. One of the BT values is 'we work as one team'. This chapter examines how we have made this happen and what lessons have we learned.

Lessons from crisis management

Multi-teamworking – often called 'matrix management' – is the key to success in a service organisation. In the past we didn't do it because we had self-contained organisations which just didn't line up with our customers, but once we had organised ourselves to be able to deal with our customers properly we found that this was a skill we had to learn.

When BT was organised geographically there was a strong local team spirit, but this rarely crossed geographical boundaries. The one exception was that we always coped well in a crisis, as any public-service organisation tends to do. We have managed to keep this strength very firmly as part of our culture. When handling a crisis everyone forgets about job titles and team roles: if

> **'When handling a crisis you need to forget about job titles and team roles: if something needs doing the nearest person does it.'**

something needs doing the nearest person does it. Crisis management, when it works well, is one of the great examples of the kind of teamwork that is focused on the collective goal of resolving the problem. No one notices what team or department or management level anyone else belongs to unless it helps things along.

One of the crises we face from time to time is exceptionally
See Chapter 1 severe weather; the hurricane of '87 is an obvious example. We've also had to deal with the after-effects of bombs. The City of London was damaged by IRA bombs in 1991 and '93, and in '96 both the London Docklands and the centre of Manchester were bombed.

The bombing in the City in 1991 is a good example of how BT people pull together in an emergency. The explosion was on a
See Chapter 7 Friday afternoon, and the force of the blast rocked some of our own offices. In fact in one of our buildings were our duty managers who work round the clock, so we routed enquiries and problems from our normal fault reporting channels through to them. We set up an impromptu service centre there that afternoon for customers whose telecomms services were disrupted or obliterated. By the Sunday evening we had managed to re-route just about every customer's calls to wherever they wanted them to go. By Monday everyone had some kind of phone service and we spent the next week improving the arrangements, relocating entire services to new sites, and so on, so that businesses could get back to work as soon as possible.

We did much the same thing after the 1993 bomb in Bishopsgate. We used the same building to set up an emergency service centre and mobilised our engineers. This time we had a system so that we could see at a glance who all our affected customers were and where they had been relocated to.

It sounds as though the whole operation went extremely smoothly, and it did, but not without a huge amount of unrehearsed and enthusiastic work from vast numbers of BT people. Many of them phoned when they saw the evening news and volunteered to come in and help. As well as engineers we had people staffing emergency caravans, which we set up to offer help and advice, to loan or sell mobile phones and to do anything else we thought would help our customers.

In these emergencies people don't even think about their job descriptions; they work alongside people they've never met before; they bend or even break rules to get some kind of service back for a customer; they use their initiative. The managers muck in with everyone else, answering phones or whatever, and hierarchies disappear. Everyone has the authority to do whatever they need to do to get things back to normal.

Making a routine out of a crisis

Why can't we all work this way all the time? Without that level of pressure, but with that degree of focus on the joint objective. Why do we get hung up on departments and boundaries and functions? The crises spirit usually carries on for a couple of weeks after an emergency, but then things go back to 'normal'.

We have analysed what happened during crises after the event to see if we can incorporate some of the good things into everyday practice. We have succeeded in many areas. For example, we have tightened up delivery times on many products because we've discovered what we're capable of. We've built flexibility into our processes and especially by developing responsibility down the line to let people make the right

> After a crisis, analyse your performance to see how you can incorporate the best aspects of it into day-to-day operations.

decisions for their customers. It is harder to work out how to sustain team feeling.

Much of the problem is to do with personalities. People become territorial about their departments and empires, their authority and status. This is a natural part of human behaviour, but it doesn't necessarily help the organisation to run as well as it would do otherwise.

We have discovered that what causes most difficulty in a team is lack of clarity about who is responsible for what. In a cross-divisional team this problem is magnified, so it's crucial for the manager setting up the team to be clear about responsibilities. This isn't as easy as it sounds. It isn't always possible to give absolute clarity because demands change so often, especially with emerging technology. It is also important not to be too rigid, so that people's flexibility and initiative are retained. The managers who are involved in setting up teams that bridge departments and divisions have to learn to find a balance.

Be as clear as possible about people's responsibilities, while allowing for initiative.

Part of that balance comes in the choice of who to put into the team in the first place. Some people always want to take on more and more. This isn't necessarily to do with ego, although it can be, but is just the way they are made. It is important not to squash that drive. Other people are quite happy to compromise, to fit round everyone else, find out where jobs need doing and get on and do them. Both types of people are necessary to make a team work: the challengers and the compromisers. The challengers' responsibilities need to be as clearly defined as possible, and the compromisers will fill the gaps between them.

Some people challenge and others compromise. You need both types on a team.

All this is part of the move away from the traditional 'command and control' culture we have grown up with. It is no longer appropriate to order people about to get the best out of them. We have to use approaches that encourage active partic-ipation and an understanding of people's different skills and strengths. We're now teaching managers and their teams to understand learning styles, behavioural preferences and how to give and receive feedback. This is not being done to comply with some mantra or management fad, but because it has been shown to bring real benefits in the hard pressed operational world of customer service. It is part of our need to build a flexible responsive organ-isation that can bring out the very best from everyone within it. Once people are able to be flexible and strong as a team they have to have something to focus on. We have made sure that this focus is firmly and unequivocally on the customer. Everyone has to share goals and objectives focused on the cus-tomers' requirements.

> *'We're now teaching managers and their teams to understand learning styles, behavioural pref-erences and how to give and receive feedback.'*

We have now taken this a step further and organised our people who are the face, voice, eyes and ears of BT – the front-line sales, service and marketing teams – around specific customers and groups of customers. Previously these teams would probably have identified more with their own organisa-tion than with the customer, but now the customer is paramount and internal boundaries are irrelevant. These front-line teams have in their power the authority to get things done from the rest of the company – everyone jumps if the front line shouts!

Teamwork helps customers

It gives people huge encouragement to work across teams if you can show them by example how well it works. Once people can see that cross-team working helps both the customers and BT they are far more willing to try it.

Show people how team working helps customers.

The aftermath of the bombs is a good example of how it helps customers when everyone pulls together.

Our people had coped excellently in the wake of the bombs. In fact Mike Owen, the manager who set up the emergency service centre in '91 and '93, was awarded the MBE for his work in putting the telephone service back together. Our customers were well aware of what a good job we had done for them, and we knew we couldn't have done it without team-work. Even now if we have problems with any of our City customers, they will say, 'Well, we still remember what you did for us after the bomb back in '91.', and they'll take it into account. We've retained immense loyalty from customers because of that.

City businesses now trust our advice on how to cope in emergencies, because we've proved that we can do so. Virtually all major businesses, especially in the City, now have back-up arrangements for emergencies (bombing is only one risk, it could be fire, flood or any other catastrophe). They have made contingency plans to re-route calls to another site and have installed extra lines at additional cost. Our records show that we cope very well in an emergency and our customers trust us to act quickly and effectively when major incidents occur.

'City businesses now trust our advice on how to cope in emergencies, because we've proved that we can do so.'

This kind of response is rewarding for everyone involved, and reinforces for them and other BT people that forming these kinds of temporary 'virtual' teams really does work. Bombings, thank goodness, happen very rarely. But there are other events, on a smaller scale, which have the same effect.

A BT customer in Glasgow is a boiler-maker with an enormous factory – the company runs its own trains through it. The factory is based in an old building; the office block attached to it is listed. This customer had a visit one Monday from the buildings inspector, who told them that the factory was unsafe and they would have to evacuate it by the following Saturday. The problem was the weight of their antiquated communications equipment; it was causing the building to sink. We received a panic phone call from them: they had less than a week, could we help?

We needed some dedicated teamwork and co-operation and, in true BT style, everyone pulled together when faced with an emergency. Our sales teams helped to plan what was needed and we found an external planner. Our service people sorted out how they could give the customer the best service in the time. We pulled in engineers to work on the job. Our buyers got the equipment sorted out. We worked out how to get rid of the old equipment. The customer had a brand new state-of-the-art communications system by the Saturday.

Once again, teamwork was the key. So how do you get that spirit going in everyday routine work as well as in emergencies? An early example of a cross-divisional team was in 1986, when we learnt a lot of lessons that we still apply now.

Heathrow is the world's busiest airport, and it has some fairly specific needs in terms of telecommunications. Although airlines compete ferociously with each other to sell tickets, they are tremendously co-operative on the ground. The airlines operating out of Heathrow came to us and said that they would like to keep using BT, but that we were only offering them the kind of service we would offer anyone else. They told us that *they* wanted to tell *us* what kind of service we were going to give them.

They had all sorts of specialised needs:

- They needed to know that if vital phone services were lost they would be fixed in minutes, not hours. They certainly didn't want to go to the back of a queue behind other customers.

- They wanted us to do any outdoor maintenance work at night because, not unreasonably, they preferred us to stay off the runways while flights were leaving and arriving.

- They need a phone service to run air traffic control. Imagine what would happen if the phones went down without an instant back-up system.

- Security is incredibly tight. We can't send different engineers out to Heathrow every day, because if they don't have a pass it can take them four hours to get onto the site. So we needed to build in all sorts of customised services into the contract.

This was about the time that our competitors were starting to target a number of our key customers, and those at Heathrow were high on their priority list, so we couldn't afford to let the airlines down. We went to all the departments in the geographical division of BT that would be involved, and told them that we were all going to have to work the way Heathrow wanted us to. Co-operation was pretty unenthusiastic (this was back in the mid '80s when attitudes to customers weren't what they are now) so we decided that we had no choice but to pull people out of other departments and put them into Heathrow, whether their bosses liked it or not.

We took service people and systems people, engineers and telephone operators, and everyone else we needed, and put them all together in a building at Heathrow, so creating Heathrow Services. They all worked together under one management line, and we told them that they now worked for Heathrow Services first and BT second. They worked together wonderfully.

We ended up looking after the telecommunications for almost all the hotels, car parks, air traffic control and other businesses at Heathrow. It worked so well that other airports (Gatwick, Manchester, Scottish air traffic control, and so on) approached us and asked for their services to be operated through Heathrow Services. We lost fewer customers than we did almost anywhere else that our competition targeted.

We discovered that if we put teams of people together in a clearly defined role we could offer the kind of bespoke service we could never manage otherwise. With this sort of structure, whatever the customer's specific requirements are you've got someone there who can deal with them. Because of the make-up of the group you have to devolve responsibility to people at the front line. This creates better customer service, as well as giving our people more job satisfaction. Since then we have totally restructured our service centres for specific groups of companies in the same industry to give just that bespoke feel.

'...we learnt that if you bring people together once, and get them working well with a common focus, you can do what you like with reporting structures and all the rest of it.'

There was another interesting development at Heathrow a few years later. All the people at Heathrow Services had come under the then Western London section of BT, although they had come from various departments within it. After Project Sovereign they all worked for different sections of BT, so they were working across far greater organisational boundaries than before. It didn't make any difference at all. That was when we learnt that if you bring people together once, and get them working well with a common focus, you can do what you like with reporting structures and all the rest of it. You have a team as long as the group is still unified in its focus.

Once a team is working well it doesn't matter if you change the reporting structure.

Building cross-functional teams: bridging the sales versus service barriers

More recently we have taken this a stage further by bringing our customer service people and our sales people together within front-line teams. BT doesn't really 'hard sell', because that's not what our customers want. In fact in our business there is a narrow distinction between selling and service. Once we have built a good relationship with our customers, the best way to sell to them is to draw their attention to products or services that could help them. We don't try to twist arms to make people buy something they don't really want. That would damage our relationship with them and, in the long run, do us more harm than good.

See Chapter 11 for information on the incentive schemes

Our incentive schemes, such as Winning Deals and Superstars, have shown us that our service people are extremely good at this sort of selling, now that we help them to do it. Once they're on the customer's premises they can spot an opportunity or a chance to say, 'Is there anything else we can do for you?' Service people are often very natural at offering the company's products without overtly selling.

Having said all that, we need our sales people more than ever. We need them to lead the account teams, to understand the customers' business and to act as consultants and business partners – adding value to the customers' operation. We are selling *relationships* to customers; selling the idea that if they trust us we can help them to change.

There is a relatively fine line between our sales and service people. The main difference is the focus: the sales people build future business, the service people deliver excellent customer service now – first time, every time. We have therefore put our sales and service people together in the teams for our large customers.

What we don't want to do, however, is to give everyone the same job. We want them to carry on being a sales person or a service person; we're just getting them to work together on the same team. Sales and service people are different; they have different abilities. There are some people who can cross over, but the majority are much happier in one discipline or the other.

In a sense it should be possible to get people working together without officially creating a new team to do it – that is what happens in a crisis. In reality, though, it's much smoother and more efficient to put some kind of organisational structure in place. The structure helps everyone to know where they are, and it minimises the scope for interpersonal rivalries if everyone is as clear as possible about what areas of responsibility are theirs.

When we brought together the sales and service teams, the first thing we had to do was to get them each to understand the other's jobs, priorities and problems. We've achieved this by running workshops, discussing problems, focusing on issues where there's either scope for co-operation or a risk of conflict, and so on. Apart from the primary aim of each of these approaches, they all have the secondary aim of simply bringing people together so that the key people in the teams get to know each other and find out about their respective requirements to help their shared customer. Now our account people visit the service centre people and talk through problems with them, and the service people will go with the account people to meet customers together. The service people are closer to the sales people, and better able to tell them what they can and can't offer, and at what price. At the same time the sales people are in a better position to talk to the service colleagues on their team and say, 'Look – if you could just promise to do this, we'd be offering the customer a much better deal...'.

There is always going to be a degree of natural tension between sales and service people, but this can be channelled positively. The traditional idea of service people is that they prefer to maintain the status quo, because they are the ones that have to live with the contract once it's been sold. Sales people, on the other hand, are always up front trying to offer something new and different in order to clinch sales. This, not surprisingly, can make the service people nervous. Putting the two schools of thought together on the same team means that the sales people drive the service people on to offer greater and greater quality of service; it gives them the spur they need. Meanwhile the service people are making sure that the sales people have a solid grasp of the service issues that affect the customer, so that they can spot sales opportunities and act on them for the customer's benefit.

The more relevant skills you have access to on a team, the more successful that team will be. We learnt that fact – among others – from how we respond in a crisis. There must be a huge benefit in being able to construct cross-divisional teams deliberately, for specific purposes. One of the keys is to be able to make everyone's role clear whilst not constraining their flexibility. The other imperative is to make sure that the team has a clear shared objective. When a team works in this way – as it did with our first industry-specific service centre at Heathrow – the whole is greater than the sum of its parts.

> **The more relevant skills there are on a team, the more successful it will be.**

A good teamwork motivation scheme

The results of good teamwork are so important that we decided to start a campaign designed to encourage it. This is a similar idea to the sales incentive schemes, which encourage non-sales people to make the most of their customer contacts.

See Chapter 11 for details of the sales incentive schemes

The scheme started in January 1995 and is called 'Let's Play Ball'. It was the brainchild of Robert Brace, our Group Finance Director. The idea is that anyone can nominate a fellow employee who has made a significant contribution to co-operation in a team. The nominator and the nominee both receive a letter and a small token of appreciation carrying the Let's Play Ball logo. In large companies such as BT it can be difficult for the different divisions to communicate well and work together effectively. Although Let's Play Ball focuses on individual examples of co-operation, it encourages the idea of wider co-operation because it is part of a plan to improve cross-divisional co-operation within the company.

Consider using an incentive scheme to encourage team co-operation.

Let's Play Ball is a way of showing people how important we think good teamwork is, and of showing that we notice and appreciate individuals who work hard to co-operate and produce good results from team effort.

Talking the same language: TQM comes home

Whilst we are still far from perfect, it is true to say that the culture of teamwork is now ingrained as part of the modern BT. A key tool that has facilitated this was, and is, TQM.

'TQM taught us to begin the process of letting go of the old ways of relying on hierarchy and status to solve problems, and allowed us to focus on our customers.'

The common language that TQM gave us, the shared approach to problem solving, the focus on tackling the 'vital few' problems first, followed by the discipline of continuous improvement have proved invaluable. But most of all, TQM taught us to begin the process of letting go of the old ways of relying on hierarchy and status to solve problems, and allowed us to focus on our customers. It taught us that, wherever we are in the organisation, we all have customers, and it's their needs we have to meet. If the organisation gets in the way of customers' needs, it's the wrong organisation and needs to be changed. We have changed it and continue to change not just in formal reorganisations but in people coming together to fix problems as and when they occur. Such change needs to be carried out properly; the application of TQM in BT gave us the start we needed.

KEY LESSONS CHAPTER 12

The most important lessons are:

•••••

After a crisis, analyse your performance to see how you can incorporate the best aspects of it into day-to-day operations.

•••••

Don't give everyone the same job: they should each bring their own skill and expertise to the team.

•••••

In cross-divisional teams, make sure the division of responsibilities is absolutely clear.

•••••

Give everyone a shared objective and a single line of management.

•••••

If people can see how working together will benefit the customer they are far more likely to want to co-operate.

•••••

You need people on a team who constantly seek new challenges, but you also need people who are willing to compromise.

•••••

The more relevant skills you have on a team, the more successful it will be.

•••••

You need a tool to help you to change; consider what a TQM approach can bring.

•••••

Shouting from the rooftops:
celebrating success and learning to do better

After all the effort of turning around customer service performance, we want to be sure that we have something to show for it:

- *Has everyone noticed that performance has improved; if not, how can we draw their attention to it?*

- *What difference does it make to customers, and to our own people?*

We have found that there are benefits for everyone in terms of customer satisfaction, customer loyalty and morale within the organisation.

W e have come a long way in the last ten years or so. Was it worth it? What difference has it made? As far as our customers are concerned, it has made a great deal of difference. The challenge is to make sure that they realise this and not to let complacency catch us out.

Marketing good customer service

Good customer service isn't easy to market. A customer can only really appreciate it as the sum of a lot of experiences. You can bite into a chocolate, or turn on the television, but you can't test customer service in the same way. Somehow we need to make sure that the message is getting across. The more complex communications become, the more our customers need to have confidence in us. They will increasingly rely on their communications supplier to lead them through the maze of emerging technology. We need to be sure that the supplier they choose is BT.

You have to market customer service, but it isn't easy.

We now have approaching 200 licensed competitors in the UK and their competitiveness is increasing all the time. We're never going to be the cheapest, so we have to be the best. Our customers are far more aware of issues such as competition and regulation than they used to be. This enables them to demand greater value for money in terms of speed, quality and professionalism. By and large they are happy to pay that bit extra to be sure they're getting top quality service. But how do we tell people that is what they'll get if they come to us?

BT Business Class

One of the ways we've tried to get the message across is by creating an identity for our package of services to businesses that clearly differentiates it from anything our competitors offer. In 1994 we launched 'BT Business Class', a package of services – some old, some new – which we promoted strongly to our larger business customers. This wasn't a master branding that was used on TV or in the press, in fact it was partly to convince ourselves just how much 'service value' we offer. Our sales and account teams needed to be able to talk about the BT service offer. BT Business Class gave them the help they wanted.

'Customers often take service for granted unless it is spelt out to them.'

Our customers reacted very positively to BT Business Class. They liked being told what they were getting for their money, and our account teams found it much easier to get across the message about the customer services we offer. Customers often take service for granted unless it is spelt out to them.

Customers like being told exactly what they are getting for their money.

BT Business Class is only a step towards featuring messages about service much more strongly in our marketing campaigns. One of its key features is getting our relationships with customers right: building trust and confidence. Our very biggest customers have a whole team of people looking after them: account managers, systems engineers and service managers. Smaller business customers have a telephone account manager who doesn't normally make visits. Whichever end of the scale they are at, we aim to offer a single named point of contact so that customers can always talk to people they know.

'It helps that we have lost quite a lot of customers to our competitors: a considerable number of them come back to us.'

Customer experience and word of mouth

In a way it helps that we have lost quite a lot of customers to our competitors because a considerable number of them come back to us. From what they tell us, the reason is the level of service we now offer. Thus the customers' own experience, and word-of-mouth that comes as a result of that experience, are two of the very strongest methods of letting our customers know that service is now high on our priority list.

Explaining what we can do for customers

The third method is to ensure that, when our sales people and account managers are talking to customers or prospects, they explain what BT can do for them. That may sound obvious, but it is all too easy to take our own service for granted and to forget what matters to our customers.

> One service we offer is to tell our customers a lot about the calls they receive: how they are distributed through the day, how many fail to get through, and so on. We need to make sure our sales people realise that this is a big selling point. We can give our customers this kind of report every day if they want it, but we have to equip our sales people with the information to pass on to the customer.

We also need to give our services a different emphasis when we talk to most of our smaller business customers. These are customers who are often just starting to get involved with faxes, modems, e-mail and the Internet, and so on. They don't want to know about optimising networks and all the technicalities – they just want the technology to help run their businesses. They want us to take as much of the worry off their shoulders as we can. Again, this is something we can do, but we have to recognise that customers need to be told this. We have to explain our services in terms of how they help to influence the business.

Offering different levels of service

We have come a huge distance, but still have further to go, in offering customers the choice of paying more for a higher level of service. The traditional BT view, years ago, was that we were offering a public service and everyone had a right to the same service. It would have been unthinkable to give someone preferential treatment just because they could afford to pay a bit more than the next person. Times have changed, and we've changed too, but it has taken a long time to shake off our instinctive reluctance to offer people a better service if they pay more, and we still have a little way to catch up. In fact, in a competitive age, most people are happy to pay more for a better service. At the same time, people who only want half the benefits would prefer to pay only half as much to have them. One of the things we can do to help market our customer service is to create more levels of service, at different prices, for the customer to choose between.

Customers like the option of paying for a higher level of service.

We need to ensure that we apply the same marketing disciplines to service as we do to any other product. We must understand what customers want by considering:

- how much they are prepared to pay for it
- what it costs us to deliver, and
- what our competitors offer.

We can then weave this into a disciplined service portfolio.

Too often in the past service has been seen as a resource that can be used to bridge gaps in other parts of the portfolio, rather

If all this makes us sound like saints rather than business people, we're not. Of course there are still areas where we need to improve even further. Complacency in employee relations is as dangerous as it is in customer relations, but at least we think that now we have the right systems in place for people to be able to tell us when we're going wrong, and for us to be able to do something about it.

The result

The changes we have made over the last decade have brought benefits for all of us, both inside and outside the company. We have achieved huge productivity improvements every year for many years; we now work smarter, not harder. Overall our revenue is holding up, although the market is far more competitive. However, complacency must be our main concern. Customers will go on demanding more and more. Our new competitors are often smaller, nimbler and set new challenges for a large organisation. We must keep driving ourselves on, but in a way that allows the people involved to really enjoy what they do. Giving people that sense of achievement, pleasure and fun is so important.

'Giving people that sense of achievement, pleasure and fun is what management is now all about.'

Our customer service has improved as a result of both external and internal factors. The external factors which have driven us are:

- **a more demanding market;** and

- **competition.**

From an internal point of view, the factors that have driven up customer service have been:

- better analysis of what constitutes customer satisfaction
- less tolerance of failure
- greater attention to detail
- taking a real interest in the people who deliver the service at the front line and giving them the support and tools to do the job well.

The external factors are here to stay and, so long as we continue to focus on the internal areas, we will continue to improve our customer service.

There is now far more choice for our customers than there ever was in the past, and we know from all our data that customer satisfaction has steadily improved. Over the last two or three years complaints have halved and halved again. In the round it isn't a bad achievement, but if we hadn't had the driving force of getting customer service right, none of it would have happened.

The key lessons to note about communicating improved customer service are:

.....

Never take for granted your customer's understanding of the service you are giving.

.....

Two of the best methods of getting the message across to customers are word of mouth and the customers' own experience.

.....

Communicate value for money by offering the option of paying more for a higher level of service.

.....

The more satisfied the customer, the greater their loyalty.

.....

As customer service improves, job satisfaction within the organisation increases.

.....

Tell your own people about customer service successes – it improves morale and prompts further improvement.

.....

The fuzzy future

*T*he sheer enormity of the changes we face and the rate at which they will affect us all make it difficult to know what to say about the future. History will probably show that today we are at the beginning of the beginning of the Information Age, and entering one of the great discontinuities of history, comparable with the agricultural and industrial revolutions. Skills requirements, education support, lifestyles, employment patterns and trading arrangements will all change completely, and there will be no going back. People's expectations of what society can and should provide will be fundamentally different from those of today.

For BT the nature of our industry will place us at the leading edge of these changes. The challenge for us is to be creative in understanding the opportunity that this technology can offer to our customers and their business needs by building strong relationships with them. What does that mean for our traditional views of customer service? Increasingly we must become not just a good service company but a truly expert organisation.

Telecommunications will come of age in the 21st century. Vast bandwidth, new technology, the growth of multimedia services, deregulation, mobility, global communication and reducing costs will all help to develop the information society – in which individual company and community wealth is determined by the speed with which information is available, and the way in which it is used to support and determine both personal and business decisions.

Computing and telecommunications will merge to enable new multimedia services that are currently beyond most of our imaginations. These services will form the platform upon which society will base its next stage of development – a stage that, from our late 20th century viewpoint, is pretty tough to predict. We can be certain, though, that the rate of change will accelerate, and that our customers will be more concerned with how technology has an impact on their lives than with the technology itself. Customer service of the traditional kind will not be enough. Added value will more and more depend on the personal touch that offers our expertise to help customers through the change barriers.

'Customers will expect the organisation we now think of as their phone company to provide service anywhere in the world.'

Perhaps the defining characteristic of the information society will be its absolute dependence on fast easy access to information, regardless of a person's physical location. Customers will expect the organisation we now think of as their phone company to provide service anywhere in the world. National boundaries will have little meaning or influence. These developments will drive, and will be driven by, the globalisation of business, world-wide telecomms companies, deregulating markets and rapid technology development.

Growth rates are already mind blowing. The Internet has doubled in size since 1988, and had well over 50 million users at the end of 1996. The world mobile phone population has quadrupled since 1991 and is set to treble again by 2000 as mobile phones become smarter and cheaper. Vastly enhanced bandwidth means that videoconferencing costs have been reduced 100-fold in the past 10 years, with no end to this trend in sight. Movies, education and training, music, newspapers, videoconferencing, shopping, financial services and much more are already available through a single terminal.

This staggering story of the power that comes from the combination of computing and telecomms is still in its infancy. Just try to think about the full scope of teleworking, electronic commerce, on-line entertainment and tele medicine.

Predicting the future is almost beyond our imagination. It is 'fuzzy'. We can say that it is very likely that highly centralised organisations and institutions will die. Knowledge, information and, therefore, power will move to the edge, to the front line. The head office as we know it will be a historic feature of a command and control structure based on holding information at the centre of an organisation. Already in BT we make such widespread use of personal computers (on the desk and laptop) linked by mobile phone for our field engineers; they allow access at the press of a button, via an intranet (a closed user group in the Internet), to information that was previously held far from the front line. So the front-line world is

No centralised and autocratic organisation will be able to keep up in the future.

transformed from one based around the screwdriver, soldering iron and paper to one dependent on state-of-the-art technology that is fundamentally changing jobs and skills requirements.

This is happening, to varying degrees, in all businesses, large and small. Our job in BT is going to be to guide our customers through this maze of new technology, and then to deliver it at the speed, reliability and quality they want. The service package that we build around these new products and applications is going to be the key factor in giving us an edge over our competitors.

How can we approach these changes?

We need to give authority to the individuals who deal directly with customers as we move knowledge outwards in the organisation. Customer-facing people have always been the new heroes of organisations and this will increase as their skills and capabilities have more and more scope for growth. We will need to supply more training to be able to deal with that, and to cope with more change rather than less. Things aren't going to settle down, change is going to accelerate. No organisation will be able to keep up

'No organisation will be able to keep up unless it learns to stop being centralised.'

unless it learns to stop being centralised. The future trends in technology that are painted here translate to changing trends in managing people. Their roles and responsibilities will grow as they are given more authority to act commercially in their customers' interests.

Customer service will keep moving up the agenda for everyone, including us. Quality and price are now the industry norm, and service is the factor that will give a competitive edge. In BT we feel that the basics are in place. In 1994 our UK operations became the largest single organisation in the world to receive company-wide registration under the international quality standard ISO 9000 (which is all about delivering high standards of quality of service consistently). In 1996 we won the European Quality Forum Silver Award. All of this is critical for a well run company. It shows compliance with processes and procedures. But the power of the technology now adds the dimension of creativity; that is the real challenge as the complexity of our industry increases. The fuzzy future must keep pushing us upwards from simply conforming.

We need to go on retraining our people to keep them up to date with changes. The paradox is that the better we get at installing and maintaining the new technology, the more obsolete we make our traditional roles. Training and retraining is going to be a big part of the future for our people. It will be the basis of the assignment culture and is already shaping how we use our own 'Skillbank'. Learning will be a key point of everyone's working life.

See Chapter 10 for more on Skillbank and the assignment culture

As far as customer satisfaction is concerned, customers used to be impressed when we turned up on site and did clever things with coloured wires. Now it takes more to impress them, and there are fewer wires. What is important now is the time spent with the customers and the way in which we treat them. Our engineers are increasingly customer service professionals with technical skills. They talk through what they're going to do, make sure they fit in with the customer and explain any noise, inconvenience or disruption. It is the personal touches that really drive customer satisfaction up, not the wiring.

> **People will need constant training and retraining to keep them up to date.**

The new technology

Today's communication products are so much more advanced than only a few years ago – and we in BT are far better equipped to diagnose and fix problems remotely. We also can do some amazingly clever things to help our customers.

Not so long ago telephone phone-ins on television swamped our return. Today we can filter calls and route them in a way that avoids that sort of disaster. But straightforward voice telephony is increasingly being overtaken by data calls on our networks – computers talking to one another and huge flows of information. 'Movies on demand' down the phone lines are technically possible as proved by large-scale trials in East Anglia. Soon, too, one phone number for life will be the norm – no more number changes when we move house or to distinguish our fixed and mobile services. And we will get smarter in the ways we store customer information and respond to their requirements. Already we can offer our largest customers direct access to input orders straight into our systems without any BT person intervening – the zero touch business!

Lurking in all this technology is the almost certainty that there will be such step changes that we will not just keep edging things forward but will totally transform the way we conduct our business.

HAL... or remote possibility no move

We are just beginning to use voice recognition where customers can talk to and follow the commands of machines. The funny thing is that people seem to find this move acceptable as the machine responds more like a human. Straightforward service transactions will soon be totally automated. The video phone is only in its infancy but will be able to provide a 'talking heads' look and move like the real thing – perhaps customers will choose who they want them to look like! HAL the computer in 2001 A Space Odyssey is not a remote possibility. It will become part of our customer service operations.

Where have all the people gone?

In 1976 the last manual telephone exchange in the UK was closed and ordinary calls were no longer connected via an operator. If we still ran a manual exchange service today – as we did everywhere until 1958 – 3/4 of the population would be employed by BT!

Looking ahead the new technologies will mean automation but the need for customer service will require more and more expertise and professionalism for our people. But now we can choose where the investment in our people is of most value.

What does this mean for customer service?

No-one really knows what impact all this will have on customer service, but the power of the Information Age will undoubtedly drive the same changes in the service world that the world of marketing saw in the '80s. Then there was a shift from mass, largely uniform, to micro, highly individualised marketing using the power of computing to construct a database of individual preferences. The next stage will be the microservice package, which will follow the same principle. We will need ever more sophisticated systems and the people to understand and respond to customer service requirements individually. These requirements will themselves be subject to continual change, and the successful service

'The key will be creativity: creativity in building relationships, in recognising a customer's needs and in designing and delivering a solution.'

232

company will be the one whose people can build effective relationships with customers based on understanding their needs and the ability to meet them almost before the customer knows they have them. The key will be creativity: creativity in building relationships, in recognising a customer's needs and in designing and delivering a solution.

World-class service in telecommunications will not be defined by the quality of the network, or the capacity of the bandwidth – all of which will be just another commodity in the marketplace – but by the nature of the relationship between the service representative (engineer, receptionist or whoever) and the customer. As this happens the distinction between sales and service will fade. It will be the nature of the business relationship between one company and another that will determine the pattern of business between the two.

Our challenge is to develop and equip our people to operate better than anyone else – to be more creative – in a highly competitive environment. This is why we need to place so much emphasis on learning and the self-motivated workforce. To operate successfully in that sort of environment people need to have knowledge, initiative and creativity. Those attributes are something the command and control managerial style cannot deliver.

Keeping ahead

State-owned telecommunications companies all over the world are being transferred out of public hands and into the private sector. One of the reasons for this is that public-sector companies do not have the flexibility to keep up in such a fast-changing environment. They have been following BT's lead, but if we don't keep ahead they, and the huge number of new telecommunications companies that are being set up, could overtake us. The key to our survival in the market is to learn faster than our competitors.

The future is going to be about changing our approach to our jobs and our customers, changing over to new technology, changing people's attitudes... change, change, change. That is the one certainty. We know that we're well on the way now. Perhaps this is best summed up by *The New York Times* commenting in 1995 on the changes we'd made by saying: 'Few companies have re-made themselves so completely as BT plc, the state-owned company that was privatised in 1984. Since privatisation it has cut costs, shed its slow-moving bureaucratic methods and claimed a place as a dominant force in the worldwide telecommunications industry.'

**KEY
LESSONS
CHAPTER
14**

You cannot prepare specific strategies for the unforeseen, but you can make sure the basics are in place so that you react fast when changes happen:
.....

Only people can deliver customer service excellence. More and more power has to be devolved to the people who deal directly with customers.
.....

All organisations will have to move away from a centralised and autocratic style if they are to succeed.
.....

Customer service will move up the agenda.
.....

People will need constant retraining to stay up to date with changes.
.....

The future is all about change and how to manage it.
.....

The key differentiator in the market of the future will be customer relationships. Successful companies will leverage that relationship with customers built from the best of sales, service and marketing.
.....

Creativity will be the key asset for our people: the creativity to build relationships, identify customer needs and design and deliver customer solutions.
.....

Index